A new Latin Grammar

John Fletcher

A NEW
LATIN GRAMMAR

BASED ON THE RECOMMENDATIONS
OF THE JOINT COMMITTEE ON
GRAMMATICAL TERMINOLOGY

BY

E. A. SONNENSCHEIN, D.Litt.

PROFESSOR OF CLASSICS IN THE UNIVERSITY
OF BIRMINGHAM
CHAIRMAN OF THE JOINT COMMITTEE
ON GRAMMATICAL TERMINOLOGY.

OXFORD
AT THE CLARENDON PRESS
1912

HENRY FROWDE, M.A.

PUBLISHER TO THE UNIVERSITY OF OXFORD

LONDON, EDINBURGH, NEW YORK

TORONTO AND MELBOURNE

PREFACE

THIS volume and the companion volume of my French grammar are based upon the work of the Joint Committee on Grammatical Terminology whose final Report was issued last year;[1] and they are designed to make the Committee's scheme of grammar teaching available for use in schools. It is a matter of great satisfaction to observe the rapid progress of the movement to which the Committee devoted so much labour; since the publication of our Report the recommendations contained in it have been adopted either in their entirety or with some modifications by the writers of at least four English grammars, and it seems to be generally recognized that the terminology and classifications recommended by the Committee constitute a real advance in the direction of simplicity and uniformity in the teaching of grammar.

So far no Latin or French grammar has appeared on these lines; but the Committee's work is expressly designed to include in its scope the grammar of other languages besides English, and so to secure that the grammatical doctrine taught to pupils shall be all of a piece. It is as a contribution to this movement that I have undertaken the task of writing the present books. It has involved no little labour; for the

[1] *On the Terminology of Grammar*, being the Report of the Joint Committee on Grammatical Terminology; revised 1911 (John Murray, Albemarle Street, W.). The Committee contained representatives of the Classical Association, the Modern Language Association, the English Association, the Incorporated Association of Head Masters, the Head Mistresses' Association, the Incorporated Association of Assistant Masters in Secondary Schools, the Incorporated Association of Assistant Mistresses in Public Secondary Schools, the Association of Preparatory Schools, and two co-opted members.

objects of the Committee cannot be attained by a mere mechanical substitution of one term for another. The whole scheme of grammar teaching had to be thought out from a new point of view. Grammatical ideas are far more than mere labels ; they are abstracts and brief chronicles of theories and doctrines ; so that the choice of a term means the choice of one grammatical conception in preference to another. This being so, the importance of a uniform system of grammatical terminology in schools becomes obvious ; to teach pupils half a dozen different names for the same thing is to demand of them that they shall carry in their heads half a dozen different ways of regarding the point in question, or to tempt them to carry nothing in their heads, but rather to reject all gram-matical terms as mere sound and fury, signifying nothing. The principle that where the same grammatical feature presents itself in different languages of the same family it should be described by the same name will be generally conceded. But it is also true that where these languages differ in their usage, their differences should be stated in terms which will be in-telligible to the pupil ; and this cannot be secured except on the basis of a common system of terminology. To start the study of a new language with a new stock of grammatical ideas is a fundamental mistake.

This Latin grammar, however, contains many things for which the Joint Committee is in no sense responsible. In the first place, the outline drawn by the Committee had to be filled in by the adoption of some terms not expressly countenanced therein ; and secondly, I have introduced into my book several features which stand in no relation to the work of the Com-mittee, but which have presented themselves to me in the course of a long experience of teaching Latin as desirable innovations.

(1) It is generally recognized that the rigid separation of syntax from accidence involves many disadvantages ; on the other hand it would not be desirable to present a complete syntax to pupils in the first stage of learning. I have steered

a middle course by giving a simple account of some of the prominent uses of forms as introductory matter to the study of the forms themselves ;[1] and I have called this part of the book 'Forms and their chief meanings'. I have intentionally made the accidence brief and simple, on the principle approved by the Curricula Committee of the Classical Association.[2] *Omne supervacuum pleno de pectore manat.* The details of accidence are relegated to an Appendix as matter of far less importance and interest to the beginner than the fundamental features of sentence construction.[3]

(2) I have throughout called attention to the similarities of Latin to English, and to French ; for I assume that nearly all pupils learning Latin have already begun or are beginning the study of French. It seems to have been too much forgotten by writers of Latin grammars that French sometimes throws light on Latin,[4] and that the English derivatives formed from Latin words may be turned to account in the learning of Latin forms. This I have tried to do wherever possible.[5]

(3) In dealing with the principal parts of verbs I have introduced what I believe to be a substantial improvement. For the first time, so far as I know, the forms of the Perfect Active have been reduced to rule by means of a classification according to the final sound of the stem from which they are formed.

---

[1] e.g. §§ 11–13 on the meanings of the cases, and §§ 125–38 on the meanings of the voices, moods, tenses; verb-adjectives and verb-nouns ; the chief uses of the pronouns are given in §§ 101–24.

[2] *Recommendations of the Classical Association on the Teaching of Latin and Greek* (London, John Murray, 1912), pp. 29 f.

[3] It is hardly necessary to say that great care has been paid to correctness of statement in regard to the details of accidence included. Some of the authorities used in this part of the book are referred to in the Appendix.

[4] That French may be turned to account in the study of Latin is shown throughout my Syntax. But I would also call attention to the fact that the scanning of Latin verse would be greatly facilitated by the learning of a simple rule of syllable division in French ; see French Grammar, § 11, and compare Latin Grammar, § 9.

[5] e.g. in the examples for declension in §§ 34–9 and Appendix § xiii, and in the formation of the Perfect Participle Passive, §§ 172–237.

It seemed worth while to try how far such a *catalogue raisonne*, exhibiting the formations of the Perfect Active in all the four conjugations at a single view, might prove to be in practice the simplest method of dealing with these apparently anomalous forms, which have always been the crux of pupils learning Latin. When one realizes that the learning by heart of a list of principal parts as so many isolated forms involves the memorizing of, on a moderate estimate, 750–1000 facts, one is not surprised that the forms are not actually remembered without long practice. Incidentally the pupil will learn some historical philology ; but the purpose of my classification is not to explain how the facts came to be what they are, but simply to lead to a practical mastery of the forms ; and it is in this light that it must be judged.—The Supine is no integral part of the system of any Latin verb, except in so far as it is employed in the periphrastic Future Infinitive Passive ; it has, therefore, no proper title to the position which it has so long usurped. By substituting for it the Perfect Participle Passive we not only get rid of a multitude of bogus Supines which have been manufactured by grammarians in order to supply a fourth 'principal part', but we also teach the pupil a form which is of incomparably greater value both in itself and as an element in the formation of the compound tenses of the passive voice.

(4) The Subjunctive mood is treated on the lines indicated by my previous work on the subject.[1] I have here attempted to present the results of that investigation in a form intelligible to the beginner, and I am encouraged to think that my exposition of the mood will be found useful in practice. Here, as in several other parts of my book, I have aimed at lucidity rather than brevity. But I have not included, here or elsewhere, any usages which go beyond what a pupil comes across in his everyday reading of authors like Caesar and Virgil.

[1] *The Unity of the Latin Subjunctive : A Quest* (John Murray, Albemarle Street, W., 1910).

(5) Most of my examples in syntax are designedly taken from Caesar, and where possible from the books of the *Gallic War* most commonly read in schools. Caesar is an admirable exponent of Latin prose usage, and an interesting author if he is studied properly. But, apart from this, the advantage of teaching syntax by way of examples which may have been already met with in the course of reading is very great; and I have rarely gone for my examples beyond the range of books commonly read in schools.

(6) In the treatment of the ablative case I have adopted a principle which is new in Latin grammar, though it is implicitly recognized by all grammarians, viz. that the meanings of the ablative depend to a great extent on the meaning of the noun used and on that of the verb or adjective or adverb with which it is used (§ 12, § 428). An ablative like *hora* stands on an altogether different footing from ablatives like *Roma* and *sagitta*; and I believe this fact ought to be recognized in the earliest stages of teaching, as an aid to understanding. I have carried out the principle in §§ 429-51 of the syntax.

(7) In regard to the pronunciation of Latin, I have adopted the scheme of the Classical Association,[1] which has been officially recognized by the Board of Education and is rapidly coming into general use. In the matter of the marking of the quantities of vowels I have carried out the principle recommended by the Classical Association,[2] and recently endorsed by a resolution of the Classical Association of Scotland. In matters of phonology and syllable division I have been guided by Niedermann's *Outlines of Latin Phonetics*.[3]

I am indebted to several friends for help and counsel. With my colleague, Mr. C. D. Chambers, I have discussed almost every point dealt with in this grammar, and he has

---

[1] *The Pronunciation of Latin* (John Murray, Albemarle Street, W., 1906).
[2] *On the Teaching of Latin and Greek*, p. 2 : ' That in texts of Latin authors intended for the use of beginners the quantities of long vowels be marked, except in syllables where they would be also "long by position ".'
[3] Translated by Strong and Stewart (George Routledge and Sons, 1910).

given me much assistance in preparing parts of the MS. for press. Dr. H. Blase, of Mainz, has been so good as to read my MS. of the syntax on the Subjunctive and the Cases. He and Prof. W. R. Hardie, of Edinburgh, and Prof. R. M. Henry, of Belfast, who have read the whole of my proof, have rendered me the inestimable service of sympathetic criticism, and at many points my book has profited by suggestions they have made. Mr. W. E. P. Pantin, Secretary of the Joint Committee on Grammatical Terminology, has read part of my proof, and to him too I owe several useful hints. My former pupil, Dr. Henry Thomas, of the British Museum, has done me the kindness of reading the MS. of my Subjunctive and suggesting various modifications of detail.

My best thanks are also due to the officials of the Clarendon Press for the help they have given me in the production of the book.

E. A. S.

CONTENTS

PART I—ACCIDENCE

FORMS AND THEIR CHIEF MEANINGS

PART I. ACCIDENCE

INTRODUCTION

1 LATIN is a member of the great Indo-European family of languages, to which English also belongs. Hence many Latin constructions and some Latin forms are similar to English constructions and forms.

French is an altered form of Latin. Hence French, too, stands in a close relation to English. Moreover, after the Norman Conquest many French words were taken over into English, and the forms and constructions of Norman French had an influence in moulding the structure of the English language. In this way English was brought into a still closer relation to French and Latin. And since that date the vocabulary of English has been enriched by the introduction of a large number of Latin and French words.

We shall see that Latin, French, and English have much in common—a fact which is due partly to their common ancestry, partly to the influence which French and Latin have had on English.

2 **Comparison of Latin with modern languages.** When we compare an ordinary Latin sentence with its English or French translation, we notice two important differences, apart from the differences in the words used.

Populus Rōmānus nātiōnēs barbarās Britanniae
The nation Roman the tribes barbarous of Britain

expedītiōnibus Caesaris nōn dēbellāverat :
by the expeditions of Caesar not had subdued:

i. e. *The Roman nation had not subdued the barbarous tribes of Britain by (by means of) the expeditions of Caesar.*

Haec hodiē facere nōn possum :
These things to-day do not I can :

i. e. *I cannot do these things to-day.*

Note that

(i) the order of the words is quite different ;

(ii) some of the English words have no Latin words to correspond to them : 'the', 'of', 'by', 'had', 'things', 'I'.

3   (i) **Order of Words.** · The normal Latin order differs from the normal English order in two important respects.[1]

RULE 1. Most adjectives, when not specially emphatic, come immediately *after* the noun to which they belong in sense, as in French : e. g. *Rōmānus* after *populus, barbarās* after *nātiōnēs* ; cf. French *le peuple romain, les peuples bar-bares.*

RULE 2. Adverbs and objects usually come *before* (most adverbs *immediately* before) the words to which they belong in sense : e. g. *nōn* (adverb) and *nātiōnēs barbarās Britanniae* (object) both before *dēbellāverat* ; *haec* (object) and *hodiē* (adverb) both before *facere* ; *facere* (object) before *possum* ; *nōn* (adverb) before *possum.*

These rules apply also, for the most part, to words and groups of words which are *equivalent* to adjectives and adverbs ; for example, they apply to cases of nouns used adjectivally or adverbially ; thus we have *Caesaris* ' of Caesar ' (adjectival = 'Caesarian') after *expedītiōnibus,* and *expedītiōnibus* (adverbial) before *dēbellāverat.*

The second rule causes the chief difficulty to the English reader of Latin. For in any group of Latin words containing an adverb or an object, the most important word, that on which the sense depends, comes *at the end* of the group, and not at the beginning, as generally in English. But in English, too, the Latin order is sometimes found, especially in poetry :

> How happy is the blameless vestal's lot
> *The world forgetting, by the world forgot.* (POPE.)

The reader of Latin must therefore learn to break up Latin sentences into *groups of words that go together* :

Populus Rōmānus | nātiōnēs barbarās Britanniae | expedī-tiōnibus Caesaris | nōn dēbellāverat. The art of reading Latin depends on forming the habit of breaking up sentences

---

[1] By the ' normal order ' is meant the usual order in prose ; the order in verse is much freer.

in this way, and of expecting the words to come in the order demanded by the rules.

4   (ii) **English words not expressed by separate words in Latin.**   Note the following points :

(*a*) Latin has no articles, definite or indefinite : thus *expedītiō* might mean either 'an expedition' or 'the expedition'.

(*b*) The subject of a Latin finite verb is often only indicated by the inflexion of the verb : e. g. *possum*, 'I can', *possumus*, 'we can.'   But Latin also has pronouns, which may be used in the nominative case for the sake of emphasis or contrast : e. g. *ego possum, tū nōn potes*, '*I* can, *you* cannot' (French *moi, je peux* ; *toi, tu ne peux pas*).

(*c*) The compound tenses of the active voice of English verbs are expressed by simple tenses of Latin : *dēbellāverat*, 'had subdued', *dēbellābat*, 'was subduing', *dēbellābit*, 'will subdue.'

(*d*) The meaning of some prepositions may be expressed in Latin by the inflexion of a noun or pronoun.   Thus in § 2 'of' and 'by' are expressed by the inflected forms called the *genitive case* and the *ablative case* ('*by* the expeditions *of* Caesar', *expedītiōnibus Caesaris*).   Other English prepositions whose meaning may be expressed in certain phrases by a Latin case without a preposition are 'to', 'for', 'from', 'with', 'at', 'on', 'in' ; see §§ 11, 12.

But Latin also has prepositions, which are sometimes necessary to express the sense, especially in prose ; for example, 'an expedition has been prepared by Caesar' would be in Latin 'expedītiō *ā Caesare* parāta est' ; even 'of' may in certain phrases be expressed by a preposition, e. g. 'one of many', 'ūnus *dē multīs*' (compare French *de*). And the meaning of the prepositions 'before', 'after', 'across', 'without', and many others is always expressed by a preposition in Latin (*ante, post, trans, sine*, &c.).

Pronunciation of Latin.

5   The Latin vowels had much the same sounds as they have in French, Italian, and German. The chief difference between Latin and French is that the Latin *u* was pronounced like *oo* in English, not like the French *u* in *lune*.

In the following English words the vowels have nearly the same sounds as the Latin *a, e, i, o, u* :

ăhā, dĕmēsne, ĭntrīgue, sŏrrōw, cŭckōō.

ā like French *â* in *pâte* or English *a* in *father* : e. g. **māter**.

ă (the same sound shortened) like French *a* in *pas* or the first *a* in English *aha* : e. g. **păter**.

ē like French *é* in *été*, but lengthened ; or English *a* in *fate* without the faint *i*-sound at the end : e. g. **mē**. The Lat. ē was what is called a 'close ē '.

ĕ like English *e* in *fret* or French *e* in *nette* : e. g. **tĕnĕt**. The Latin ĕ was what is called an 'open ĕ '.

ī like *i* in English *machine*, French *rire* or *île* : e. g. **īmus**.

ĭ like *i* in English *in, pit* : e. g. **regĭt**.

ō like French *ô* in *môle* or French *eau* in *beau* ; or English *o* in *home* without the faint *u*-sound at the end : e. g. **Rōma**.

ŏ like *o* in English *hot* or French *mol* : e. g. **hŏminem**.

ū like English *oo* in *too* or French *oû* in *goûte* : e. g. **tū**.

ŭ (the same sound shortened) like English *oo* in *took* or French *ou* in *goutte* : e. g. **consŭl**.

y (a Greek letter, used only in foreign words) like French *u* in *lune* : sometimes long, e. g. **Lȳdia** ; sometimes short, e. g. **tȳrannus**.

6   Diphthongs (double vowel sounds) are produced by running two different vowel sounds together so as to make a single long syllable.

The Latin diphthongs were pronounced somewhat as follows :

ae like English *ai* in *aisle*: e. g. **taedae**.

au like English *ou* in *loud* : e. g. **laudō**.

ei like English *ey* in *grey* : e. g. eia (Interjection).

eu like English *ew* in *new* : e. g. seu, heu.

oe like English *oi* in *boil* : e. g. poena.

ui like French *oui* ('yes') : e. g. huic.   The word *cui* (dat. sing. of *quis* and *quī*) was sometimes pronounced as two short syllables, *cŭĭ*, like the two vowels of the English *ruin*.

7   The consonants were pronounced by the Romans much as they are pronounced in English, except the following :

c, always like English *c* in *can* (= *k*) : e. g. canō, cecinī; condiciō, scit.

g, always like English *g* in *good* :   e. g. regō, regis, regam, regēs, regunt; regiō.

s, always like English *s* in *seal*, *gas* : e. g. sūs, rosa.

z (a Greek letter, used only in foreign words), probably like English *dz* in *adze* : e. g. Zephyrus, gaza.

t, always like English *t* in *ten* : tenet, nātiō, fortia.

i consonant (sometimes written *j*), like English *y* in *yoke* : e. g. iugum, iacere, cūius, hūius, ēius.

u consonant (generally written *v*), like English *w* in *wall*, *wine* : e. g. vallum, vīnum.

qu and ngu before a vowel were pronounced as in the English *queen, anguish* (not like the French *qu* in *qui, que*) : e. g. quī, anguis.   Similarly, *su* was pronounced like English *sw* in *sweet* in the three words suāvis, suādeō, suescō, and their derivatives.

Doubled consonants (*ll, mm, nn, rr, tt*, &c.) were both pronounced : e. g. col·lis, Cot·ta.

Quantity of Syllables.

8   By the quantity of a syllable is meant the amount of time which is taken to pronounce it.   A long syllable is considered to be equal in duration to two short syllables.

A syllable is **long** in two cases :

(i) when it contains a long vowel or diphthong : e. g. *mē, mātrēs, rēgī, taedae, laudō* ;

(ii) when it contains a short vowel followed by two or

more consonants other than a mute (*c, g; t, d; p, b*) or *j* and a liquid (*r, l*): *dant, trabs, condunt, aiment.* The double consonants *x* (= *cs*) and *z* (= *dz*, § 7) count as two consonants; thus *dux* and the first syllable of *gaza* are long.

The letter *h* and the *u* in *qu* do not count as consonants. Thus the first syllable of *adhūc, loquor, neque,* &c., is short.

A syllable is **short** when its vowel-sound is short and is followed either by no consonant or by only one consonant: *ego, -que, dat, dabat, rapere.* Syllables in which a short vowel-sound is followed by a mute or *f* and a liquid are properly short, except when the mute and the liquid belong to different parts of a compound word, as in *abripere, neglegere.*

9 In order to understand the reason for these rules it is necessary to consider the division of Latin words into syllables, *as pronounced.* The rules for syllable division are (as in French) : [1]

(i) A single consonant is pronounced with the following vowel: *mā-ter, ca-dit, bo-nus, nō-men.*

(ii) Two or more consonants are divided between two syllables, except when the first consonant is a mute or *f* and the second one of the liquids *r* or *l*. In this case the two consonants are easily combined, and are therefore pronounced together at the beginning of a syllable (except in compounds): *la-crima, a-grum, pa-trem, va-fra, lo-cu-plēs, A-tlās,* &c.

From these rules of syllable division the quantity of syllables is at once intelligible. A syllable is long when it ends (i) with a long vowel or diphthong, (ii) with two or more consonants (*trabs, hiems, dant*) or a double consonant (*dux*), (iii) with a single consonant followed by a syllable which begins with a consonant (*ar-ma, ad-sum, con-dit, vac-ca, bel-lus, ab-ripere, con-trahō*). In this case the first consonant is separated from the second by a slight pause.

All other syllables are short: viz. (i) those ending with a short vowel (*e-go, be-ne, ma-le, pi-a, a-grī, pa-tre,* &c.); (ii) those

---

[1] See French Gram. § 11.—The rule of the Roman grammarians which led to divisions like *ma-gnus, ae-stās, di-ctus* has been shown to be mistaken.

containing a short vowel followed by a single consonant (*dat*) and not followed by a syllable beginning with a consonant.

In connected discourse (prose or verse) the words are run on together, so that the first syllable of the next word counts as the next syllable, within the limits of the sentence or clause or, in verse, generally of the line.

In this grammar long vowels are marked (ā, ē, ī, ō, ū), except where they are followed by two or more consonants such as themselves make the syllable long, apart from the length of the vowel.[1] **Short vowels have no mark over them,** except for some special reason (as in § 5). **Diphthongs, being necessarily long, are also not marked.**

) **Accent.** All Latin words of more than one syllable had an accent (stress), which did not necessarily fall on a long syllable. In words of three or more syllables, if the last syllable but one was long it was also accented ; if short, the accent fell on the last syllable but two : thus *vocábō, honéstus* ; but *vocávĕrit, honéstĭor, hómĭnis, homĭnĭbus.*

In words of two syllables the first was accented, whether it was long or short : thus *máter, pắter, vŏ́cō, Mắsās.*

The words *-que,* 'and', *-ve,* ' or', *-ne* (used in asking questions) and *-cum* ' with ' counted as part of the word to which they were attached in speaking and writing ; and the accents fell in accordance with the above rules : thus *Mūsásque, patérve, vocóne ?* ; but *Mứsăque, rósăve, mihíne ?.*

In words that had lost a syllable the accent might fall on the last syllable remaining : e. g. *tantón* (for *tantóne*), *istínc* (for *istún-ce*). But apart from such cases no Latin words of two or more syllables were accented on the last syllable. Contrast French.

---

[1] When a word, whose vowel is marked long on the above principle, enters into composition with another word, the mark of length is retained ; e. g. *nōnne, mōsque, ūndecim, vēndō.*

FORMS AND THEIR CHIEF MEANINGS

General meanings of the Cases.

11   Most Latin nouns, pronouns, and adjectives have inflected forms called 'cases', which differ from one another in meaning, though not always in form.   Note that (i) all neuter nouns, pronouns, and adjectives have the same form in the nominative, vocative, and accusative cases, both in the singular and in the plural number; (ii) all nouns have the same form in the dative as in the ablative plural; (iii) the vocative does not differ from the nominative in form, except in the singular number of nouns and adjectives of the 2nd declension in *us* (§§ 16, 18, 22).

The general meanings of the nominative, vocative, accusative, genitive, and dative cases are the same as in English :

Nominative. **Patria mihi** est **Britannia.** **My country** *is*
 (lit. *To me the country is*) **Britain.**

Vocative. **Tē, patria, amō.** *I love thee,* **my country.**

Accusative. **Patriam amō.** *I love* **my country.**

Genitive. **Lītora patriae relinquō.** *I am leaving* **my country's** *shores* (or *the shores* **of my country**).

 Vincet amor patriae. *The love* **of country** *will prevail.*

Dative. **Patriae lībertātem dedit.** *He gave* **his country** *freedom,* or *He gave freedom* **to his country.**

 Nōn tibi ipsī sed **patriae** nātus es. *You are born not for yourself but* **for your country.**

12   The ABLATIVE is a case peculiar to Latin. Its meaning
depends partly on the meaning of the noun used and of the
verb with which it is used. Thus with a verb denoting 'to
expel' the abl. may express the idea of 'from': **patriā** ex-
pulsus est, 'he has been expelled **from his country**'. The
abl. of a noun denoting an instrument may express the idea
of 'with', or 'by means of': aquilam **sagittā** necāvit, 'he
killed an eagle **with (or by means of) an arrow**'. The abl.
of a noun denoting a period of time may express the idea of
'at', 'on', 'in': **prīmā hōrā** diēī, '**at the first hour** of the
day'; hōc diē, '**on this day**'; hōc annō, '**in this year.**'

   Note that the abl. of a noun denoting a material object
could not express the idea of 'on' or 'in' in prose: for
instance *prīmā mensā* could not mean 'on the first table',
nor could *hōc hortō* mean 'in this garden'. In these and
similar instances the abl. would take a preposition in prose:
in prīmā mensā, in hōc hortō. Similarly, *ex patriā* (or *ā patriā*)
venit, 'he comes from his native land'; *cum patre vīvit,* 'he
lives with his father'; *ā patre amātur,* 'he is loved by his
father.'

13   Names of towns and a few other nouns (including names
of small islands which had only one town of importance in
them, after which they were called) have also a LOCATIVE CASE
denoting 'at', 'in', or 'on'; see § 55.

DECLENSION OF NOUNS AND ADJECTIVES

14   Latin nouns are arranged in five declensions, according to
the endings of the genitive singular and the genitive plural:

	Ending of Gen. Sing.	*Ending of Gen. Plur.*
1st Declension	ae	ārum
2nd „	ī	ōrum
3rd „	is	um
4th „	ūs	uum
5th „	ĕī	ērum

   Latin adjectives have forms similar to (though not exactly
the same as) those of nouns.

B 2

Nouns of the First Declension.

15   insula, f., *island*.

	Singular	*Plural*
N., V.	insula	insulae
Acc.	insulam	insulās
Gen.	insulae	insulārum
Dat.	insulae	} insulīs
Abl.	insulā	

EXAMPLES FOR DECLENSION —

Fem.: fuga, *flight*; hōra, *hour*; iniūria, *injury*; via, *road*; victōria, *victory*; Iūlia, *Julia.*

Masc.: agricola, *husbandman*; nauta, *sailor*; perfuga, *deserter*; Catilīna, *Catiline.*

Nouns of the Second Declension.

16   dominus, m., *owner*   bellum, n., *war*

	Sing.	*Plur.*	*Sing.*	*Plur.*
Nom.	dominus	} dominī		
Voc.	domine		} bellum	} bella
Acc.	dominum	dominōs		
Gen.	dominī	dominōrum	bellī	bellōrum
Dat.	} dominō	} dominīs	} bellō	} bellīs
Abl.				

Examples for declension are given in § 21. For nouns in *ius, ium* see § 22.

17   magister, m., *teacher*   puer, m., *boy*

	Sing.	*Plur.*	*Sing.*	*Plur.*
N., V.	magister	magistrī	puer	puerī
Acc.	magistrum	magistrōs	puerum	puerōs
Gen.	magistrī	magistrōrum	puerī	puerōrum
Dat.	} magistrō	} magistrīs	} puerō	} puerīs
Abl.				

Examples for declension are given in § 21.

Vir, m., *man* (as distinct from *woman*) is declined as follows :
Sing. virum, virī, virō ; *Plur.* virī, virōs, virōrum, virīs.

Adjectives like nouns of the 2nd and the 1st declension.

18   1. cārus, cāra, cārum, *dear* (like *dominus, insula, bellum*, p. 20)

	Singular			Plural		
	masc.	*fem.*	*neut.*	*masc.*	*fem.*	*neut.*
N.	cārus	cāra	cārum	} cārī	cārae	cāra
V.	cāre	cāra	cārum			
Ac.	cārum	cāram	cārum	cārōs	cārās	cāra
G.	cārī	cārae	cārī	cārōrum	cārārum	cārōrum
D.	cārō	cārae	cārō	} cārīs	cārīs	cārīs
Ab.	cārō	cārā	cārō			

19   2. crēber, crēbra, crēbrum, *frequent* (like *magister* in the masc.)

	Singular			Plural		
	masc.	*fem.*	*neut.*	*masc.*	*fem.*	*neut.*
N. *V.*	} crēber	crēbra	crēbrum	} crēbrī	crēbrae	crēbra
Ac.	crēbrum	crēbram	crēbrum	crēbrōs	crēbrās	crēbra
G.	crēbrī	crēbrae	crēbrī	crēbrōrum	crēbrārum	crēbrōrum
D.	crēbrō	crēbrae	crēbrō	} crēbrīs	crēbrīs	crēbrīs
Ab.	crēbrō	crēbrā	crēbrō			

20   3. līber, lībera, līberum, *free* (like *puer* in the masc. Here the *e* of the nom. sing. is retained throughout)

	Singular			Plural		
	masc.	*fem.*	*neut.*	*masc.*	*fem.*	*neut.*
N. *V.*	} līber	lībera	līberum	} līberī	līberae	lībera
Ac.	līberum	līberam	līberum	līberōs	līberās	lībera
G.	līberī	līberae	līberī	līberōrum	līberārum	līberōrum
D.	līberō	līberae	līberō	} līberīs	līberīs	līberīs
Ab.	līberō	līberā	līberō			

Examples for declension (like 1, 2, 3) are given in § 21.

Examples for Declension (Nouns and Adjectives, pp. 20, 21).

21 Like **dominus**: Masc. amīcus, *friend*; annus, *year*; numerus, *number*.—Fem. fāgus, *beech*; ulmus, *elm* (names of trees).

Like **bellum**: Neut. perīculum, *danger, peril*; proelium, *battle*; signum, *standard*; consilium, *plan, counsel*.

Like **cārus, a, um**: bonus, a, um, *good*; antīquus, a, um, *ancient*; vacuus, a, um, *empty*; idōneus, a, um, *fitted*; tertius, a, um, *third*; datus, a, um, *given*; tuus, a, um, *your*; tantus, a, um, *so great*; quantus, a, um, *how great?*; and all superlatives in -issimus, a, um.

Like **magister (magistr·)** and **crēber, crēbr·a, crēbr·um** are declined most nouns and adjectives of the 2nd decl. in *er*: e.g. arbiter, m., *witness*; faber, m., *carpenter* or *smith*; minister, m., *servant*; ager, m., *field*; liber, m., *book*; aeger, aegr-a, -um, *sick*; integer, integr-a, -um, *whole, entire*; pulcher, pulchr-a, -um, *fine*; sacer, sacr-a, -um, *sacred*; noster, nostr-a, -um, *our*.

Like **puer** and **līber, a, um** are declined only a few nouns and adjectives: chiefly (1) līberī (no sing.), m., *children*, lit. 'free-born ones'; (2) asper, a, um, *rough*; lacer, a, um, *torn*; miser, a, um, *unhappy*; tener, a, um, *tender*; (3) compounds of -fer and·-ger, like aquilifer, m., *standard-bearer*; armiger, m., *armour-bearer*; frūgifer, a, um, *fruit-bearing*.

Nouns in ius, ium.

22 1. Nouns (but not adjectives) in **ius** or **ium** properly form the gen. sing. in ī in prose (in verse often in ·iī):

e.g. fīlius, m., *son*, fīlī; negōtium, n., *business*, negōtī; except proper names, e.g. Clōdius, gen. Clōdiī.

2. Proper names in **ius** and the noun **fīlius** form the voc. sing. in *ī*:

e.g. Vergilius, Vergilī; Gāius (three syllables), Gāī.

3. **Deus**, m., *god*, has its voc. sing. = nom. sing., and generally contracts two syllables into one in the nom., voc., dat., and abl. plural: *dī*, *dīs*; gen. sometimes *deum*.

Nouns of the Third Declension.

23   Class A (Consonant stems with gen. plur. in ·um).
Those nouns of the 3rd decl. which have one more syllable
in the genitive singular than in the nominative singular and
only one consonant before the ending of the gen. sing. form
the genitive plural in **um**.

24   (i) Nominative singular formed without any suffix.

MASCULINES AND FEMININES

victor, m., *victor.*   nātiŏ, f., *tribe.*

	Sing.	*Plur.*	*Sing.*	*Plur.*
N., V.	victor	} victŏr-ēs	nātiŏ	} nātiōn-ēs
Acc.	victŏr-em		nātiōn-em	
Gen.	victŏr-is	victŏr-um	nātiōn-is	nātiōn-um
Dat.	victŏr-ī	} victŏr-ibus	nātiōn-ī	} nātiōn-ibus
Abl.	victŏr-e		nātiōn-e	

25   NEUTERS

nōmen, n., *name.*   tempus, n., *time.*

	Sing.	*Plur.*	*Sing.*	*Plur.*
N., V., A.	nōmen	nōmin-a	tempus	tempor-a
Gen.	nōmin-is	nōmin-um	tempor-is	tempor-um
Dat.	nōmin-ī	} nōmin-ibus	tempor-ī	} tempor-ibus
Abl.	nōmin-e		tempor-e	

26   (ii) Nominative singular formed with the suffix -*s* (before
which a dental disappears).

CHIEFLY FEMININE

hiems, f., *winter.*   cīvitās, f., *state.*

	Sing.	*Plur.*	*Sing.*	*Plur.*
N., V.	hiem-s	} hiem-ēs	cīvitā-s	} cīvitāt-ēs
Acc.	hiem-em		cīvitāt-em	
Gen.	hiem-is	hiem-um	cīvitāt-is	cīvitāt-um
Dat.	hiem-ī	} hiem-ibus	cīvitāt-ī	} cīvitāt-ibus
Abl.	hiem-e		cīvitāt-e	

Examples for declension (like i, ii) are given in §§ 34–9.

27   **Class B (Vowel stems with gen. plur. in ·i·um).** Those
nouns of the 3rd decl. which have **either** the same number of
syllables in the gen. sing. as in the nom. sing. **or** two consonants before the ending of the gen. sing. form the genitive
plural in **ium.**[1]

28   (i) With the same number of syllables in the gen. sing. as
in the nom. sing.

nāvis, f., *ship.*   caedēs, f., *massacre.*

	Sing.	Plur.	Sing.	Plur.
N., V.	nāvi-s	nāvēs	caedē-s	caedēs
Acc.	nāvem	nāvēs	caedem	caedēs
Gen.	nāvis	nāvium	caedis	caedium
Dat.	nāvī	} nāvibus	caedī	} caedibus
Abl.	nāve		caede	

Obs. The abl. sing. of words like *nāvis* often ends in -*ī*, and
the acc. plur. of nouns like *nāvis* and *caedēs* in -*īs*.

29   (ii) With two consonants before the ending of the gen.
sing. (which has one more syllable than the nom. sing.).

urbs, f., *city.*   gens, f., *clan.*

	Sing.	Plur.	Sing.	Plur.
N., V.	urb-s	urbēs	gen-s	gentēs
Acc.	urbem	urbēs	gentem	gentēs
Gen.	urbis	urbium	gentis	gentium
Dat.	urbī	} urbibus	gentī	} gentibus
Abl.	urbe		gente	

Obs. The acc. plur. of nouns like *urbs* and *gens* often ends
in -*īs*.

30   (iii) Neuters in *e* with the same number of syllables in the
gen. sing. as in the nom. sing., and those which have dropped
the *e* of the nom. sing. and so end in *al* or *ar.* Note the abl.
sing. and nom. plur.

---

[1] Most of these nouns come from stems in *i* (*nāvi-, urbi-, insigni-,* &c.).

insigne, n., *badge.*   animal, n., *animal.*

	Sing.	Plur.	Sing.	Plur.
N., V., A.	insigne	insignia	animal	animālia
Gen.	insignis	insignium	animālis	animālium
D., Ab.	insignī	insignibus	animālī	animālibus

Most of these neuters were originally adjectives. Thus *animal* (originally *animāle*) meant 'possessed of life', from *anima.*

Examples for declension (like i, ii, iii) are given in §§ 40–5.

Adjectives like nouns of the 3rd declension.

Adjectives of this kind are declined like the nouns of Class B on the opposite page, excepting that the ablative singular always ends in ī (not *e*).

(1) brevis, m., f., breve, n., *short, brief* (like *nāvis* § 28, and *insigne* § 30).

	Singular		Plural	
	masc. and fem.	neut.	masc. and fem.	neut.
N., V.	brevi-s	breve	brevēs	brevia
Acc.	brevem	breve	brevēs	brevia
Gen.	brevis		brevium	
Dat. Abl.	brevī		brevibus	

(2) ācer, m., ācris, f., ācre, n., *keen,* differs from *brevis, breve* only in the nom. sing. masc.

	Singular			Plural	
	masc.	fem.	neut.	masc. and fem.	neut.
N., V.	ācer	ācri-s	ācre	ācrēs	ācria
Acc.	ācrem	ācrem	ācre	ācrēs	ācria
Gen.		ācris		ācrium	
Dat. Abl.		ācrī		ācribus	

33 (3) ingen̦s, m., f., n., *huge* (like *gens* § 29 in the masc. an̦
fem. Note̦ the nom. and acc. sing. neut.)

		Singular		Plural	
		masc. and fem.	*neut.*	*masc. and fem.*	*neut.*
N., V.		ingen-s	ingen-s	ingentēs	ingentia
Acc.		ingentem	ingen-s	ingentēs	ingentia
Gen.		ingentis		ingentium	
Dat.		ingentī		ingentibus	
Abl.					

Obs. The acc. plur. (masc. and fem.) of adjectives like th
above (1, 2, 3) often ends in -*īs*.

Examples for declension are given in §§ 46–8.

Examples of nouns of the 3rd declension

34 **Class A.** The only difficulty in words of this class
especially those which end in *s*, is to find out the stem of th
word from the form of the nominative singular ; in many c
these words the English derivatives, formed from the stem
provide a key.

(1) Like **victor** (§ 24).

(*a*) with long vowel in stem : imperātor, m., *general*, an̦
many others in *tor* (derived from the stems of verbs ; *imperāto*
= *is quī imperat*); clāmor, m., *shout*; honor *or* honōs, m.
honour; sōl, m., *sun*.

(*b*) with short vowel in stem : Caesar, m., *Caesar*; agger
m., *mound*; consul, m., *consul*; arbor, f., *tree*; mulier, f.
woman.

To this group belong a number of words with nom. sing
ending in *s*, which is part of the stem, appearing as *r* in th
other cases :

mōs, m., *custom*	[moral]	STEM mōr-
flōs, m., *flower*	[floral]	STEM flōr-
pulvis, m., *dust*	[pulverize]	STEM pulver-

(2) Like nātiō (§ 24). Here the stem ends in *n* :

(*a*) with long *ō* in last syllable of stem : ēruptiō, f., *sortie* ; legiō, f., *legion* ; ōrātiō, f., *speech* ; ratiō, f., *reason* ; regiō, f., *region* ; sermō, m., *discourse* [sermon].

(*b*) with short *i* in last syllable of stem :

longitūdō, f., *length*	[longitudinal]	STEM longitūdin-
multitūdō, f., *multitude*	[multitudinous]	STEM multitūdin-
ordō, m., *rank*	[ordinary]	STEM ordin-

So consuētūdō, f., *habit*, STEM consuētūdin- ; homō, m., *man*, STEM homin-.

(3) Like nōmen (§ 25) : agmen, n., *army on the march, advancing column* ; crīmen, n., *accusation* ; flūmen, n., *river* ; caput, n., *head* [capital], STEM capit-.

(4) Like tempus (§ 25). The final *s* is part of the stem, as in *mōs* above. The last syllable of the stem of these neuters is generally short.

corpus, n., *body*	[corporal]	STEM corpor-
decus, n., *ornament*	[decorate]	STEM decor-
lītus, n., *shore*	[litoral]	STEM lītor-
genus, n., *kind*	[general]	STEM gener-
latus, n., *side*	[lateral]	STEM later-
onus, n., *burden*	[onerous]	STEM oner-
opus, n., *work*	[operate]	STEM oper-
pondus, n., *weight*	[ponderous]	STEM ponder-
vulnus, n., *wound*	[vulnerable]	STEM vulner-
iūs, n., *right*	[jurist]	STEM iūr-
rūs, n., *country*	[rural]	STEM rūr-
ōs, n., *mouth*	[oral]	STEM ōr-
cadāver, n., *corpse*	[cadaverous]	STEM cadāver-
rōbur, n., *strength*	[cor-roborate]	STEM rōbor-

38 (5) Like **hiems** (§ 26).

plebs, f., *rabble*	[plebeian]	STEM	plēb-
princeps, m., *chief*	[principal]	STEM	princip-
pax (x = cs), f., *peace*	[pacify]	STEM	pāc-
lex (x = gs), f., *law*	[legal]	STEM	lēg-
vox, f., *voice*	[vocal]	STEM	vōc-
dux, m. or f., *leader*	[ducal]	STEM	duc-
iūdex, m., *judge*	[judicial]	STEM	iūdic-
rādix, f., *root*	[radical]	STEM	rādīc-
rex, m., *king*	[regal]	STEM	rēg-

39 (6) Like **cīvitās** (§ 26). A dental (*t* or *d*) or *n* of the ster has been dropped before the suffix *s*.

aestās, f., *summer*; calamitās, f., *disaster*; lībertās, f., *liberty*

mīles, m. or f., *soldier*	[military]	STEM	mīlit-
hospes, m. or f., *host*	[hospitable]	STEM	hospit-
quiēs, f., *rest*	[quiet]	STEM	quiēt-
salūs, f., *welfare*	[salutary]	STEM	salūt-
virtūs, f., *valour*		STEM	virtūt-
custōs, m. or f., *guardian*	[custodian]	STEM	custōd-
sacerdōs, m. or f., *priest* (*-ess*)	[sacerdotal]	STEM	sacerdōt
lapis, m., *stone*	[dilapidated]	STEM	lapid-
obses, m. or f., *hostage*		STEM	obsid-
laus, f., *praise*	[laudable]	STEM	laud-
palūs, f., *marsh*		STEM	palūd-
pēs, m., *foot*	[biped]	STEM	ped-
sanguis, m. *blood*	[sanguinary]	STEM	sanguin-

40 **Class B.**

(1) Like **nāvis** (§ 28):
classis, f., *fleet*; fīnis, m., *end*; hostis, m. or f., *enemy* collis, m., *hill*; fūnis, m., *rope*; orbis, m., *circle*.

41 (2) Like **caedēs** (§ 28):
aedēs (plur.), f., *house*; nūbēs, f., *cloud*; mōlēs, f., *mass* clādēs, f., *disaster*; famēs, f., *hunger*; sēdēs, f., *seat*.

42 (3) Like **urbs** (§ 29):
arx, f., *stronghold*, gen. arc-is; falx, f., *sickle*, gen. falc-is.

(4) Like **gens** (§ 29):

(a) with *nt* before the ending of the gen. sing.: cliens, m. or f., *client*; mens, f., *mind*; mons, m., *mountain*.

(b) with other consonants before the ending of the gen. sing.: ars, f., *art*, art-is; pars, f., *part*, part-is; mors, f., *death*, mort-is; cohors, f., *cohort*, cohort-is; nox, f., *night*, noct-is.

(5) Like **insigne** (§ 30):

cubīle, n., *lair*; ovīle, n., *sheep-fold*; mare, n., *sea*; penetrāle, n., *inner sanctuary*.

(6) Like **animal** (§ 30):

tribūnal, n., *platform*; vectīgal, n., *tax*; calcar, n., *spur*; exemplar, n., *pattern*.

EXAMPLES OF ADJECTIVES LIKE NOUNS OF THE 3RD DECLENSION

(1) Like **brevis, breve** (§ 31):

facilis, e, *easy*; fortis, e, *brave*; gravis, e, *heavy*; inermis, e, *unarmed*; omnis, e, *all*; ūtilis, e, *useful*; tālis, e, *such* (= *of such a kind*); quālis, e, *of what kind?*.

(2) Like **ācer, ācris, ācre** (§ 32):

alacer, cris, cre, *lively*; celeber, bris, bre, *celebrated*; equester, tris, tre, *equestrian*; volucer, cris, cre, *winged*; and the adjectives September, October, November, December (bris, bre), *e.g.* mense Septembrī, *in September*.

(3) Like **ingens** (§ 33):

frequens, *numerous*; praesens, *present*; potens, *powerful*; prūdens, *prudent*; recens, *recent*.

Also some with only one consonant before the ending of the gen. sing., e. g. audax, gen. audācis, *audacious*; fēlix, gen. fēlīcis, *lucky*; vēlox, gen. vēlōcis, *swift*; Arpīnās, gen. Arpīnātis, *belonging to Arpinum*; optimātēs (plur.), *aristocratic*, as a noun, *aristocrats*; praeceps, gen. praecipitis (from caput, capit-), *headlong*; teres, gen. teretis, *shapely*. Similarly (without *s* in the nom. sing.) pār, gen. paris, *equal*; impār, gen. imparis, *unequal*.

DECLENSION OF COMPARATIVES

49 Adjectives in the comparative degree are declined like the nouns on p. 23 (not like those on pp. 24, 25); thus the ablative singular ends in **e**, the genitive plural in **um**, the neuter nominative plural in **a**.

[The formation of the nominative singular in *ior, ius* is given in § 66: *e.g.* cār-ior, -ius, *dear-er*; brev-ior, -ius, *short-er, brief-er.*]

	Singular		*Plural*	
	masc. and fem.	*neut.*	*masc. and fem.*	*neut.*
N., V.	cārior	cārius		
Acc.	cāriōr-em	cārius	cāriōr-ēs	cāriōr-a
Gen.	cāriōr-is		cāriōr-um	
Dat.	cāriōr-ī			
Abl.	cāriōr-e		cāriōr-ibus	

50 *Plūs*, 'more' (§ 71), is declined from the stem *plūr-*, as follows:

	Neuter Singular	*Plural*	
		masc. and fem.	*neut.*
Nom., Acc.	plūs	plūr-ēs	plūr-a
Gen.	plūr-is	plūr-ium	
Dat., Abl.	none	plūr-ibus	

The compound *complūr-ēs* (masc. and fem.), *complūr-a* (neut.), 'several,' found only in the plural, is declined in the same way: *complūr-ium, complūr-ibus.*

Nouns of the Fourth Declension.

51   exercitus, m., *army.*   cornū, n., *horn.*

	Sing.	*Plur.*	*Sing.*	*Plur.*
N., V.	exercitus	exercitūs	cornū	cornua
Acc.	exercitum		cornū	
Gen.	exercitūs	exercituum	cornūs	cornuum
Dat.	exercituī (*or* ū)	exercitibus	cornū (*or* uī)	cornibus
Abl.	exercitū		cornū	

EXAMPLES OF NOUNS OF THE 4TH DECLEN.

1. Like **exercitus.**

MASC.: adventus, *arrival*; impetus, *attack*; metus, *fear*; ūsus, *use*; currus, *chariot.*

FEM.: Īdūs (plur.), *the Ides*; manus, *hand.*

2. Like **cornū.** NEUT.: genū, *knee.*

domus, f., *house, home*, belongs partly to the 2nd decl.

	Singular	Plural
N., V.	domus	domūs
Acc.	domum	**domōs** (*2nd decl.*) *or* domūs (*4th*)
Gen.	domūs	**domōrum** (*2nd*) *or* domuum (*4th*)
Dat.	domuī	
Abl.	**domō** (*2nd decl.*)	domibus
Loc.[1]	**domī** (*2nd decl.*)	

Nouns of the Fifth Declension.

rēs, f., *thing, affair.*

	Singular	Plural
N., V.	rēs	
Acc.	rem	rēs
Gen.	reī	rērum
Dat.	˙reī	
Abl.	rē	rēbus

The only nouns of importance belonging to the 5th decl. besides rēs[2] are diēs, *day* (generally masc.), and the following feminines, none of which have all cases of the plural in use: aciēs, *line of battle*; faciēs, *shape, face*; fidēs, *fidelity*; perniciēs, *destruction*; plānitiēs, *plain*; speciēs, *appearance*; spēs, *hope.* Those which have an *i* before the *ēs* of the nom. sing. have a long *e* in the gen. and dat. sing., e. g. *diēī, aciēī.*

A shorter form of the gen. and dat. sing. is sometimes found: *diē, aciē.*

[1] See § 13 and § 55.

[2] The combination *rēs publica* (sometimes written as one word *rēspublica*), literally 'the public interest', 'the common weal', means *republic, commonwealth*, or *constitution.* The plural *rēs publicae* (found in all the cases) means *republics, commonwealths*, or *constitutions*, and should never be translated 'public affairs', which meaning is expressed by the singular number.

THE LOCATIVE CASE (see § 13)

55   The endings of the **Locative,** which is used to denote
'at', 'in', or 'on' (i. e. to answer the question 'Where?')
are as follows :—

in Singulars of the 1st decl. **ae** : Rōmae, *at Rome* ; mīlitiae
on military service:

in Singulars of the 2nd decl. **ī** : Beneventī, *at Beneventum*
Brundisiī, *at Brundisium* ; domī, *at home* (§ 52), bellī, *in war*
humī, *on the ground.*

In all other nouns the locative has the same form as the
ablative : thus—

Singulars of the 3rd decl. : Carthāgine, *at Carthage* ; Tībure
at Tibur ; rūre, *in the country* ; Neāpolī, *at Naples* (§ 28, Obs.)

Names of towns of plural form :

1st decl. : Athēnīs, *at Athens* (nom. Athēnae) ; Cannīs, *a
Cannae.*

2nd decl. : Philippīs, *at Philippi* ; Gabiīs, *at Gabii.*

3rd decl. : Gādibus, *at Gades.*

GENDER OF NOUNS [1]

56   The rule for the gender of NOUNS DENOTING PERSONS is
the same as in French, and there are no exceptions to it
of any importance :

Nouns that denote a MALE PERSON are **masculine** ;

Nouns that denote a FEMALE PERSON are *feminine.*

The gender of these words depends on their *meaning,* and
has nothing to do with their *form* or *declension.*

Thus MASC.: **agricola,** farmer ; **Sulla,** Sulla ; **Horātius**
Horace ; **puer,** boy ; **vir,** man, husband ; **pater,** father
frāter, brother ; **rex,** king ; **senex,** old man ; **Cupīdō,** the
god Cupid.

FEM.: *puella,* girl ; *Cornēlia,* Cornelia ; *rēgīna,* queen

---

[1] On this and the two following pages masculines are printed in heavy
type, feminines in *italics*, and neuters in *CAPITALS.*

mulier, woman ; *uxor*, wife ; *soror*, sister ; *māter*, mother ;
Venus, the goddess Venus ; *anus*, old woman.

7 Nouns which may denote persons of either sex are masculine
or feminine according to their application : e. g. **parens meus,**
my father ; *parens mea*, my mother ; **sacerdōs castus,** a holy
priest ; *sacerdōs longaeva*, an aged priestess ; **cīvis Rōmānus**
or *cīvis Rōmāna*, a Roman citizen. Similarly masc. or fem. :
comes, *companion* ; dux, *guide* ; hospes, *host* or *hostess* ; hostis,
enemy ; mīles, *warrior*.

8 NOTE. (i) This rule does not apply to nouns which denote
a *collection* of persons ; these follow the rules for the separate
declensions given below : e. g. *nātiō* (fem.), tribe ; *plebs* (fem.),
the commons ; *cōpiae* (fem.), forces (plur. of *cōpia*, supply);
AUXILIA (neut.), auxiliary forces (plur. of *AUXILIUM*, aid).

(ii) Words like the following do not properly denote
persons, though they are sometimes applied to persons :
MANCIPIUM, chattel (neut., sometimes applied to slaves);
dēliciae, delight (= darling).[1]

The gender of nouns NOT DENOTING PERSONS may be mostly
found by the following rules.[2]

9 I. Those of the 1st declension are all feminine, e. g.
hōra, hour ; *insula*, island ; *īra*, anger ; *rīpa*, bank ; *vīta*, life.

10 II. Those of the 2nd declension in **us** or **er** are nearly all
masculine, e. g. **annus,** year ; **hortus,** garden ; **numerus,**
number ; **ager,** field ; **liber,** book : those of the 2nd declension
in *UM* are all neuter, e. g. *DŌNUM*, gift ; *VĪNUM*, wine.

11 III. 1. Those of the 3rd declension which form the nom.
sing. by adding the suffix *s* to the stem are mostly feminine :
e. g. *hiem-s*, winter ; *cīvitā-s*, state ; *salū-s*, welfare ; *virtū-s*,
virtue (Class A (ii), § 26) ; *nāvi-s*, ship ; *caedē-s*, massacre
(Class B (i), § 28) ; *urb-s*, city ; *gen-s*, clan ; *cohor-s*, cohort
(Class B (ii), § 29).

[1] In a play of Plautus a lady is humorously called ' my delight, my life,
apple of my eye, tip of my lip, my salvation, my honey, my heart, my little
cream cheese '.
[2] The chief exceptions to these rules are given in the Appendix.

C

62 2. Those of the 3rd declension which form the nom. sing. without the addition of the suffix *s* are—

feminine if the nom. sing. ends in *tiō, tūdō, gō* :

e. g. *nātiō*, tribe ; *ōrātiō*, oration ; *multitūdō*, multitude, *orīgō*, origin ; *imāgō*, image (Class A (i), § 24).

Most other nouns in *tō* and *dō* are also feminine :

e. g. *legiō*, legion ; *formīdō*, terror.

NEUTER if the nom. sing ends in *MEN, US, UR, E,* $\{^{AL}_{AR}$:

e. g. *NŌMEN*, name ; *TEMPUS*, time ; *RŌBUR*, strength (Class A (i), § 25) ; *INSIGNE*, badge ; *MARE*, sea ; *ANIMAL*, animal ; *EXEMPLAR*, pattern (Class B (iii), § 30).

Note that these neuters in *us* differ from the feminines in *us* of § 39 in two ways : firstly, the *u* of the neuters is generally short, that of the feminines is always long ; secondly, the neuters have an *r* before the ending of gen. sing. Contrast *TEMPŬS, TEMPŎR-IS*, and *GENŬS, GENER-IS* with *salū-s, salūt-is.*

masculine in all other cases :

e. g. **labor,** labour ; **agger,** mound ; **sōl,** sun ; **mōs,** custom ; **pulvis,** dust ; **sermō,** discourse (Class A (i), § 24).

☞Test the above rule by referring to the nouns on pp. 26–9.

63 IV. Those of the 4th declension in **tus** and **sus** are all masculine :

e. g. **exercitus,** army ; **mōtus,** motion ; **ūsus,** use.

So too are most of the others of the 4th decl. in **us** ;

e. g. **currus,** chariot ; **gradus,** step.

The two or three of the 4th declension in *ū* are all neuter :

e. g. *GENŪ*, knee.

64 V. Those of the 5th declension are all feminine, except *diēs* (§ 54).

---

65 The above rules apply in general to nouns denoting kinds of animals, except that none of these are neuter. Those which would be neuter according to the above rules are masculine : e.g. **mūs,** mouse ; **vultur,** vulture. But some nouns denoting kinds of animals are masc. when they denote the male, and fem. when they denote the female : e. g. **bōs,** bull ; *bōs,* cow. Some have different forms to denote the two sexes : e. g. **equus,** horse ; *equa,* mare.

COMPARISON OF ADJECTIVES

56 The Comparative is regularly formed by adding *ior* (masc. and fem.), *ius* (neut.) to the part of the positive which remains when the ending of the genitive singular is removed.

The Superlative is generally formed by adding to the same part of the positive the endings *issimus* (masc.), *issima* (fem.), *issimum* (neut.) :

Positive	*Gen. Sing.*	*Comparative*	*Superlative*
cārus *dear*	cār-ī	cār-**ior,** -**ius** *dearer, too dear rather dear*	cār-**issimus** *dearest, most dear very dear*
brevis	brev-is	brev-**ior,** -**ius**	brev-**issimus**
ūtilis	ūtil-is	ūtil-**ior,** -**ius**	ūtil-**issimus**
nōbilis	nōbil-is	nōbil-**ior,** -**ius**	nōbil-**issimus**
ingens	ingent-is	ingent-**ior,** -**ius**	ingent-**issimus**

57 But in some adjectives the superlative is formed by adding the endings *imus* (masc.), *ima* (fem.), *imum* (neut.)—

(1) to the same part of the positive, with the final letter (*l*) doubled, in the four adjectives *facilis, gracilis, humilis, similis* ('easy', 'slender', 'lowly', 'like') and their compounds (*difficilis,* 'difficult', *dissimilis,* 'unlike') :

facilis	facil-is	facil-**ior,** -**ius**	facil-l-**imus**

(2) to the nom. sing. masc., with the final letter (*r*) doubled, in all adjectives whose nom. sing. masc. ends in *er* : thus—

līber	līber-ī	līber-**ior,** -**ius**	līber-r-**imus**
pulcher	pulchr-ī	pulchr-**ior,** -**ius**	pulcher-r-**imus**
ācer	ācr-is	ācr-**ior,** -**ius**	ācer-r-**imus**
celer	celer-is	celer-**ior,** -**ius** ·	celer-r-**imus**

68   Many verb-adjectives (present and perfect participles) have degrees of comparison formed regularly: e. g. amans, *loving*, amant-ior, amant-issimus ; parātus, *prepared, ready*, parāt-ior, parāt-issimus.

69   Adjectives in *us* preceded by a vowel making a separate syllable (*e-us, ı-us, u-us*) generally form the comparative and superlative by means of the adverbs *magis*, ' more ', and *maximē*, ' most ' :

pius, *faithful*   magis pius, a, um   maximē pius, a, um
idōneus, *suitable*   magis idōneus, a, um   maximē idōneus, a, um

70   A similar form of speech is always used to express the ideas of ' less ' and ' least ' :

cārus, *dear*   minus cārus, a, um   minimē cārus, a, um

For the declension of comparatives see § 49; superlatives are declined like other adjectives in *us, a, um*, § 18.

Irregular Comparatives and Superlatives

71 bonus, *good*   mel·ior, ·ius, *better*   optimus, *best*
malus, *bad*   pēior, pēius,[1] *worse*   pessimus, *worst*
magnus, *great*   māior, māius,[1] *greater*   maximus, *greatest*
parvus, *small*   min·or, ·us, *smaller*   minimus, *smallest*
multus, *much*   plūs (n.), *more*[2]   plūrimus, *most*
multī, *many*   plūr·ēs, ·a, *more*   plūrimī, *very many*
iuvenis, *young*   iūn·ior, *younger*   [nātū minimus, *younge*
senex, *aged*   sen·ior, *elder*   [nātū maximus, *eldest*]
novus, *new*   [recent·ior, ·ius, *fresher*]   novissimus, a, um, *last*
vetus (veter-), *old*   [vetust·ior, ·ius, *older*]   veterrimus, *oldest*
propinquus, *near*   prop·ior, ·ius, *nearer*   proximus, *nearest, nexı*

72   In the case of the following comparatives and superlatives the corresponding positive adjective does not exist, or is rare[3]:

---

[1] Two syllables (with *i* pronounced as *y*, § 7).

[2] The singular *plūs* is used like a noun : plūs vīnī, *more wine* (lit. *more of wine*). For the declension of *plūs* see § 50.

[3] In this list only the masc. is given; the fem. and neut. are formed regularly.

dēterior, *worse*	dēterrimus, *worst*
exterior, *outer*	extrēmus, *outermost*
inferior, *lower*	īmus infimus } *lowest*
interior, *inner*	intimus, *inmost*
posterior, *later*	postrēmus, *last*
prior, *former*	prīmus, *first*
superior, *higher*	suprēmus summus } *highest*
ulterior, *farther*	ultimus, *farthest*

FORMATION OF ADVERBS FROM ADJECTIVES

13 I. From adjectives declined like nouns of the 2nd declension (§§ 18–20) adverbs are mostly formed by adding *ē* to the part of the positive which remains when the ending of the gen. sing. is removed :—

Adjective	*Gen. Sing.*	*Adverb*
14 doctus *learned*	doct-ī	doct-ē *learnedly*
pulcher *fine*	pulchr-ī	pulchr-ē *finely*
līber *free, frank*	līber-ī	līber-ē *freely, frankly*

But in some cases *ō* is added instead of *ē* :

citus, *swift*; cito (shortened)
crēber, *frequent*; crēbrō
falsus, *false*; falsō
meritus, *deserved*; meritō
necessārius, *necessary*; necessāriō

rārus, *rare*; rārō
sērus, *late*; sērō
subitus, *sudden*; subitō
tūtus, *safe*; tūtō

Distinguish the following formations :
vērus, *true*; vērē, *truthfully*; vērō, *in truth, indeed*; vērum, *but, yet* (a conjunction).

certus, *certain*; certē, *at any rate* (ego certē sciō, *I at any rate know*); certō, *for certain* (certō sciō, *I know for certain*).

prīmus, *first*; prīmō, *at first* (of time; opposed to posteā, *afterwards*); prīmum, *first, in the first place* (French *premièrement*), cf. § 77.

75 II. From adjectives declined like nouns of the 3rd decl. (§§ 31–3) adverbs are mostly formed by adding *iter* to the part of the positive which remains when the ending of the gen. sing. is removed :—

brevis, *brief*	brev-is	brev-iter, *briefly*
fēlix, *lucky*	fēlīc-is	fēlīc-iter, *luckily*

Note audax, *bold*   audāc-is   audac-ter, *boldly*

76 But when the adjective has *nt* before *is* in the gen. sing., the adverb is formed by adding *er* instead of *iter*:

prūdens, *prudent*   prūdent-is   prūdent-er, *prudently*

77 III. Many adverbs are supplied by the accusative singular neuter of adjectives, especially adjectives of quantity and number: multum, *much*; aliquantum, *considerably*; nimium, *too much*; paulum, paululum, *a little*; quantum, *how much*; tantum, *so much* (or *only just so much*, hence *only*); sōlum, *only*; prīmum, *first, in the first place*; secundum, *secondly*; tertium, *thirdly*, &c. So also (from facilis) facile, *easily*, and all comparative adverbs (§ 78).

COMPARISON OF ADVERBS

78 The Comparative of adverbs formed from adjectives is supplied by the accusative singular neuter of the comparative adjective: the Superlative is formed by adding *ē* to the part of the superlative adjective which remains when the ending of the gen. sing. is removed :—

Positive	*Comparative*	*Superlative*
vērē, *truthfully*	vēr-ius, *more truthfully*	vērissim-ē, *most truthfully*
pulchrē, *finely*	pulchr-ius, *more finely*	pulcherrim-ē, *most finely*
crēbrō, *frequently*	crēbr-ius, *more frequently*	crēberrim-ē, *most frequently*
breviter, *briefly*	brev-ius, *more briefly*	brevissim-ē, *most briefly*

79 The following are irregular (either in the positive or in the comparative and superlative):

bene,[1] *well*	melius, *better*	optimē, *best*
male,[1] *badly*	pēius, *worse*	pessimē, *worst*
magnopere,[2] *greatly*	magis, *more*	maximē, *most*
multum, *much*	plūs, *more*	plūrimum, *most*
nōn multum } *little* parum	minus, *less*	minimē, *least*

diū, *long* (of time)	diūtius, *longer*	diūtissimē, *longest*
nūper, *lately*	[wanting]	nūperrimē, *most recently*
[wanting]	potius, *rather*	potissimum, *especially*
prope, *near*	propius, *nearer*	proximē, *next*
saepe, *often*	saepius, *oftener*	saepissimē, *oftenest*

80   NUMERAL ADJECTIVES

	CARDINAL some declinable	ORDINAL all declinable
I	ūnus, a, um (§ 86)	prīmus, a, um
II	duo, duae, duo (§ 89)	secundus, a, um *or* alter, alter-a, -um
III	trēs, tria (§ 89)	tertius, a, um
IV	quattuor	quartus, a, um
V	quinque	quintus, a, um
VI	sex	sextus, a, um
VII	septem	septimus, a, um
VIII	octō	octāvus, a, um
IX	novem	nōnus, a, um
X	decem	decimus, a, um
XX	vīgintī	vīcensimus, a, um
XXX	trīgintā	trīcensimus, a, um
XL	quadrāgintā	quadrāgensimus, a, um
L	quinquāgintā	quinquāgensimus, a, um
LX	sexāgintā	sexāgensimus, a, um
LXX	septuāgintā	septuāgensimus, a, um
LXXX	octōgintā	octōgensimus, a, um
XC	nōnāgintā	nōnāgensimus, a, um
C	centum	centensimus, a, um

[1] Note the short final *e* in these adverbs.
[2] *Magnopere = magnō opere* (from *opus* ' work', 3rd decl.).

CC	ducentī, ae, a [1]	ducentensimus, a, um
CCC	trecentī, ae, a	trecentensimus, a, um
CCCC	quadringentī, ae, a	quadringentensimus, a, um
D	quingentī, ae, a	quingentensimus, a, um
DC	sescentī, ae, a	sescentensimus, a, um
DCC	septingentī, ae, a	septingentensimus, a, um
DCCC	octingentī, ae, a	octingentensimus, a, um
DCCCC	nōngentī, ae, a	nōngentensimus, a, um
M	mille (§ 83)	millensimus, a, um

Compound forms of Numeral Adjectives.

(1) The numerals 11–19 :

		Cardinal.	Ordinal.
81	XI	ūndecim	ūndecimus
	XII	duodecim	duodecimus
	XIII	tredecim	tertius decimus
	XIV	quattuordecim	quartus decimus
	XV	quindecim	quintus decimus
	XVI	sēdecim	sextus decimus
	XVII	septendecim	septimus decimus
	XVIII	duodēvīgintī [2]	duodēvīcensimus
	XIX	ūndēvīgintī [2]	ūndēvīcensimus

82 (2) In compound numbers from 20–100 the smaller number is generally placed first with *et* 'and' (as in the English 'one-and-twenty'), but the other order without *et* (like 'twenty-one') is often found; in compound numbers above 100 the larger number is generally placed first (without *et*) :—

	Cardinal.	Ordinal.
XXI	ūnus (a, um) et vī-gintī *or* vīgintī ūnus (a, um)	ūnus (a, um) et vīcensi-mus (a, um) *or* vīcensi-mus (a, um) prīmus (a, um)
XXVIII	duodētrīgintā [2]	duodētrīcensimus (a, um)
XXIX	ūndētrīgintā [2]	ūndētrīcensimus (a, um)
CXXXIII	centum trīgintā trēs (tria)	centensimus (a, um) trī-censimus (a, um) ter-tius (a, um)

[1] The hundreds are declined regularly in the plural.

[2] Numbers compounded with 8 and 9 are generally expressed by means of *dē*, denoting subtraction ('two from twenty', 'one from twenty', &c.): except 98 *octō et nōnāgintā*, 99 *novem et nōnāgintā*.

Where *ūnus* occurs in compound numbers, it does not agree in number (though it does in gender and case) with the plural noun, e.g. *centum ūnus pedēs,* '101 feet'.

83 (3) Numbers above 1,000.

The numeral *mille,* 'thousand', is indeclinable in the singular and is an adjective: e.g. *mille hominēs,* 'a thousand men', *cum mille hominibus,* 'with a thousand men'; but the plural *mīlia,* 'thousands' (used in multiples of 1,000), is a neuter noun of the 3rd declension, declined like the plural of *insigne* (p. 25)—*mīlia, mīlium, mīlibus;* and it takes the genitive after it: e.g. *duo mīlia hominum,* lit. 'two thousands of men', i.e. '2,000 men'; *cum duōbus mīlibus hominum,* 'with 2,000 men'. But compound numbers containing hundreds as well as thousands (e.g. '3,333 men') do not need the genitive: *tria mīlia trecentī trīgintā trēs hominēs* or *tria mīlia hominum et trecentī trīgintā trēs.*

84 DISTRIBUTIVE ADJECTIVES	NUMERAL ADVERBS
answering the question 'how many apiece?' (*quotēnī?*)	answering the question 'how many times?' (*quotiens?*)
singulī, ae, a, *one apiece*	semel, *once*
bīnī, ae, a, *two apiece*	bis, *twice*
ternī (trīnī), ae, a, *three apiece*	ter, *thrice*
quaternī, ae, a, *four apiece*	quater, *four times*
quīnī, ae, a, *five apiece*	quinquiens, *five times*
sēnī, ae, a, *six apiece*	sexiens, *six times*
septēnī, ae, a, *seven apiece*	septiens, *seven times*
octōnī, ae, a, *eight apiece*	octiens, *eight times*
novēnī, ae, a, *nine apiece*	noviens, *nine times*
dēnī, ae, a, *ten apiece*	deciens, *ten times*
ūndēnī, ae, a, *eleven apiece*	ūndeciens, *eleven times*
duodēnī, ae, a, *twelve apiece*	duodeciens, *twelve times*
ternī dēnī, ae, a, *thirteen apiece*	terdeciens, *thirteen times*
duodēvīcēnī, ae, a, *eighteen apiece,* § 81	duodēvīciens, *eighteen times*

The others can be found from the cardinals by changing the ending: thus—

vīcēnī, ae, a, *20 apiece*
vīcēnī (ae, a) singulī (ae, a)
  21 apiece
trīcēnī, ae, a, *30 apiece*
quadrāgēnī, ae, a, *40 apiece*
  &c. (-*gēnī* for -*gintā*, § 80)
centēnī, ae, a, *100 apiece*
ducēnī, ae, a, *200 apiece*
trecēnī, ae, a, *300 apiece*
quadringēnī, ae, a, *400 apiece*
  &c. (-*gēnī* for -*gentī*, § 80)

vīciens, *20 times*
semel et vīciens, *21 times*
trīciens, *30 times*
quadrāgiens, *40 times*
  &c. (-*giens* for -*gintā*, § 80)
centiens, *100 times*
ducentiens, *200 times*
trecentiens, *300 times*
quadringentiens, *400 times*
  &c. (-*iens* for -*ī*, § 80)

Note—

singula mīlia, *1,000 apiece*	mīliens
bīna mīlia, *2,000 apiece*	bis mīliens
centēna mīlia, *100,000 apiece*	centiens mīliens
deciens centēna mīlia, *1,000,000 apiece*	deciens centiens mīliens

85 The distributives, except *singulī, ae, a,* are sometimes used as cardinals : (i) with plural nouns which have. singular meaning : bīna castra, *two camps*; (ii) in multiplication : bis bīna sunt quattuor, *twice two is* (or *are*) *four*; deciens centēna mīlia sestertium (gen. plur.), *ten times a hundred thousand sesterces* (= a million sesterces); (iii) in poetry, denoting a group : bīna pōcula, *a pair of cups.*

DECLENSION OF CERTAIN NUMERAL ADJECTIVES

86 **ūnus, sōlus, tōtus, ullus, nullus** (gen. sing. -ius, dat. sing. -ī).

ūnus, ūna, ūnum, *one* (or *alone, only*)

	Singular			Plural		
	masc.	*fem.*	*neut.*	*masc.*	*fem.*	*neut.*
Nom.	ūnus	ūna	ūnum	ūnī	ūnae	ūna
Voc.	ūne	ūna	ūnum	ūnī	ūnae	ūna
Acc.	ūnum	ūnam	ūnum	ūnōs	ūnās	ūna
Gen.		ūnīus		ūnōrum	ūnārum	ūnōrum
Dat.		ūnī			ūnīs	
Abl.	ūnō	ūnā	ūnō			

87 The plural of *ūnus* is used (1) in the sense of 'alone': *ūnī ex omnibus Sēquanī,* 'the Sequani alone of all'; *trēs ūnōs passūs ambulāvit,* 'he walked only three steps': (2) with

nouns whose plural has singular meaning, e. g. *ūna castra,*
'one camp'; *ūnae litterae,* 'one letter' (= *ūna epistula*).

88 'Like *ūnus, a, um* are declined the following adjectives of
kindred meaning:

sōlus	tōtus	ullus [1]	nullus [1]
alone	*whole*	*any at all*	*not any at all*

All these adjectives (including *ūnus*) are sometimes found with
a short *i* in the gen. sing. (*-ius*) in the poets, that form being more
convenient for some kinds of verse.—For examples showing the
meaning of *ullus* see § 116.

89 **duo, duae, duo,** *two*   **trēs, tria,** *three*

	masc.	fem.	neut.	masc. and fem.	neut.
Nom.	duo	duae	duo	trēs	tria
Acc.	duōs *or* duo	duās	duo		
Gen.	duōrum	duārum	duōrum	trium	
	or duum		*or* duum		
Dat. Abl.	}duōbus	duābus	duōbus	tribus	

90 Like *duo, duae, duo* is declined *ambō, ambae, ambō,* 'both'.

91 **alter, uter, neuter** (gen. sing. **-ius,** dat. sing. **-ī**).[2]

Alter, altera, alterum *one of the two* or *the second*

	Singular			Plural		
	masc.	fem.	neut.	masc.	fem.	neut.
Nom.	alter	altera	alterum	alterī	alterae	altera
Acc.	alterum	alteram	alterum	alterōs	alterās	altera
Gen.		alterīus		alterōrum	-ārum	-ōrum
Dat.		alterī				
Abl.	alterō	alterā	alterō		alterīs	

92 *Alter, a, um* always refers to *one of two* persons or things;
alterō oculō captus, *blinded in one eye.* When repeated,

---

[1] *Ullus* is a diminutive of *ūnus; nullus* is formed by prefixing *ně* 'not'.

[2] The gen. sing. of *alter, uter,* and *neuter* is often found with a short *i* in
the poets; cf. above on *ūnus, sōlus, tōtus, ullus* (§ 88).

the first *alter* means 'the one of the two', the second 'the other of the two': alter erat Rōmānus, alter Gallus.

The plural *alterī, ae, a* means 'one of two parties'; or, when repeated, 'the one of the two parties' . . . 'the other of the two parties': alterī erant Rōmānī, alterī Gallī.

93 The following adjectives of number are declined like *alter, altera, alterum*, except that the *e* of the nom. sing. masc. disappears in all the other forms:

(1) uter, utra, utrum, *which of the two?* (interrogative): utrō oculō captus erat?

Or *whichever of the two* (relative, cf. § 115): uter eōrum vītā superāverit, ad eum pars utrīusque pervenit, 'whichever of them survives, to him falls the share of both'.

The plural *utrī, ae, a* means 'which of the two parties?', or 'whichever of the two parties'.

94 So too is declined the first part of the compounds of *uter*, e. g. uter-que, utra-que, utrum-que, *either of the two = both*; utrōque oculō captus = ambōbus oculīs captus.

The plurals of such compounds refer to two *parties*.

95 (2) neuter, neutra, neutrum, *neither of the two*; plural neutrī, ae, a, *neither of the two parties*.

PERSONAL PRONOUNS

96   **First Person** (i. e. the person speaking).

	Singular		Plural	
Nom.	ego	*I*	nōs	*we*
Acc.	mē	*me*	nōs	*us*
Gen.	meī	*of me*	nostrī nostrum	*of us* *of us*
Dat.	mihi	*me, to me*	nōbīs	*us, to us*
Abl.	mē	*me*	nōbīs	*us*

97 **Second Person** (i. e. the person spoken to).

	Singular		Plural	
N., V.	tū	*thou* [1]	vōs [2]	*you, ye*
Acc.	tē	*thee*	vōs	*you, ye*
Gen.	tuī	*of thee*	{vestrī	*of you*
			{vestrum	*of you*
Dat.	tibi	*thee, to thee*	vōbīs	*you, to you*
Abl.	tē	*thee*	vōbīs	*you*

[1] or *you* (denoting one person).   [2] not used to denote one person.

98 The acc., gen., dat., and abl. of the 1st and the 2nd person may be used **reflexively,** i. e. may refer to the doer of the action denoted by the verb; they are then translated by *myself, thyself* (*yourself*), *ourselves, yourselves*: mē occīdam, *I will kill myself*; tē amās, *you love yourself* (= you are selfish).

99 **Third Person** (i. e. the person spoken of: *he, she, it*; *they*).

	Singular			Plural		
	masc.	*fem.*	*neut.*	*masc.*	*fem.*	*neut.*
Nom.	is	ea	id	iī	eae	ea
Acc.	eum	eam	id	eōs	eās	ea
Gen.		ēius		eōrum	eārum ·	eōrum
Dat.		eī		}	iīs	
Abl.	eō	eā	eō	}		

The *nom. sing.* and *plur.* is used only for the sake of emphasis or contrast.

The nom. and dat. and abl. plur. are sometimes spelled· eī, eīs.

100 In the third person there is, as in French, a separate

reflexive form for the acc., gen., dat., and abl. cases:

	Sing. and Plur. ; masc., fem., and neut.
Acc.	sē *or* sēsē *himself, herself, itself; themselves*
Gen.	suī *of himself, of herself, of itself; of themselves*
Dat.	sibi *to* (or *for*) *himself,* &c.
Abl.	sē *or* sēsē *himself,* &c.

EXAMPLES :—

Catō sē occīdit. *Cato killed himself* (committed *sui*-cide).

Homō nōn sibi sōlī nātus est, sed patriae. *A man is born not for himself alone, but for his country.*

101 Of the above forms of the genitive case (§§ 96–100) only *ēius* and *eōrum, eārum* have possessive meaning : liber ēius, *the book of him = his book.* The genitives in *ī* are used chiefly as genitives of the object ; mementō meī, *remember me* or *be mindful of me* ; memor sum tuī, *I am mindful of you* ; amor suī, *the love of self* ; odium vestrī, *the hatred of you = the feeling of hatred against you.* The genitives *nostrum* and *vestrum* are used chiefly as genitives of partition ; quis nostrum ? *who of us ?,* nēmō vestrum, *no one of you.*

The possessive meaning in the 1st and 2nd persons, and in the 3rd person when reflexive, is expressed by possessive adjectives (§ 103).

THE EMPHASIZING ADJECTIVE *IPSE*

102 **ipse** m., **ipsa** f., **ipsum** n., *-self,* differs from *sē* (§ 100) in two respects :

(i) it is an **emphasizing adjective or pronoun** ; *sē* is a reflexive pronoun : e. g. Brūtus fīliōs suōs ipse occīdit. *Brutus himself put his own sons to death.* Mulierem ipsam vīdī. *I saw the woman herself.*

(ii) it may agree with a pronoun (generally not expressed) of the 1st or 2nd as well as of the 3rd person, whereas *sē* refers only to the 3rd person : Ipse fēcī. *I did it myself.* Ipse fēcistī. *You did it yourself.* Ipse dixit. *He said it himself.* Ipsī diximus. *We said it ourselves,* &c.

	Singular			Plural		
Nom.	ipse	ipsa	ipsum	ipsī	ipsae	ipsa
Acc.	ipsum	ipsam	ipsum	ipsōs	ipsās	ipsa
Gen.		ipsīus		ipsōrum	ipsārum	ipsōrum
Dat.		ipsī				
Abl.	ipsō	ipsā	ipsō		ipsīs	

POSSESSIVE ADJECTIVES

03   Declined like other adjectives in *us, a, um* and *er, ra, rum* (§§ 18, 19), except that the voc. sing. masc. of *meus* is *mī*.

1st PERSON :   meus, a, um, *my* or (reflexive) *my own* ;
  noster, nostra, nostrum, *our* or (reflex.) *our own* ;

2nd PERSON :   tuus, a, um, *your* or (reflex.) *your own* ;
  vester, vestra, vestrum, *your* or (reflex.) *your own*;

3rd PERSON :   suus, a, um, *his own, her own, its own, their own* (reflex.).

EXAMPLES :

pater noster, patria nostra, consilium nostrum.

Līberōs meōs occīdit.   *He has killed my children.*

Mē et līberōs meōs occīdam.   *I will kill myself and my own children.*

Brūtum et fīliōs ēius (§ 101) occīdam.   *I will kill Brutus and his sons.*

Brūtus fīliōs suōs occīdit.   *Brutus killed his own sons.*

DEMONSTRATIVE ADJECTIVE AND PRONOUN

04   hic m., haec f., hoc n., *this*

	Singular			Plural		
Nom.	hic[1]	haec	hoc[1]	hī	hae	haec
Acc.	hunc	hanc	hoc	hōs	hās	haec
Gen.		hūius		hōrum	hārum	hōrum
Dat.		huic				
Abl.	hōc	hāc	hōc		hīs	

[1] The nom. sing. masc. and neut. are generally long syllables : see note at the foot of next page.

The *c* at the end of most of the above forms (§ 104) is a demonstrative suffix with the same force as the French *ci* in *ceci* and *celui-ci*; thus Lat. *hic* is literally 'this here'.

For the pronunciation of *hūius* and *huic* see § 7 and § 6.

All the following adjectives and pronouns (demonstrative, interrogative, indefinite, and relative, §§ 105–19) have the neuter nominative and accusative singular in d.[1]

OTHER DEMONSTRATIVE ADJECTIVES AND PRONOUNS

105 ille m., illa f., illud n., *that, yon*

	Singular			*Plural*		
Nom.	ille	illa	illud	illī	illae	illa
Acc.	illum	illam	illud	illōs	illās	illa
Gen.		illīus		illōrum	illārum	illōrum
Dat.		illī			illīs	
Abl.	illō	illā	illō			

106 iste m., ista f., istud n., *that, that of yours,* is declined exactly like *ille, illa, illud.*

107 is m., ea f., id n., *that, the* (unemphatic)

	Singular			*Plural*		
Nom.	is	ea	id	iī	eae	ea
Acc.	eum	eam	id	eōs	eās	ea
Gen.		ēius		eōrum	eārum	eōrum
Dat.		eī			iīs	
Abl.	eō	eā	eō			

[1] The demonstrative *hic, haec, hoc* (§ 104) had originally the *d*-formation in the neut. sing., and this explains how it is that *hoc* is a long syllable, though its vowel is short. The original form *hod-ce* became *hoc-ce, hocc*; and though the last *c* was dropped in writing it was pronounced before vowels, making the syllable long (see § 9, ii). The nom. sing. masc. *hic* became a long syllable by imitation of the neuter.

8   ī-dem m., ea-dem f., ĭ-dem n., *the same*
(literally, *that very one*)

	Singular			Plural		
Nom.	ĭdem	eadem	idem	īdem	eaedem	eadem
Acc.	eundem	eandem	idem	eōsdem	eāsdem	eadem
Gen.		ēiusdem		eōrundem	eārundem	eōrundem
Dat.		eīdem		} īsdem		
Abl.	eōdem	eādem	eōdem			

9   **alius m., alia f., aliud n.,** *other, another*

	Singular			Plural		
Nom.	alius	alia	aliud	aliī	aliae	alia
Acc.	alium	aliam	aliud	aliōs	aliās	alia
Gen.		alīus[1]		aliōrum	aliārum	aliōrum
Dat.		aliī		} aliīs		
Abl.	aliō	aliā	aliō			

[1] The gen. sing. is rarely used, being commonly replaced either by the adjective *aliēnus, a, um* or by the gen. of *alter, a, um* (§ 91) : aes. aliēnum, *debt,* lit. *money belonging to another*; domus alterīus, *one's neighbour's house.*

alius . . . alius, *one . . . another* : alius alium interfēcit.

INTERROGATIVE PRONOUN AND ADJECTIVE

10 **quis (mostly pron.)** \ **qui (mostly adj.)** } m., **quae** f., **quid (always pron.)** \ **quod (always adj.)** } n., *who ?, which ?, what ?*

The acc., gen., dat., and abl. are either pronouns or adjectives.

	Singular			Plural		
Nom.	{ quis \ quī	quae	{ quid \ quod	quī	quae	quae
Acc.	quem	quam	{ quid \ quod	quōs	quās	quae
Gen.		cūius		quōrum	quārum	quōrum
Dat.		cui		} quibus		
Abl.	quō	quā	quō			

Exx. : Quis vocat ? *Who is calling ?*

Quī puer vocat ? *What boy is calling ?*

Quae puella vocat? *What girl is calling ?*

All the forms in the above table except *quis* and *quid* may be not interrogative but exclamatory : quī sermōnēs! *what talk* (*there will be*)*!*

For the pronunciation of *cūius* and *cui* see § 7 and § 6.

INDEFINITE PRONOUNS AND ADJECTIVES

111   The Latin indefinite pronouns and adjectives are closely connected in form with the interrogatives (§ 110), but in meaning with numerals.   They denote *indefinite* number.[1]

(1) **quis** (quī) m., **quae** f., **quid** (quod) n., *anyone, any* ; declined like the interrogative (§ 110), except that the nom. sing. fem. and the nom. and acc. plur. neut. are generally shortened to *quă.*

Used after words like *sī,* 'if', *nisi,* 'unless', *nē,* 'not' or 'lest', *num,* 'whether' :

Sī quis quid rūmōre accēperit, ad magistrātum dēferat. *If anyone hears anything by report, he is to inform the magistrate.*

Nē qua multitūdō trans Rhēnum trādūcātur. *Let no mass of men be led across the Rhine.*

112   (2) Compounds of the above (§ 111) with an indeclinable part.

Forms in -*quis* and -*quid* are generally pronouns : forms in ·*quī,* ·*quae* (or -*qua*), -*quod* generally adjectives.

aliquis **aliquī** } m., **aliqua** f.,   **aliquid** **aliquod** } n. *someone, some.*

Exx. : Aliquem ad mē mitte. *Send someone to me.*

Cum aliquod bellum incidit, omnēs pugnant. *When some war arises, they all fight.*

---

[1] Other words of the same kind are *nēmō,* 'no one' and *nihil,* 'nothing', derived from *nĕ* 'not' and *hemō* (an Old Latin form of *homō,* ' man '), *hīlum,* 'a whit': *nēmō* = not a man ; *nihil* = not a whit.

13 quīdam m., quaedam f., quiddam (quoddam) n., *a certain, some* : declined with *n* instead of *m* before *d*.

Exx. : Quendam ad sē vocat. *He calls a certain man to him.*

Cum quibusdam adulescentibus conloquitur. *He converses with some young men.*

14 quīvīs m., quaevīs f., quidvīs (quodvīs) n.
quīlibet m., quaelibet f., quidlibet (quodlibet) n. } *any you like*
= *every* (·vīs from *volō*).

Exx. : Quīlibet haec facere potest. *Anyone* (= *every one*) *can do this.*

Nōn cuivīs hominī contingit adīre Corinthum. *It is not every one's good luck to visit Corinth.*

15 quisquam m. and f., quicquam (for quidquam) n. ; used like the English *anyone at all*, chiefly in negative and interrogative sentences (no plural).

Exx. : Nē quemquam ōderīs. *Do not hate anyone at all.*

Cūr quicquam sibi postulat ? *Why does he demand anything at all for himself ?*

16 The adjective which corresponds in meaning (= *any at all*) is *ullus, a, um* (declined like *ūnus, a, am*, § 86).

Exx. : Neque ullam vōcem exprimere poterat. *Nor could he utter a single word.*

Sine ullō maleficiō abībimus. *We shall depart without any wrong-doing at all.*

17 quisque m., quaeque f., quidque (quodque) n., *each one, each.*

Exx. : Quaerunt quid quisque eōrum dē quāque rē audierit. *They inquire what each one of them has heard about each matter.*

Māteria cūiusque generis in Britanniā est. *There is timber of each* (= *every*) *kind in Britain.*

18 quispiam m., quaepiam f., quidpiam (quodpiam) n., *someone or other.*

Exx. : Cum quaepiam cohors ex orbe excesserat, hostēs refugiēbant. *Whenever some cohort or other quitted the circle, the enemy fled.*

Dixerit quispiam . . . *Somebody is likely to say . . .*

RELATIVE PRONOUN AND ADJECTIVE

119 The relative pronoun and adjective are connective; i. e. they introduce a new clause with a verb of its own, like a conjunction. The word in the other clause to which the relative refers is called the antecedent.

quī m., quae f., quod n., *who, which*

	Singular			*Plural*		
Nom.	quī	quae	quod	quī	quae	quae
Acc.	quem	quam	quod	quōs	quās	quae
Gen.		cūius		quōrum	quārum	quōrum
Dat.		cui			quibus	
Abl.	quō	quā	quō			

The relative need not stand as near as possible to its antecedent, as it does in French and generally in English :

Examples :

Cōrus ventus nāvigātiōnem impediēbat, quī in hīs locīs flāre consuēvit. *The NW. wind, which is wont to blow in these parts, was stopping navigation.*

Pulvis in eā parte vidēbātur in quam (*or* quam in partem) legiō iter fēcerat. *Dust was seen in that* (or *the*) *direction in which the legion had marched.*

Cum quibusdam adulescentibus conloquitur, quōrum erat princeps Litaviccus atque frātrēs ēius. *He converses with certain young men, the chief of whom were Litaviccus and his brothers.*

120 In the above instances the clause introduced by the relative is subordinate ; in the following it is co-ordinate :

Magnum numerum obsidum imperat : quibus adductīs Morinōs in fidem recēpit. *He demands a great number of hostages : which having been brought to him* (= and when they had been brought to him), *he admitted the Morini to his protection* (B. G. iv. 22. 2). Instead of *quibus adductīs* Caesar might have

written *et his adductis* or *qui* (= et hi) *cum adducti essent.*
Compare B. G. vii. 5. 4.

21   NOTES.—1. An old ablative (sing. and plur., all genders) is
qui, which is generally used as an adverb meaning 'how' or
'why', but sometimes as a rel. pron., *e. g.* quicum, *with whom.*

2. Another form of the dat. and abl. plur. is *quis* (in poets).

3. Latin has two generalizing relatives, meaning 'whoever',
'whatever': (i) quicumque m., quaecumque f., quodcumque
n.—compounds of *qui, quae, quod,* § 119; (ii) quisquis m., f.,
quidquid n.—doubled form of an old-fashioned relative *quis,
quid.*

22   TABLE OF CORRESPONDING WORDS

In the following table—

(1) the relatives correspond to the demonstratives; e. g.
Tantam eōrum multitūdinem interfēcērunt quantum fuit diēī
spatium. *They killed* as great *a number of them* as *was the
length of the day.*[1] Duae nāvēs eōsdem portūs quōs reliquae
capere nōn potuērunt. *Two ships could not make* the same
ports as *the rest.* Dixērunt sē ibi futūrōs esse ubi Caesar
voluisset. *They said they would be* there where *Caesar
wished.*

(2) The adverbs correspond to the pronouns—demonstrative to demonstrative and relative to relative: for instance,
ibi *there* (= in eō locō) corresponds to is *that,* and ubi *where*
(= quō in locō) to quī *which.*

23   Note the English word 'as' in the table:

(i) with relative or conjunctive meaning (in the second
and the fourth columns);

(ii) with demonstrative meaning (in the first and the
third columns).

---

[1] i. e. 'as the day was long'. The sentence means that the number of the
slain was proportionate to the length of the day.

124 Demonstrative Pronouns and Adjectives	Relative Pronouns and Adjectives	Demonstrative Adverbs	Relative Adverbs and Subordinating Conjunctions
hic, haec, hoc, *this*		hīc, *here* hūc, *hither* hinc, *hence*	
ille, illa, illud *that, yon*		illīc, *there* illūc, *thither* illinc, *thence*	
is, ea, id *that, the*	quī, quae, quod *who, which*	ibi, *there* eō, *thither* inde, *thence*	ubi, *where* quō, *whither* unde, *whence*
īdem, eadem, idem *the same*		ibīdem, *in* eōdem, *to* indidem, *from* } *the same place*	
iste, ista, istud *that of yours*		istīc, *there* istūc, *thither* istinc, *thence*	
tantus, a, um *so great, as great*	quantus, a, um *as*	tantopere *so much*	quantopere *as*
tālis, e *of such a kind*	quālis, e *as*	tam, *so* (before adjectives and adverbs) ita, sīc, adeō, *so* (before verbs)	quam, *as* ut, *as*
tot, *so many, as many*	quot, *as*	totiens, *so many times, as many times*	quotiens, *as*

THE VERB

I. Meanings of Voices, Moods, and Tenses.

125 **Voices.** There are two voices in Latin:

1. The **Active Voice,** which is used either transitively or intransitively:

    nuntium vocat, *he calls the messenger* (trans.).
    quis vocat ? *who is calling ?* (intrans.).

2. The **Passive Voice** :

nuntius vocātur, *the messenger is called.*

vocātur ad arma, *there is a call to arms* (impersonal passive construction ; literally *it is called to arms*).

6 **Moods and their Tenses.**

1. The **Indicative Mood** relates to matters of fact :

vocat, *he is calling.*

num vocat ? *is he calling ?*

7 There are six tenses of the Indicative.

The Present, the Past Imperfect and the Future are tenses of incomplete action :

Present : vocat, *he is calling*[1] or *he calls* (habitually).

Past Imperfect : vocābat, *he was calling* or *he called* (habitually = *he used to call*).

Future : vocābit, *he will call* or *will be calling.*

8 The Perfect, the Past Perfect and the Future Perfect are tenses of completed action :

Perfect : vocāvit, used either (i) as a Present Perfect, marking the action as completed at the time of speaking : *he has called* ;

or (ii) as a Past Historic, marking the action as having taken place in the past (i.e. before the time of speaking) : *he called.*[2]

Past Perfect : vocāverat, *he had called.*

Future Perfect : vocāverit, *he will have called.*

9 2. The **Imperative Mood** is used like the English imperative, and has in addition a 3rd person (sing. and plur.). It has two forms of the 2nd person (singular and plural) :

a short form : vocā ⎰
a long form : vocātō ⎱ *call.*

---

[1] The Present is most commonly translated by the English Present Continuous, except in verbs that denote a *state* as distinct from an *act.*

[2] Used like the French Past Historic : *il appela, il s'écria.*

130   3. The **Subjunctive Mood** has the same kind of meaning as the English subjunctive, but is more widely used.[1] It has four tenses, which are translated in different ways, according to the context in which they stand. Their uses will be given later (Syntax, §§ 318-67). Meanwhile note the following translations, which, though they are not applicable to all usages, express the fundamental meanings of the tenses of the subjunctive, and will serve as a clue to their more difficult uses :—

> **Present Subj.**: vocet, *he call, he is to call, he shall call.* Compare the Fut. Indic.: vocābit, *he will call*, which expresses no more than future time. The Pres. Subj. combines the idea of obligation with that of future time.

> **Perfect Subj.**: vocāverit, *he have called, he shall have called*. Compare the Fut. Perf. Indic. (which has the same form in this person) : vocāverit, *he will have called.*

The Past and the Past Perfect Subjunctive have the corresponding meanings in past time :

> **Past Subj.** : vocāret, *he was to call, he should call.*
> (a kind of Future in the past)

> **Past Perf. Subj.** : vocāvisset, *he should have called.*
> (a kind of Future Perfect in the past)

---

[1] Examples of the English Present Subjunctive (from Shakespeare) denoting what *is to be done*.—Call him my king ? (= Am I to call him my king?).—Somebody call (= somebody is to call, let somebody call) my wife.— Now call we (= let us call) our high court of parliament.—Look you call (= look: you are to call) me Ganymede.—Past Subjunctive (from a daily paper) :—No cabinet would be able to endure the odium attaching to a government which called upon us to make peace on such terms (*called = should call*)

131   But in some uses the *shall*-meaning of the tenses of the subjunctive is modified: sometimes they denote what *would be done* or *would have been done* under certain conditions:

vocem, vocēs, vocet   } *I should (you would, he*
vocārem, vocārēs, vocāret } *would) call.*
vocāvissem, vocāvissēs, vocāvisset, *I should (you would, he would) have called.*

In some subordinate clauses they may be translated by English indicatives of the corresponding tense: e. g. Quis vocet (vocāverit) nesciō. *I do not know who is calling (has called).*

132   II. **Meanings of Verb · Adjectives and Verb · Nouns** (formed from the stem of the verb).

1. The three **Participles**, called (i) Present (ii) Perfect (iii) Future, mark the action as (i) *going on* or *not completed* (ii) *completed* (iii) *in prospect*:

Present Participle Active: vocans (-nt-), *calling.*
Perfect Participle Passive: vocātus, a, um, *called.*
Future Participle Active: vocātūrus, a, um, *about to call.*

Note the absence of a Perfect Participle Active, a Present Participle Passive and a Future Participle Passive.

133   2. The **Gerund Adjective** is a passive verb-adjective, marking the action as *to be done*: vocandus, a, um, *to-be-called*:

Nuntius revocandus est. *The messenger is to be called back* (= must be called back).

Mīlitēs ab opere revocandī erant. *The soldiers had to be* (lit. *were to be) called back from their work.*

The nom. sing. neut. of the gerund adjective is used with a tense of *esse* in an impersonal passive construction (cf. § 125, 2):

Magnā vōce vocandum est. *We must call* (lit. *It is to be called) with a loud voice.*

Magnā vōce vocandum erat. *We had to call* (lit. *It was to be called) with a loud voice.*

In some cases the Gerund Adjective may be translated by an English adjective in *-able* or *-ible*, where these adjectives have passive meaning :

liber laudandus, *a laudable book, a praiseworthy book.*
homō contemnendus, *a contemptible person.*

134   3. The **Infinitives** called (i) Present (ii) Perfect (iii) Future mark the action as (i) *going on* or *not completed* (ii) *completed* (iii) *in prospect* :

ACTIVE	PASSIVE
Present Infin. : vocāre, *to call, to be calling.*	vocārī, *to be called.*
Future Infin. : vocātūrus (a, um) esse, *to be about to call.*	vocātum īrī (§ 137), *to be about to be called.*
Perfect Infin. : vocāvisse, *to have called.*	vocātus (a, um) esse, *to have been called.*

135   4. The **Gerund** is an Active Verb-Noun of the neuter gender, corresponding to the English verb-noun in *-ing*, and denoting *the act of —ing* ; it is used only in the singular number and chiefly in the genitive and the ablative cases :

vocandī causā, *for the sake of calling.*
vocandō, *by calling.*

It has no nominative case.[1]

136   5. The **Supine in -um** is the Accusative Case of a Verb-Noun of the 4th declension (Nom. vocātus, *a calling, a call*) ; the Accusative here denotes the end in view or purpose :

vocātum, *to call* (lit. *with a view to calling*).
Vēnērunt rogātum ut sibi ignosceret. *They came to ask that he should pardon them.*

137   The combination of the Supine in -um with the Present Infinitive Passive of *eō* ' I go ' is equivalent to a Future Infinitive Passive :[2]

Nōn crēdō mīlitēs revocātum īrī. *I don't think that the*

---

[1] The form in *-um* given in the following tables (§ 139, &c.) is the Accusative, which is used after certain prepositions (chiefly *ad*).
[2] This construction is impersonal : see Syntax, § 377.

soldiers will be called back (lit. *I do not believe there to
be a going with a view to calling back the soldiers*).
Many verbs have no supine in -um.

38   A few verbs have also a **Supine in ·ū,** which is an Ablative
or Dative or Locative case of a Verb-Noun of the 4th declension ; but supines in -ū are very rare :
     facile factū, *an easy thing to do.*
     Difficile dictū est. *It is difficult to say.*

The following tables show the principal translations
of the moods, tenses, verb-nouns, and verb-adjectives in
the active voice of two verbs: (1) the verb *vocō,* '**I call,**'
(2) the verb *sum,* '**I am,**' which is used in two ways:

     (i) with full meaning, in sentences like *Sum pius Aenēās*
'I am the faithful Aeneas'; *Est profectō deus quī quae nōs
gerimus audit et videt* 'There is (= *exists*) assuredly a god
who hears and sees what we are doing' (Plautus, *The Captives,*
313).

     (ii) as an auxiliary verb, which, when joined with the Perfect
Participle Passive, forms the tenses of completed action of the
Passive Voice (§ 158).

VOCO—Active Voice

139 | Tenses of incomplete action—Stem vocā·

INDICATIVE	IMPERATIVE
Present	
vocō *I am calling*	
vocās *you are calling*	vocā, vocātō *call*
vocat *he is calling*	vocātō *let him call*
vocāmus *we are calling*	
vocātis *you are calling*	vocāte, vocātōte *call*
vocant *they are calling*	vocantō *let them call*
or *I call*, &c., § 127	
	SUBJUNCTIVE
Future	**Present**
vocābō *I shall call*	vocem
vocābis *you will call*	vocēs
vocābit *he will call*	vocet
vocābimus *we shall call*	vocēmus
vocābitis *you will call*	vocētis
vocābunt *they will call*	vocent
or *I shall be calling*, &c., § 127	*For the meanings see* §§ 130, 131
Past Imperfect	**Past**
vocābam *I was calling*	vocārem
vocābās *you were calling*	vocārēs
vocābat *he was calling*	vocāret
vocābāmus *we were calling*	vocārēmus
vocābātis *you were calling*	vocārētis
vocābant *they were calling*	vocārent
or *I called* (habitually), = *used to call*, &c., § 127	*For the meanings see* §§ 130, 131

VERB-ADJS.	**Pres. Part.** vocans (-nt-) *calling*	**Fut. Part.** vocātūrus, a, um *about to call*
VERB-NOUNS	**Pres. Infin.** vocāre *to call*	**Fut. Infin.** vocātūrus (a, um) esse *to be about to call*
	Gerund vocandum [*the act of*] *calling*	**Supine** vocātum [*with a view*] *to call*

VOCO—ACTIVE VOICE (continued)

40

Tenses of completed action—Stem vocāv-	
INDICATIVE	*IMPERATIVE*
PERFECT	
vocāvī *I have called*	
vocāvistī *you have called*	
vocāvit *he has called*	[None]
vocāvimus *we have called*	
vocāvistis *you have called*	
vocāvērunt (-ēre) *they have called*	
or *I called*, &c., § 128	*SUBJUNCTIVE*
FUTURE PERFECT	PERFECT
vocāverō *I shall have* ⎫	vocāverim
vocāveris [1] *you will have* ⎪	vocāverīs [2]
vocāverit *he will have* ⎪ *called*	vocāverit
vocāverimus [1] *we shall have* ⎬	vocāverīmus [2]
vocāveritis [1] *you will have* ⎪	vocāverītis [2]
vocāverint *they will have* ⎭	vocāverint
	For the meanings see §§ 130, 131
PAST PERFECT	PAST PERFECT
vocāveram *I had* ⎫	vocāvissem
vocāverās *you had* ⎪	vocāvissēs
vocāverat *he had* ⎪ *called*	vocāvisset
vocāverāmus *we had* ⎬	vocāvissēmus
vocāverātis *you had* ⎪	vocāvissētis
vocāverant *they had* ⎭	vocāvissent
	For the meanings see §§ 130, 131
VERB-ADJ.	[None]
VERB-NOUN	PERF. INFIN. vocāvisse *to have called*

[1] *ĭ often lengthened.*   [2] *ī often shortened.*

The same statements apply in all other verbs [see Appendix].

SUM

141 | Tenses of incomplete action

INDICATIVE	IMPERATIVE
PRESENT	
sum *I am*	
es *you are*	es, estō *be*
est *he is*	estō *let him be*
sumus *we are*	
estis *you are*	este, estōte *be*
sunt *they are*	suntō *let them be*

	SUBJUNCTIVE
FUTURE	PRESENT
erō *I shall be*	sim *I be*
eris *you will be*	sīs *you be*
erit *he will be*	sit *he be*
erimus *we shall be*	sīmus *we be*
eritis *you will be*	sītis *you be*
erunt *they will be*	sint *they be*
	[*Other translations in* §§ 130, 131]
PAST IMPERFECT	PAST
eram *I was*	essem *I were*
erās *you were*	essēs *you were*
erat *he was*	esset *he were*
erāmus *we were*	essēmus *we were*
erātis *you were*	essētis *you were*
erant *they were*	essent *they were*
	[*Other translations in* §§ 130, 131]

VERB-ADJ.	[No Pres. Part.] FUT. PART. futūrus, a, um *about to be*
VERB-NOUNS	PRES. INFIN. esse FUT. INFIN. {fore [1] {futūrus (a, um) esse *to be* *to be about to be* [No Gerund]

[1] *Fore* is the only non-compounded fut. infin. which exists in Latin. It also serves as a fut. infin. to *fīo* (§ 246). From the same stem comes a by-form of the Past Subjunctive : forem, forēs, foret ; forent = *I should be, you would be,* &c.

SUM (continued)

42	Tenses of completed action—Stem fu·	
	INDICATIVE	*IMPERATIVE*

<table>
<tr><td colspan="2">

INDICATIVE

PERFECT

fuī *I have been*
fuistī *you have been*
fuit *he has been*
fuimus *we have been*
fuistis *you have been*
fuērunt (-ēre) *they have been*
   or *I was, you were, he was*, &c., § 128
</td><td>

IMPERATIVE

[None]
</td></tr>
</table>

FUTURE PERFECT   *SUBJUNCTIVE*

FUTURE PERFECT	SUBJUNCTIVE — PERFECT
fuerō *I shall have been*	fuerim
fueris *you will have been*	fuerīs
fuerit *he will have been*	fuerit
fuerimus *we shall have been*	fuerīmus
fueritis *you will have been*	fuerītis
fuerint *they will have been*	fuerint
	For the meanings see §§ 130, 131
PAST PERFECT	PAST PERFECT
fueram *I had been*	fuissem
fuerās *you had been*	fuissēs
fuerat *he had been*	fuisset
fuerāmus *we had been*	fuissēmus
fuerātis *you had been*	fuissētis
fuerant *they had been*	fuissent
	For the meanings see §§ 130, 131

VERB-ADJ.	[None]
VERB NOUN	PERF. INFIN. fuisse *to have been*

143 III. Formation of moods, tenses, verb-adjectives and verb-nouns.

The personal inflexions of the active voice in all tenses of the indicative and subjunctive, except the perfect indicative, are as follows :

Sing.	1.	·ō or ·m	Plur. 1.	·mus
	2.	·s	2.	·tis
	3.	·t	3.	·nt

See the tables of *vocō* and *sum* (§§ 139–42).

Two of these inflexions are seen in English verbs—the *m* of the 1st pers. sing. in the verb 'am', and the *t* of the 3rd pers. sing. in forms like 'love*th*'. Three of them survive in some French verbs : *tu cour-s, il cour-t, ils coure-nt.*

144 The four conjugations.

Latin verbs are divided into four conjugations,[1] which are distinguished by their characteristic vowels (seen in the present infinitive active) :

1st CONJ.	Pres. Infin. Act.	vocāre,	*to call*
2nd CONJ.	„ „ „	habēre,	*to have, to hold*
3rd CONJ.	„ „ „	regĕre,	*to rule, to guide*
4th CONJ.	„ „ „	audīre,	*to hear*

145 By removing the *re* of the pres. infin. act. may be found the **stem** from which the tenses of incomplete action are formed, and which is found unchanged in most forms :

EXAMPLES :

	Stem	Imperative Active	Imperative Passive	Past Subj. Act.	Past Subj. Pass.
1st CONJ.	**vocā·**	vocā	vocā-re	vocā-rem	vocā-rer
2nd CONJ.	**habē·**	habē	habē-re	habē-rem	habē-rer
3rd CONJ.	**rege·**	rege	rege-re	rege-rem	rege-rer
4th CONJ.	**audī·**	audī	audī-re	audī-rem	audī-rer

---

[1] These do not include a very important group of verbs which belong partly to the 4th, partly to the 3rd Conjugation (Mixed Conjugation, § 159).

But in many of the forms belonging to the tenses of incomplete action the stem suffers modifications; in some forms its final vowel is shortened, as in *voca-t, habe-t, audi-t*; in others it is changed, as in *regi-t, regu-nt.* Some of the forms of the 3rd and 4th conjugations are got from imitation of the 2nd conjugation; so *regē-bam, audi-ē-bam.* It is, therefore, necessary to learn these tenses separately in the separate conjugations. They are given side by side in §§ 149, 150 for purposes of comparison.

6 The tenses of completed action have exactly the same endings in all the four conjugations, which differ only in the formation of the stem from which these tenses come. Here all the conjugations can be learned together: see § 151.

17 The stem of the perfect tenses active is formed—

in most verbs of the 1st and 4th conjugations by adding the suffix *v* to the stems in *ā* and *ī*: **vocā-v-, audī-v-;**

in most verbs of the 2nd conjugation by adding *v* to the stem in *ē* (here shortened to *ĕ*); but the *v* amalgamates with the *ĕ* so as to form *ŭ*: **habu-;**

in most verbs of the 3rd conjugation from a stem which has no final vowel, e. g. *reg-.* To this stem the suffix *s* is very commonly added: **rex-** (for *reg-s-*).[1]

18 The stem of the perfect participle passive is formed—

in most verbs of the 1st and 4th conjugations by adding the suffix *t*[2] to the stems in *ā* and *ī*: **vocā-t-, audī-t-;**

in most verbs of the 2nd conjugation by adding *t* to the stem in *ē* (here shortened to *ĭ*): **habi-t-;**

in most verbs of the 3rd conjugation by adding *t* to a stem which has no final vowel: **rec-t-** (for *reg-t-*).

---

[1] Other ways of forming the perf. act. and the perf. part. pass. are given in §§ 171, 172.

[2] This *t* is the same as the *t* or *d* which is used to form the past participle of most English verbs: dwel*t*, los*t*, hear*d*. The *t* which is found in the future participle active and the supine is of different origin, being the same as that which is used in nouns of the 4th declension. Hence these forms have no sense of completion: vocātūrus = *about to call*, not *about to have called*.

THE FOUR CONJUGATIONS—ACTIVE VOICE

149	**Tenses of incomplete action**			
	1st CONJ.	2nd CONJ.	3rd CONJ.	4th CONJ.
STEM	vocā-, *call*	habē-, *have, hold*	rege-, *rule*	audī-, *hear*

INDICATIVE

	1st CONJ.	2nd CONJ.	3rd CONJ.	4th CONJ.
PRESENT	vocō	habeō	regō	audiō
	vocās	habēs	regis	audīs
	vocat	habet	regit	audit
	vocāmus	habēmus	regimus	audīmus
	vocātis	habētis	regitis	audītis
	vocant	habent	regunt	audiunt
FUTURE	vocābō	habēbō	regam	audiam
	vocābis	habēbis	regēs	audiēs
	vocābit	habēbit	reget	audiet
	vocābimus	habēbimus	regēmus	audiēmus
	vocābitis	habēbitis	regētis	audiētis
	vocābunt	habēbunt	regent	audient
PAST IMPERFECT	vocābam	habēbam	regēbam	audiēbam
	vocābās	habēbās	regēbās	audiēbās
	vocābat	habēbat	regēbat	audiēbat
	vocābāmus	habēbāmus	regēbāmus	audiēbāmus
	vocābātis	habēbātis	regēbātis	audiēbātis
	vocābant	habēbant	regēbant	audiēbant

VERB-ADJECTIVES AND VERB-NOUNS

	1st CONJ.	2nd CONJ.	3rd CONJ.	4th CONJ.
PR. PT.	vocans (-nt-)	habens (-nt-)	regens (-nt-)	audiens (-nt-)
FUT. PT.	vocātūrus, a, um	habitūrus, a, um	rectūrus, a, um	audītūrus, a, um
PR. INF.	vocāre	habēre	regere	audīre
GER.	vocandum	habendum	regendum	audiendum
FUT. INF.	vocātūrus (a, um) esse	habitūrus (a, um) esse	rectūrus (a, um) esse	audītūrus (a, um) esse
SUP.	vocātum	habitum	rectum	audītum

The Four Conjugations—Active Voice (continued)

	1st Conj.	2nd Conj.	3rd Conj.	4th Conj.
Stem	**vocā-,** *call*	**habē-,** *have*	**rege-,** *rule*	**audī-,** hear

Tenses of incomplete action (continued)

IMPERATIVE

	1st Conj.	2nd Conj.	3rd Conj.	4th Conj.
S. 2	vocā	habē	rege	audī
	vocātō	habētō	regitō	audītō
3	vocātō	habētō	regitō	audītō
P. 2	vocāte	habēte	regite	audīte
	vocātōte	habētōte	regitōte	audītōte
3	vocantō	habentō	reguntō	audiuntō

SUBJUNCTIVE

Present				
	vocem	habeam	regam	audiam
	vocēs	habeās	regās	audiās
	vocet	habeat	regat	audiat
	vocēmus	habeāmus	regāmus	audiāmus
	vocētis	habeātis	regātis	audiātis
	vocent	habeant	regant	audiant

Past				
	vocārem	habērem	regerem	audīrem
	vocārēs	habērēs	regerēs	audīrēs
	vocāret	habēret	regeret	audīret
	vocārēmus	habērēmus	regerēmus	audīrēmus
	vocārētis	habērētis	regerētis	audīrētis
	vocārent	habērent	regerent	audīrent

THE FOUR CONJUGATIONS—ACTIVE VOICE (continued)

151

Tenses of completed action
Stems vocāv-, habu-, rex-, audīv-

INDICATIVE	IMPERATIVE

INDICATIVE

PERFECT

vocāv-, habu-, rex-, audīv-
S. 1. -ī   P. 1. -imus
   2. -istī   2. -istis
   3. -it   3. -ērunt
                  or -ēre

IMPERATIVE

[None]

SUBJUNCTIVE

FUTURE PERFECT

vocāv-, habu-, rex-, audīv-
S. 1. -erō   P. 1. -erimus [1]
   2. -eris [1]   2. -eritis [1]
   3. -erit   3. -erint

PERFECT

vocāv-, habu-, rex-, audīv-
S. 1. -erim   P. 1. -erīmus [2]
   2. -erīs [2]   2. -erītis [2]
   3. -erit   3. -erint

PAST PERFECT

vocāv-, habu-, rex-, audīv-
S. 1. -eram   P. 1. -erāmus
   2. -erās   2. -erātis
   3. -erat   3. -erant

PAST PERFECT

vocāv-, habu-, rex-, audīv-
S. 1. -issem   P. 1. -issēmus
   2. -issēs   2. -issētis
   3. -isset   3. -issent

VERB-NOUN

PERFECT INFINITIVE

vocāv-, habu-, rex-, audīv-
-isse

THE PASSIVE VOICE

152 The passive forms of the tenses of incomplete action (indicative, imperative, and subjunctive) may be found from the active forms in all the four conjugations by adding the following endings and making some changes (i, ii, iii below):

---

[1] *i* often lengthened (§ 140).   [2] *ī* often shortened (§ 140).

Endings.—Indic., Subj. and short forms of the Imperative:

S. 1. r	P. 1. r	In P. 2 **mini** is
2. **ris** or **re**		substituted for
3. **ur**	3. **ur**	-*tis* and -*te*

Long forms of the Imperative, 2nd and 3rd persons, r.

(i) where the active form ends in a consonant and the passive ending begins with *r*, the last consonant of the active is dropped; (ii) the stem vowels, *a, e, i* of the 1st, 2nd, and 4th conjugation recover their length in some of the forms in which they are shortened in the active; (iii) a final *ō* in the active is shortened to *ŏ* in the passive; (iv) a short *ĭ* before *s* in the active becomes *ĕ* in the passive.

Examples: vocō, vocŏ-r ; vocem, voce-r (*m* dropped);
vocāmus, vocāmu-r (*s* dropped).
vocās, vocā-ris (*s* dropped); vocātis, vocā-minī.
vocat, vocāt-ur (*a* long); vocant, vocant-ur.
vocā, vocā-re ; vocāte, vocā-minī.
vocābis, vocābe-ris ; regis, rege-ris.

53 The passive tenses of completed action are formed by combining the perfect participle passive with tenses of the verb *sum* (§ 141). The participle, being an adjective, agrees in gender number and case with the subject of the sentence or clause: populus Rōmānus ad arma vocātus est, *the Roman nation has been* (lit. *is*) *called to arms*; māter Gracchōrum vocāta est Cornēlia, *the mother of the Gracchi was called Cornelia*; nūmina magna vocāta sunt, *the great deities were invoked*. The sense of completed action is given not by the verb *sum* but by the participle: vocātus sum, *I am a called person* (i. e. a person who has been called). Compare in English 'All these articles are sold'='All these articles have been sold'. *Vocātus sum* is properly a present perfect (= Engl. *I have been called*), but it came to have the same double use as the perfect active (§ 128); as a past historic it is translated *I was called*.

VOCOR—Passive Voice

154 | Tenses of incomplete action—Stem vocā-

INDICATIVE	IMPERATIVE
Present	
vocor *I am being called*	
vocāris[1] *you are being called*	vocāre, vocātor *be called*
vocātur *he is being called*	vocātor *let him be called*
vocāmur *we are being called*	
vocāminī *you are being called*	vocāminī *be called*
vocantur *they are being called*	vocantor *let them be called*
or *I am called*, &c., § 127	

	SUBJUNCTIVE
Future	**Present**
vocābor *I shall be called*	vocer
vocāberis[1] *you will be called*	vocēris[1]
vocābitur *he will be called*	vocētur
vocābimur *we shall be called*	vocēmur
vocābiminī *you will be called*	vocēminī
vocābuntur *they will be called*	vocentur
	For the meanings see §§ 130, 131

Past Imperfect	**Past**
vocābar *I was being*	vocārer
vocābāris[1] *you were being* ⎞	vocārēris[1]
vocābātur *he was being*	vocārētur
vocābāmur *we were being*	vocārēmur
vocābāminī *you were being*	vocārēminī
vocābantur *they were being* ⎠ *called*	vocārentur
or *I was called* (habitually) = *used to be called*, § 127	*For the meanings see* §§ 130, 131

VERB-ADJ.	Gerund Adj. vocandus, a, um *to-be-called*

VERB-NOUNS	Pres. Infin. vocārī *to be called*
	Fut. Infin. vocātum īrī *to be about to be called* ·

[1] Or with -*re* for -*ris* (vocāre, vocābere, vocābāre, vocēre, vocārēre).

VOCOR—Passive Voice (continued)

55	· Tenses of completed action—Compounded with Perf. Part. Pass.

INDICATIVE

PERFECT

vocātus sum *I have*
vocātus es *you have*
vocātus est *he has*
vocātī sumus *we have* | *been called*
vocātī estis *you have*
vocātī sunt *they have*
　or *I was called*, &c., § 153

FUTURE PERFECT

vocātus erō *I shall have*
vocātus eris *you will have*
vocātus erit *he will have* | *been called*
vocātī erimus *we shall have*
vocātī eritis *you will have*
vocātī erunt *they will have*

PAST PERFECT

vocātus eram *I had*
vocātus erās *you had*
vocātus erat *he had* | *been called*
vocātī erāmus *we had*
vocātī erātis *you had*
vocātī erant *they had*

IMPERATIVE

[None]

SUBJUNCTIVE

PERFECT

vocātus sim
vocātus sīs
vocātus sit
vocātī sīmus
vocātī sītis
vocātī sint

PAST PERFECT

vocātus essem
vocātus essēs
vocātus esset
vocātī essēmus
vocātī essētis
vocātī essent

For the meanings see
§§ 130, 131

In all the above forms the participle may be masc., fem., or neut.

SING. vocātus, a, um　　PLUR. vocātī, ae, a

VERB-ADJ.	PERF. PART. vocātus, a, um *called, having been called*
VERB-NOUN	PERF. INFIN. vocātus (a, um) esse *to have been called*

The Four Conjugations—Passive Voice

156	Tenses of incomplete action			
STEM	1st Conj. vocā·	2nd Conj. habē·	3rd Conj. rege·	4th Conj. audī·

INDICATIVE

	1st Conj.	2nd Conj.	3rd Conj.	4th Conj.
PRESENT	vocor	habeor	regor	audior
	vocāris[1]	habēris[1]	regeris[1]	audīris[1]
	vocātur	habētur	regitur	audītur
	vocāmur	habēmur	regimur	audīmur
	vocāminī	habēminī	regiminī	audīminī
	vocantur	habentur	reguntur	audiuntur
FUTURE	vocābor	habēbor	regar	audiar
	vocāberis[1]	habēberis[1]	regēris[1]	audiēris[1]
	vocābitur	habēbitur	regētur	audiētur
	vocābimur	habēbimur	regēmur	audiēmur
	vocābiminī	habēbiminī	regēminī	audiēminī
	vocābuntur	habēbuntur	regentur	audientur
PAST IMPERFECT	vocābar	habēbar	regēbar	audiēbar
	vocābāris[1]	habēbāris[1]	regēbāris[1]	audiēbāris[1]
	vocābātur	habēbātur	regēbātur	audiēbātur
	vocābāmur	habēbāmur	regēbāmur	audiēbāmur
	vocābāminī	habēbāminī	regēbāminī	audiēbāminī
	vocābantur	habēbantur	regēbantur	audiēbantur

VERB-ADJECTIVE AND VERB-NOUNS

	1st Conj.	2nd Conj.	3rd Conj.	4th Conj.
VERB-ADJ.	vocandus, a, um	habendus, a, um	regendus, a, um	audiendus, a, um
VERB-NOUNS	vocārī vocātum īrī	habērī habitum īrī	regī[2] rectum īrī	audīrī audītum īrī

[1] Or with -re for -ris (vocāre, habēre, regere, audīre, &c.); see note p. 70.
[2] Note the peculiar form of the Pres. Infin. in ī (regī), not, as might have been expected, in erī.

57

	Tenses of incomplete action (continued)			
STEM	1st CONJ. vocā-	2nd CONJ. habē-	3rd CONJ. rege-	4th CONJ. audī-
	IMPERATIVE			
S. 2	vocāre / vocātor	habēre / habētor	regere / regitor	audīre / audītor
3	vocātor	habētor	regitor	audītor
P. 2	vocāminī	habēminī	regiminī	audīminī
3	vocantor	habentor	reguntor	audiuntor
	SUBJUNCTIVE			
PRESENT	vocer	habear	regar	audiar
	vocēris [1]	habeāris [1]	regāris [1]	audiāris [1]
	vocētur	habeātur	regātur	audiātur
	vocēmur	habeāmur	regāmur	audiāmur
	vocēminī	habeāminī	regāminī	audiāminī
	vocentur	habeantur	regantur	audiantur
PAST IMPERFECT	vocārer	habērer	regerer	audīrer
	vocārēris [1]	habērēris [1]	regerēris [1]	audīrēris [1]
	vocārētur	habērētur	regerētur	audīrētur
	vocārmur	habērēmur	regerēmur	audīrēmur
	vocārēminī	habērēminī	regerēminī	audīrēminī
	vocārentur	habērentur	regerentur	audīrentur

58   The **tenses of completed action** are formed by compound-ing the Perf. Part. Pass. with a tense of *esse* 'to be'. The participle may be masc., fem., or neut., and sing. or plur.

See table on next page.

[1] Or with *-re* for *-ris* (vocēre, habeāre, regāre, audīre; vocārēre, habērēre, regerēre, audīrēre.).

170 PRINCIPAL PARTS OF VERBS OF ALL CONJUGATIONS [1]

The Principal Parts given in the following list are—

1. The Present Indicative Active, 1st Pers. Sing.
2. The Present Infinitive Active.
3. The Perfect Indicative Active, 1st Pers. Sing.
4. The Perfect Participle Passive. This form is given in the *masculine gender* whenever the Perf. Part. Pass. can be used in all three genders: e. g. *vocātus* from *vocō*. But in verbs whose Perf. Part. Pass. can only be used in the impersonal passive construction, the form is given in the *neuter gender*: e. g. *mansum* from *maneō*, *fautum* from *faveō*. The active voice of the verbs to which these participles in *-um* belong is used intransitively or with a dative. In the few verbs which have no Perf. Part. Pass. (masc., fem., or neut.) the Future Participle Active is given as the 4th Principal Part. [2]

The 3rd Conjugation is taken first because the most important Perfects to be mentioned under the 1st, 2nd, and 4th Conjugations are formed in the same way as those of the 3rd Conjugation.

Formation of the Perfect Active.

171 (i) RULE 1. [3] **All Perfects Active which are formed from stems ending in one of the vowels *a*, *e*, *i*, or *o* are formed with the suffix *v*:** e. g. 1st conj. *vocā-*, *vocāv-*;

---

[1] In the list which follows (§§ 173-237) only the most important verbs are included. Others are given in the alphabetical list in the Appendix.

[2] The Supine in *-um* is generally taken as the 4th Principal Part. But the Perf. Part. Pass. is a far more important form than the Supine; and, moreover, many verbs have no Supine in actual use. The Supine may be formed by changing *-us* of the Perf. Part. Pass. into *-um*.

[3] The rules given here in heavy type have no exceptions.

4th conj. *audī-, audīv-* ; 2nd conj. *complē-, complēv-* ; *habē-, habu-* (for *habēv-*, § 147) ; 3rd conj. *pa-sc-, pāv-* ; *cre-sc-, crēv-* ; *sci-sc-, scīv-* ; *no-sc-, nōv-*.[1]

(ii) RULE 2. **All Perfects Active which are formed from stems ending in the vowel *u* or the consonant *v* or in *nd* are formed without any suffix**; e.g. 3rd conj. *statu-, statu-* ; *volv-, volv-* ; *dēfend-, dēfend-* ; 2nd conj. *mov-, mōv-* ; *pend-, pepend-*.[1]

(iii) Perfects Active which are formed from stems ending in a consonant other than *v* or *nd* are formed in three different ways (*a*, *b*, and *c*, below):

either (*a*) with the suffix *s*: e.g. 3rd conj. *scrīb-, scrips-*.

If the stem ends in a guttural, the guttural generally amalgamates with the *s*: e.g. 3rd conj. *reg-, rex-* (§ 147); 2nd conj. *aug-, aux-* ; 4th conj. *vinc-, vinx-*.

But (RULE 3) **if a liquid precedes the guttural, the guttural is always dropped before the suffix *s* of the Perf. Act.**: e.g. 3rd conj. *sparg-, spars-* ; 2nd conj. *indulg-, induls-* ; 4th conj. *fulc-, fuls-*.

RULE 4. **If the stem ends in a dental, the dental is dropped before the suffix *s* or turned into another *s***: e.g. 3rd conj. *claud-, claus-* ; *cēd-, cess-* ; 2nd conj. *rīd-, rīs-*.

or (*b*) with the suffix *u* (chiefly when the stem ends in *l* or *m*): e.g. 3rd conj. *col-, colu-* ; *trem-, tremu-*.

or (*c*) without any suffix: e.g. 3rd conj. *vert-, vert-* ; *leg-, lēg-* ; *ag-, ēg-* ; *curr-, cucurr-*.

2 The stem of the Perfect Participle Passive is formed—

(i) by adding the suffix *t* to a stem ending in a vowel or in any consonant except a dental : 1st conj. *vocā-, vocāt-* ; 2nd conj. *complē-, complēt-* ; *habe-, habit-* ; 4th conj. *audī-, audīt-* ; *ven-, vent-* ; 3rd conj. *reg-, rect-* (§ 148); *scrīb-,*

---

[1] Note that here the stem from which the Perf. Act. stem is formed is not the same as that from which the tenses of incomplete action are formed (cf. §§ 178, 198, 199, 201). So too in many verbs of the 1st, 2nd, and 4th conjugations; see §§ 208, 213, 223.

The Four Conjugations—Passive Voice (continued)

PERF. INDIC.

S. vocātus, habitus, } sum, es, est
rectus, audītus

P. vocātī, habitī, } sumus, estis, sunt
rectī, audītī

FUT. PERF. INDIC.

S. vocātus, habitus, } erō, eris, erit
rectus, audītus

P. vocātī, habitī, } erimus, eritis, erunt
rectī, audītī

PAST PERF. INDIC.

S. vocātus, habitus, } eram, erās, erat
rectus, audītus

P. vocātī, habitī, } erāmus, erātis, erant
rectī, audītī

PERF. SUBJ.

S. vocātus, habitus, } sim, sīs, sit
rectus, audītus

P. vocātī, habitī, } sīmus, sītis, sint
rectī, audītī

PAST PERF. SUBJ.

S. vocātus, habitus, } essem, essēs, esset
rectus, audītus

P. vocātī, habitī, } essēmus, essētis, essent
rectī, audītī

VERB-ADJECTIVE	*VERB-NOUN*
Perfect Participle	Perfect Infinitive

	Perfect Participle	Perfect Infinitive	
1st Conj.	vocātus, a, um	vocātus, a, um	
2nd Conj.	habitus, a, um	habitus, a, um	esse
3rd Conj.	rectus, a, um	rectus, a, um	
4th Conj.	audītus, a, um	audītus, a, um	

THE MIXED CONJUGATION

59 In the following important verbs in *iō* the present infinitive, the past subjunctive, and most of the persons of the present indicative and imperative belong to the 3rd conjugation (with the stem-vowel *i* or *e* short), while the rest of the tenses of incomplete action bel ong to the 4th conj.

capiō, **capere**, cēpī, captus, *take.*
cupiō, **cupere**, cupīvī, cupītus, *desire.*
faciō,[1] **facere**, fēcī, factus, *make.*
fugiō, **fugere**, fūgī, fugitūrus, *flee.*
iaciō, **iacere**, iēcī, iactus, *throw.*
pariō, **parere**, peperī, partus, *produce, bring forth.*
rapiō, **rapere**, rapuī, raptus, *seize.*
sapiō, **sapere**, sapīvī —— *be sensible.*

And compounds of *quatiō* and *·spiciō* :

con-cutiō, **·cutere**, ·cussī, ·cussus, *shake violently.*
con-spiciō, **·spicere**, ·spexī, ·spectus, *catch sight of.*

60 **Tenses of incomplete action—Active voice.**

	INDICATIVE	*IMPERATIVE*
	PRESENT	
	S. capiō P. **capimus**	
	capis **capitis**	S. **cape, capitō** P. **capite**
	capit capiunt	**capitō** capiuntō
		SUBJUNCTIVE
	FUTURE	PRESENT
	capiam, capiēs, capiet, *&c.*	capiam, capiās, capiat, *&c.*
	PAST IMPERFECT	PAST
	capiēbam, capiēbās, capiēbat, *&c.*	**caperem, caperēs, caperet,** *&c.*
VERB-ADJS.	PRES. PART. **capiens** (-nt-)	FUT. PART. **captūrus,** a, um
VERB-NOUNS	PRES. INFIN. **capere**	FUT. INFIN. **captūrus** (a, um) esse
	GERUND capiendum	SUPINE captum

[1] *Faciō* forms the imperative 2nd sing. *fac* (without the final *e*).

161 **Tenses of incomplete action—Passive voice.**

INDICATIVE		*IMPERATIVE*	
PRESENT			
S. capior	P. capimur		
caperis[1]	capiminī	S. capere, capitor	P. capiminī
capitur	capiuntur	capitor	capiuntor
		SUBJUNCTIVE	
FUTURE		PRESENT	
capiar, capiēris,[1] capiētur, &c.		capiar, capiāris,[1] capiātur, &c.	
PAST IMPERFECT			
capiēbar, capiēbāris,[1] capiē-bātur, &c.		caperer, caperēris,[1] caperē-tur, &c.	

VERB-ADJ.	GERUND ADJ. capiendus, a, um	
VERB-NOUNS	PRES. INFIN. **capī**	FUT. INFIN. captum īrī

[1] Or with *-re* for *-ris*; compare notes on pp. 70, 72, 73.

Tenses of completed action – Active voice.

162 PERFECT INDIC. cēpī, cēpistī, cēpit, &c.

SUBJ. cēperim, cēperīs,[1] cēperit, &c.

FUT. PERF. INDIC. cēperō, cēperis,[1] cēperit, &c.

PAST PERF. INDIC. cēperam, cēperās, cēperat, &c.

SUBJ. cēpissem, cēpissēs, cēpisset, &c.

VERB-NOUN—PERF. INFIN. cēpisse.

Tenses of completed action—Passive voice.

163 PERFECT INDIC. captus sum, captus es, captus est, &c.

SUBJ. captus sim, captus sīs, captus sit, &c.

FUT. PERF. INDIC. captus erō, captus eris, captus erit, &c.

PAST PERF. INDIC. captus eram, captus erās, captus erat, &c.

SUBJ. captus essem, captus essēs, captus esset, &c.

VERB-ADJ.—PERF. PART. captus, a, um.

VERB-NOUN—PERF. INFIN. captus (a, um) esse.

[1] See notes on p. 61.

DEPONENT VERBS

54 Deponent verbs are verbs whose indicative, subjunctive, and imperative are passive in form, but active in meaning, and whose only active forms are those of the present participle, future participle, future infinitive, supine, and gerund. The gerund adjective of deponents is passive in meaning, as in other verbs.

Deponents are the only Latin verbs which have three participles and three infinitives with active meaning.

	PARTICIPLES	INFINITIVES
PRES.	horta-ns (-nt-), *exhorting.*	hortā-rī, *to exhort.*
PERF.	hortāt-us, -a, -um, *having exhorted.*	hortāt-us (-a, -um) esse, *to have exhorted.*
FUT.	hortāt-ūrus, -ūra, -ūrum, *about to exhort.*	hortāt-ūrus (-ūra, -ūrum) esse, *to be about to exhort.*

55 Some deponents had originally a reflexive meaning, i. e. denoted an action done to oneself, e. g. orīrī, *to raise oneself,* French *se lever;* hence *to arise;* ūtī, *to serve oneself,* French *se servir* (argentō meō ūsus est, *il s'est servi de mon argent*); vescī, *to feed oneself.*

56 The tenses of incomplete action of deponent verbs are exactly like those of the four regular conjugations (*vocor, habeor, regor, audior,* §§ 156, 157), except in three deponents which belong to the mixed conjugation (§ 161):

> ad-gredior, -gredī, -gressus, *attack:* so too other compounds of gradior : con-gredior, in-gredior, *&c.*
>
> morior, morī, mortuus (fut. part. moritūrus), *die.*
>
> patior, patī, passus, *suffer.*

57 Orior, orīrī, ortus (fut. part. oritūrus), *arise,* is peculiar ; it belongs to the 4th conj., but is conjugated like *capior* in the pres. indic. and imperative, and in the past subj. forms *orerer* as well as *orīrer.* Its gerund adjective *oriundus* (never *oriendus*) has the meaning of a present or perfect participle : dīs oriundus, *springing* or *sprung from the gods.*

The following tables show all the forms and meanings of a deponent of the 1st conjugation.

Examples in other conjugations : vereor, *I fear* (2nd conj.) ; fungor, *I discharge* (3rd conj.) ; potior, *I get possession of* (4th conj.).

CONJUGATION OF A DEPONENT VERB

168 | Tenses of incomplete action

INDICATIVE	*IMPERATIVE*
PRESENT	
hortor, *I am exhorting*	
hortāris,[1] *you are exhorting*	hortāre, hortātor, *exhort*
hortātur, *he is exhorting*	hortātor, *let him exhort*
hortāmur, *we are exhorting*	
hortāminī, *you are exhorting*	hortāminī, *exhort*
hortantur, *they are exhorting*	hortantor, *let them exhort*
or *I exhort*, &c., § 127	
	SUBJUNCTIVE
FUTURE	PRESENT
hortābor, *I shall*	horter
hortāberis,[1] *you will*	hortēris [1]
hortābitur, *he will*	hortētur
hortābimur, *we shall*	hortēmur
hortābiminī, *you will*	hortēminī
hortābuntur, *they will*	hortentur
or *I shall be exhorting*	*For the meanings see* §§ 130, 131
PAST IMPERFECT	PAST
hortābar, *I was*	hortārer
hortābāris,[1] *you were*	hortārēris [1]
hortābātur, *he was*	hortārētur
hortābāmur, *we were*	hortārēmur
hortābāminī, *you were*	hortārēminī
hortābantur, *they were*	hortārentur
or *I exhorted* (habitually = *used to exhort*)	*For the meanings see* §§ 130, 131

(Future column marked: *exhort*)
(Past Imperfect column marked: *exhorting*)

VERB-ADJS.	PRES. PART. hortans (-nt-), *exhorting* GERUND ADJ. hortandus, a, um, *to-be-exhorted*	FUT. PART. hortātūrus, a, um, *about to exhort*

VERB-NOUNS	PRES. INFIN. hortārī, *to exhort* GERUND hortandum, [*the act of*] *exhorting*	FUT. INFIN. hortātūrus (a, um) esse, *to be about to exhort* SUPINE hortātum, [*with a view*] *to exhort*

[1] Or with -*re* for -*ris* (hortāre, hortābere, hortābāre, hortēre, hortārēre); cf. notes on pp. 70, 72, 73.

CONJUGATION OF A DEPONENT VERB (continued)

	Tenses of completed action	
	INDICATIVE	*IMPERATIVE*

INDICATIVE

PERFECT

hortātus {
sum, *I have exhorted*
es, *you have exhorted*
est, *he has exhorted*
}

hortātī {
sumus, *we have exhorted*
estis, *you have exhorted*
sunt, *they have exhorted*
}

or *I exhorted, § 153 and § 128*

FUTURE PERFECT

hortātus {
erō, *I shall have*
eris, *you will have*
erit, *he will have*
}

hortātī {
erimus, *we shall have*
eritis, *you will have*
erunt, *they will have*
} *exhorted*

PAST PERFECT

hortātus {
eram, *I had*
erās, *you had*
erat, *he had*
}

hortātī {
erāmus, *we had*
erātis, *you had*
erant, *they had*
} *exhorted*

IMPERATIVE

[None]

SUBJUNCTIVE

PERFECT

hortātus {
sim
sīs
sit
}

hortātī {
sīmus
sītis
sint
}

For the meanings see §§ 130, 131

PAST PERFECT

hortātus {
essem
essēs
esset
}

hortātī {
essēmus
essētis
essent
}

For the meanings see §§ 130, 131

In all the above forms the participle may be masc., fem., or neut.

SING. hortātus, a, um   PLUR. hortātī, ae, a

VERB-ADJ.	PERF. PART. hortātus, a, um, *having exhorted*
VERB-NOUN	PERF. INFIN. hortātus (a, um) esse, *to have exhorted*

170 PRINCIPAL PARTS OF VERBS OF ALL CONJUGATIONS [1]

The Principal Parts given in the following list are—

1. The Present Indicative Active, 1st Pers. Sing.
2. The Present Infinitive Active.
3. The Perfect Indicative Active, 1st Pers. Sing.
4. The Perfect Participle Passive. This form is given in the *masculine gender* whenever the Perf. Part. Pass. can be used in all three genders : e. g. *vocātus* from *vocō*. But in verbs whose Perf. Part. Pass. can only be used in the impersonal passive construction, the form is given in the *neuter gender*: e. g. *mansum* from *maneō*, *fautum* from *faveō*. The active voice of the verbs to which these participles in *-um* belong is used intransitively or with a dative. In the few verbs which have no Perf. Part. Pass. (masc., fem., or neut.) the Future Participle Active is given as the 4th Principal Part.[2]

The 3rd Conjugation is taken first because the most important Perfects to be mentioned under the 1st, 2nd, and 4th Conjugations are formed in the same way as those of the 3rd Conjugation.

Formation of the Perfect Active.

171 (i) RULE 1.[3] **All Perfects Active which are formed from stems ending in one of the vowels *a*, *e*, *i*, or *o* are formed with the suffix *v* : e. g. 1st conj. *vocā-*, *vocāv-* ;**

---

[1] In the list which follows (§§ 173-237) only the most important verbs are included. Others are given in the alphabetical list in the Appendix.

[2] The Supine in *-um* is generally taken as the 4th Principal Part. But the Perf. Part. Pass. is a far more important form than the Supine ; and, moreover, many verbs have no Supine in actual use. The Supine may be formed by changing *-us* of the Perf. Part. Pass. into *-um*.

[3] The rules given here in heavy type have no exceptions.

4th conj. *audī-*, *audīv-*; 2nd conj. *complē-*, *complēv-*; *habē-*, *habu-* (for *habēv-*, § 147); 3rd conj. *pa-sc-*, *pāv-*; *cre-sc-*, *crēv-*; *sci-sc-*, *scīv-*; *no-sc-*, *nōv-*.[1]

(ii) RULE 2. **All Perfects Active which are formed from stems ending in the vowel *u* or the consonant *v* or in *nd* are formed without any suffix; e.g. 3rd conj.** *statu-*, *statu-*; *volv-*, *volv-*; *dēfend-*, *dēfend-*; 2nd conj. *mov-*, *mōv-*; *pend-*, *pepend-*.[1]

(iii) Perfects Active which are formed from stems ending in a consonant other than *v* or *nd* are formed in three different ways (*a*, *b*, and *c*, below):

either (*a*) with the suffix *s*: e.g. 3rd conj. *scrib-*, *scrips-*.

If the stem ends in a guttural, the guttural generally amalgamates with the *s*: e.g. 3rd conj. *reg-*, *rex-* (§ 147); 2nd conj. *aug-*, *aux-*; 4th conj. *vinc-*, *vinx-*.

But (RULE 3) **if a liquid precedes the guttural, the guttural is always dropped before the suffix *s* of the Perf. Act.**: e.g. 3rd conj. *sparg-*, *spars-*; 2nd conj. *indulg-*, *induls-*; 4th conj. *fulc-*, *fuls-*.

RULE 4. **If the stem ends in a dental, the dental is dropped before the suffix *s* or turned into another *s*:** e.g. 3rd conj. *claud-*, *claus-*; *cēd-*, *cess-*; 2nd conj. *rīd-*, *rīs-*.

or (*b*) with the suffix *u* (chiefly when the stem ends in *l* or *m*): e.g. 3rd conj. *col-*, *colu-*; *trem-*, *tremu-*.

or (*c*) without any suffix: e.g. 3rd conj. *vert-*, *vert-*; *leg-*, *lēg-*; *ag-*, *ēg-*; *curr-*, *cucurr-*.

2   The stem of the Perfect Participle Passive is formed—

(i) by adding the suffix *t* to a stem ending in a vowel or in any consonant except a dental : 1st conj. *vocā-*, *vocāt-*; 2nd conj. *complē-*, *complēt-*; *habe-*, *habit-*; 4th conj. *audī-*, *audīt-*; *ven-*, *vent-*; 3rd conj. *reg-*, *rect-* (§ 148); *scrib-*,

---

[1] Note that here the stem from which the Perf. Act. stem is formed is not the same as that from which the tenses of incomplete action are formed (cf. §§ 178, 198, 199, 201). So too in many verbs of the 1st, 2nd, and 4th conjugations; see §§ 208, 213, 223.

F

scrip-t- (*p* for *b*); *consul-, consul-t-*; *inser-, inser-t-*; *cre-sc-, crē-t-*; *no-sc-, nō-t-*.

(ii) by adding the suffix *s* to a stem ending in a dental. In this case the dental is either dropped or turned into another *s* before the suffix *s*: *claud-, clau-s-*; *dēfend-, dēfen-s-*; *vert-, ver-s-*; *mitt-, mis-s-*; *sed-, sess-*.

But there are some exceptions to the above rule; these are printed in heavy type in the following list of Principal Parts. The best guide to the formation of the Perfect Participle Passive is the English derivative which is formed from it.

THIRD CONJUGATION

1. **Verbs in gō, guō** (pronounced *gwō*) **or hō.**

173   (*a*) Most of these form the Perf. Act. stem with the suffix *s*:

reg-ō   -ere   rex-ī   rect-us   [direction]   *rule*

So tegō, *cover*; intellegō, *understand*; neglegō, *disregard*.

dī-lig-ō	-ere	-lex-ī	-lect-us	[predilection]	*love*
ad-flīg-ō	-ere	-flix-ī	-flict-us	[affliction]	*dash down*
fīg-ō	-ere	fix-ī	**fix-us**	[suffix]	*fix*
iung-ō	-ere	iunx-ī	iunct-us	[junction]	*join*
cing-ō	-ere	cinx-ī	cinct-us	[succinct]	*surround*

So ex-stinguō, *quench* [whence English 'extinct'].

fing-ō   -ere   finx-ī   fictus   [fiction]   *fashion*

So pingō, *paint*; stringō, *tighten*.

| trah-ō | -ere | trax-ī | tract-us | [traction] | *draw* |
| veh-ō | -ere | vex-ī | vect-us | [invective] | *carry* |

174   The guttural is dropped after a liquid [Rule 3, § 171].

| merg-ō | -ere | mers-ī | **mers-us** | [immerse] | *dip* |
| sparg-ō | -ere | spars-ī | **spars-us** | [sparse] | *scatter* |

175   (*b*) The following in *gō* form the Perf. Act. stem withou a suffix:

| ag-ō | -ere | ēg-ī | act-us | [action] | *drive, do* |
| leg-ō | -ere | lēg-ī | lect-us | [collection] | *gather* |

frang-ō	-ere	frēg-ī [1]	fract-us	[fraction]	*break*
pang-ō	-ere	pepig-ī [1]	pact-us	[compact]	*fix*
tang-ō	-ere	tetig-ī [1]	tact-us	[contact]	*touch*
pung-ō	-ere	pupug-ī [1]	punct-us	[puncture]	*prick*

2. Verbs in cō, quō (pronounced *kwō*).

76   (*a*) Perf. Act. stem formed with the suffix *s* :

dīc-ō [2]	-ere	dix-ī	dict-us	[diction]	*say*
dūc-ō [2]	-ere	dux-ī	duct-us	[reduction]	*lead*
coqu-ō	-ere	cox-ī	coct-us	[decoction]	*cook*

77   (*b*) Perf. Act. stem formed without a suffix :

vinc-ō	-ere	vīc-ī [1]	vict-us	[victory]	*conquer*
re-linqu-ō	-ere	-līqu-ī [1]	-lict-us	[derelict]	*leave*
parc-ō	-ere	peperc-ī	**pars-ūrus** [3]	[parsimony]	*spare*

78   (*c*) The following verbs in *scō* form the Perf. Act. from a stem ending in a vowel (viz. the vowel that precedes the *sc*), with the suffix *v* [Rule 1, § 171] :

pasc-ō	-ere	pāv-ī	**past-us**	[pasture]	*feed*
ad-suesc-ō	-ere	-suēv-ī	-suēt-us		*be accustomed*

So cresco, *grow*; quiesco, *go to rest.*

scisc-ō	-ere	scīv-ī	scīt-us	[plebiscite]	*decree*
nosc-ō	-ere	nōv-ī	nōt-us	[notion]	*get to know*

79   But *disco* and *posco* are peculiar :

disc-ō	-ere	didic-ī	——		*learn*
posc-ō	-ere	poposc-ī	postulāt-us [4]	[postulate]	*demand*

80   All other verbs in *escō* take a Perf. from the 2nd Conj. :

e.g. languesc-ō	-ere	langu-ī		*grow weak*
abolesc-ō	-ere	abolēv-ī (§ 221)		

81   **3. Verbs in ŭō or vō.** Most of these form the Perf. Act. from a stem ending in *u* or *v*, without a suffix [Rule 2, § 171] :

statu-ō	-ere	statu-ī	statūt-us	[statute]	*set up*

[1] Formed from a stem which has no *n* before the guttural (*frag-, pag-, tag-, pŭg-, vic-, reliqu-*).
[2] Imperative and sing. *dīc, dūc* ; cf. *fac,* § 159, *fer,* § 241..
[3] The Perf. Pass. of *parcō* is generally supplied by *temperātum est* from the verb *temperō,* 1st Conj.   [4] From the verb *postulō,* 1st Conj.

So exu-ō, *take off*; imbu-ō, *tinge*; minu-ō, *lessen*; tribu-ō, *assign*; metu-ō (no part. pass.), *fear*.

ru-ō	-ere	ru-ī	-rut-us [1]		*tumble*
			ruit-ūrus		
solv-ō	-ere	solv-ī	solūt-us	[solution]	*loosen*

So volv-ō, *roll*.

182 But *vīv-ō*, *stru-ō*, and *flu-ō* form the Perf. Act. from a stem ending in a guttural (not seen in the Pres. Indic.), with the suffix *s* :

vīv-ō	-ere	vix-ī	victūrus	[victuals]	*live*
stru-ō	-ere	strux-ī	struct-us	[construction]	*pile up*
flu-ō	-ere	flux-ī	**flux**-us [2]	[influx]	*flow*

4. Verbs in dō.

183   (*a*) Most of these verbs, except those in *ndō* (§ 186), form the Perf. Act. stem with the suffix *s* [Rule 4, § 171] :

ē-vād-ō	-ere	-vās-ī	-vās-um	[evasion]	*go out*
claud-ō	-ere	claus-ī	claus-us	[clause]	*shut*
dīvid-ō	-ere	dīvīs-ī	dīvīs-us	[division]	*divide*

So laed-ō, *hurt*; plaud-ō, *clap*; lūd-ō, *play*; trūd-ō, *thrust*.

cēd-ō	-ere	cess-ī	cess-um	[concession]	*yield*

184   (*b*) The following form the Perf. Act. stem without a suffix :

ed-ō	esse	ēd-ī	-ēs-us		*eat*
con-sīd-ō	-ere	-sēd-ī	-sess-um	[session]	*seat oneself*
cad-ō	-ere	cecid-ī	cās-ūrus	[occasion]	*fall*
caed-ō	-ere	cecīd-ī	caes-us		*fell, slay*
crēd-ō	-ere	crēdid-ī	crēdit-us	[credit]	*trust*

185   Like *crēdō* are all compounds of *dare* (§ 210), if formed with a preposition of one syllable, *e. g.* abdō, *hide*; addō, *add*; condō, *found*; ēdō, *give out, utter*; indō, *put in*; perdō, *lose*; prōdō, *betray*; reddō, *give back*; subdō, *put under*; trādō, *hand down*; similarly vēndō, *sell* (from vēnum dō, *I offer for sale*).

---

[1] In transitive compounds : *dī-rutus*, 'destroyed'; *ob-rutus*, 'buried'.
[2] *Fluxus* means ' flowing ', ' slackened ', ' lax '.

86   (c) All verbs in *ndō* form the Perf. Act. stem without a suffix [Rule 2, § 171]:

dē-fend-ō -ere -fend-ī -fens-us [defensive] *defend*

So a-scendō, *climb*; ac-cendō, *kindle*; prehendō, *grasp*.

pand-ō	-ere	pand-ī	pass-us		*spread out*
pend-ō	-ere	pepend-ī	pens-us	[pension]	*weigh, pay*
tend-ō	-ere	tetend-ī	**tent**-us	[attention]	*stretch*
fund-ō	-ere	fūd-ī [1]	fūs-us	[fusion]	*pour*
scind-ō	-ere	scid-ī [1]	sciss-us	[scissors]	*tear*

5. Verbs in tō.

87   (a) Perf. Act. stem formed with the suffix *s*:

mitt-ō	-ere	mīs-ī	miss-us	[mission]	*send*
flect-ō	-ere	flex-ī	flex-us	[flexible]	*bend*
nect-ō	-ere	nexu-ī [2]	nex-us	[connexion]	*bind*

88   (b) Perf. Act. stem formed without a suffix:

vert-ō	-ere	vert-ī	vers-us	[version]	*turn*
sist-ō	-ere	-stit-ī [3]	stat-us [4]	[station]	*stop* (tr. and
			(= *fixed*)		intr.)

89   (c) *Petō* forms its Perf. Act. from a stem ending in *ī* (added to *pet-*), with the suffix *v* [Rule 1, § 171]:

pet-ō -ere petīv-ī petīt-us [petition] *aim at*

6. Verbs in bō, pō.

90   (a) Perf. Act. stem formed with the suffix *s*:

scrīb-ō -ere scrips-ī script-us [description] *write*

So nūbō, *marry*; carpō, *pluck.*

91   (b) Perf. Act. stem formed without a suffix:

bib-ō	-ere	bib-ī	pōtāt-us [5]	[potation]	*drink*
			pōt-us [6]	[potion]	
rump-ō	-ere	rūp-ī	rupt-us	[rupture]	*burst*

---

[1] Formed from a stem which has no *n* before the *d* (*fud-*, *scid-*).

[2] *nexu-ī* is a double Perfect formed by adding *u* to *nex-*.

[3] Chiefly in compounds like *con-stitī, re-stitī.*

[4] From the stem *sta-*.

[5] From the verb *pōtō*, 1st Conj.

[6] Often active in meaning (= 'having drunk') like the English 'drunken'.

192 (c) Perf. Act. stem formed with the suffix *u* :

prō-cumb-ō	-ere	-cubu-ī	-cubit-um	*fall forward*
strep-ō	-ere	strepu-ī	-—-	*make a noise*

7. Verbs in lō.

193 (a) All verbs in *llō* form the Perf. Act. stem without a suffix :

vell-ō	-ere	vell-ī	vuls-us	[convulsion]	*pluck*
fall-ō	-ere	fefell-ī	fals-us[1]	[false]	*deceive*
pell-ō	-ere	pepul-ī	puls-us	[compulsion]	*push*
per-cell-ō	-ere	-cul-ī	-culs-us		*cast down*
toll-ō	-ere	sus-tul-ī	sub-lāt-us		*lift*

194 (b) All other verbs in *lō* form the Perf. Act. stem with the suffix *u* :

al-ō	-ere	alu-ī	alt-us		*nourish*
col-ō	-ere	colu-ī	cult-us	[culture]	*cultivate*
consul-ō	-ere	consulu-ī	consult-us	[juris-consult]	*consult*

So occulō, *hide* ; and compare volō, nōlō, mālō, § 242.

8. Verbs in mō, nō.

195 (a) Perf. Act. stem formed with the suffix *u* :

trem-ō	-ere	tremu-ī	——	*tremble*

So gem-ō, *groan* ; fremō, *make a noise.*

gign-ō[2]	-ere	genu-ī	genit-us	[genitive]	*beget*

196 (b) Perf. Act. stem formed without a suffix :

em-ō	-ere	ēm-ī	empt-us	[redemption]	*buy, take*
can-ō	-ere	cecin-ī	cantāt-us[3]	[incantation]	*sing*

197 (c) Perf. Act stem formed with the suffix *s* :

prem-ō	-ere	press-ī	**press-us**	[pressure]	*press*
con-temn-ō	-ere	-temps-ī	-tempt-us	[contemptible]	*despise*
prōm-ō	-ere	promps-ī	prompt-us	[prompt]	*take forth*
sūm-ō	-ere	sumps-ī	sumpt-us	[consumption]	*take up*

---

[1] The meaning 'deceived' is generally expressed by *dēceptus.*
[2] For gi-**gen**-ō.
[3] From the verb *cantō,* 1st Conj.

98   (d) The following verbs in *nō* form their Perf. Act. from
a stem ending in a vowel (*e, a* or *i*), with the suffix *v* [Rule 1,
§ 171].

cern-ō   -ere   crēv-ī   -crēt-us[1]   [discretion]   *distinguish*

So spernō, *scorn*.

stern-ō   -ere   strāv-ī   strāt-us   [prostration]   *strew, lay low*
sin-ō   -ere   sīv-ī   sit-us   [site]   *permit*
pōn-ō[2]   -ere   poṣu-ī   posit-us   [position]   *place*

9. Verbs in rō.

99   (a) The following form the Perf. Act. from a stem ending
in a vowel (*e* or *i*), with the suffix *v* [Rule 1, § 171].

ser-ō   -ere   sēv-ī   sat-us   *sow*
ter-ō   -ere   trīv-ī   trīt-us   [detrition]   *rub*
quaer-ō   -ere   quaesīv-ī   quaesīt-us   *seek*
ac-quīr-ō   -ere   -quīsīv-ī   -quīsīt-us   [acquisition]   *acquire*

00   (b) The following form the Perf. Act. stem variously :

ger-ō   -ere   gess-ī   ges-tus   [gesture]   *carry*
ūr-ō   -ere   uss-ī   ust-us   [combustion]   *burn* (trans.)
curr-ō   -ere   cucurr-ī   curs-um   [cursory]   *run*
ser-ō   -ere   -seru-ī[3]   sert-us   [insertion]   *twine*
fer-ō[4]   ferre   tul-ī   lāt-us   [translation]   *bear*

10. Verbs in ssō, ξō, xō.

01   (a) Verbs in *ssō* form the Perf. Act. from a stem ending
in a vowel (*i* added after the *ss*), with the suffix *v* [Rule 1,
§ 171]:

arcess-ō   -ere   arcessīv-ī   arcessīt-us   *summon*

So lacessō, *provoke* ; capessō, *catch at* ; facessō, *do eagerly* ;
incessō, *assail.*

02   (b) *Vīsō* forms the Perf. Act. without a suffix, and *texō*
with the suffix *u* :

vīs-ō   -ere   vīs-ī   ——   *visit*
tex-ō   -ere   texu-ī   text-us   [texture]   *weave*

---

[1] In compounds *dē-crētus, dis-crētus, sē-crētus.*
[2] *Pōnō* is a compound of *sinō*; its original form was *po-sinō*, Perf. *po-sīvī*,
of which *posuī* is only another form.   [3] Only in compounds, e.g. *in-seru* ī.
[4] *Ferō* forms its principal parts from three entirely different stems.

MIXED CONJUGATION (§ 159).

203   1. **Most verbs of the Mixed Conjugation form the Perf. Act. from a stem ending in a consonant (= the part of the Infinitive which comes before the ending *ere*).** In the following list the Infinitive is divided so as to show this stem.

204   (*a*) Perf. Act. stem formed without a suffix :

. capi-ō	cap-ere	cēp-ī	capt-us	[capture]	*take*
faci-ō	fac-ere	fēc-ī	fact-us	[faction]	*make*
iaci-ō	iac-ere	iēc-ī	iact-us		*throw*
fodi-ō	fod-ere	fōd-ī	foss-us	[fosse]	*dig*
fugi-ō	fug-ere	fūg-ī	fugit-ūrus	[fugitive]	*flee*
pari-ō	par-ere	peper-ī	part-us		*bring forth*

205   (*b*) Perf. Act. stem formed with the suffix *s* :

con-cuti-ō	-cut-ere	-cuss-ī	-cuss-us	[concussion]	*shake*
con-spici-ō	-spic-ere	-spex-ī	-spect-us	[inspection]	*look at*

So in-lici-ō, *lure on*; but ē-lici-ō, *lure out*, forms ē-licu-ī, ē-licit-us [elicit].

206   (*c*) Perf. Act. stem formed with the suffix *u* :

rapi-ō   rap-ere   rapu-ī   rapt-us   [rapture]   *seize*

207   2. *Cupiō* and *sapiō* form their Perf. Act. from the stems *cupī-, sapī-*, with the suffix *v* [Rule 1, § 171] like *audiō* (4th Conjugation) :

cupi-ō	cupere	cupīv-ī	cupit-us	*desire*
sapi-ō	sapere	sapīv-ī	——	*be sensible*

FIRST CONJUGATION

208   1. **Four verbs of the 1st Conjugation form the Perf. Act. from a stem ending in a consonant (= the part of the Infinitive which comes before the ending *āre*), like verbs of the 3rd Conjugation.** In the following list the Infinitive is divided so as to show this stem.

These four form the Perf. Act. stem without a suffix :

209   (*a*) *iuvō* and *lavō* without reduplication [Rule 2, § 171] :

iuv-ō	iuv-āre	iūv-ī	iūt-us	[adjutant]	*aid*
lav-ō	lav-āre	lāv-ī	laut-us		*wash*

210   (*b*) *dō* and *stō* with reduplication :

d-ō	d-are	ded-ī	dat-us	[dative]	*give*

Dō differs from all other verbs of the 1st conj. in having the stem vowel *a* short in all forms except *dās* (2nd sing. Pres. Indic. Act.) and *dā* (2nd sing. Imperative): thus *dăre*, *dătus*. Similarly *circum-dō* forms *circum-dăre*, *-dedī*, *-dătus*. But all compounds formed with a preposition of one syllable belong to the 3rd conjugation ; see § 185.

211 st-ō   st-āre   stet-ī   stāt-ūrus   [station]   *stand*

The compounds of *stō* with a preposition of one syllable form the Perf. Act. in *-stitī*, and many of them have a Fut. Part. Act., e. g. *in-stō*, *-stāre*, *-stitī*, *-ştātūrus*. *Circum-stō* forms *-stāre*, *-stetī*, ——.

212   2. **Some verbs of the 1st Conjug. form the Perf. Act. like habeō (2nd Conj.) : the most important are—**

vet-ō	vet-āre	vetu-ī	vetit-us	*forbid*

So cubō, *lie down* ; domō, *tame* [whence English 'in-domit-able '].

sec-ō	secā-re	secu-ī	sect-us	[section]	*cut*
son-ō	sonā-re	sonu-ī	sonāt-ūrus		*sound*
ton-ō	tonā-re	tonu-ī	——		*thunder*

So mic-ō, *glitter*.

SECOND CONJUGATION.

213   1. **About twenty verbs of the 2nd Conjugation form the Perf. Act. from a stem ending in a consonant (= the part of the Infinitive which comes before the ending *ēre*), like verbs of the 3rd Conjugation. In the following list the Infinitive is divided so as to show this stem.**

214   (*a*) From a stem ending in a guttural. These all take the suffix *s*, like most verbs in *gō* and *cō* of the 3rd Conjug. (§§ 173, 176):

auge-ō	aug-ēre	aux-ī	auctus	[auction]	*increase*
lūce-ō	lūc-ēre	lux-ī	——		*shine*

So lūge-ō, *mourn.*

215   The guttural is dropped after a liquid [Rule 3, § 171]:

indulge-ō   indulg-ēre   induls-ī   ——   *indulge*

So fulgeō, *flash*; urgeō, *urge.*[1]

torque-ō torqu-ēre tors-ī   tort-us [torture] *twist*

216   (*b*) From a stem ending in *d* (not preceded by *n*):

       (i) with the suffix *s* [Rule 4, § 171]:

arde-ō	ard-ēre	ars-ī	ars-ūrus	[arson]	*be on fire*
rīde-ō	rīd-ēre	rīs-ī	rīs-um[2]	[derision]	*laugh*
suāde-ō	suād-ēre	suās-ī	suās-um	[persuasion]	*advise*

217   (ii) without a suffix:

sede-ō	sed-ēre	sēd-ī	sess-um	[session]	*sit*
vide-ō	vid-ēre	vīd-ī	vīs-us	[vision]	*see*
morde-ō	mord-ēre	momord-ī	mors-us	[morsel]	*bite*

218   (*c*) From a stem ending in *nd*; always without a suffix [Rule 2, § 171].

pende-ō	pend-ēre	pepend-ī	——		*hang* (intr.)
sponde-ō	spond-ēre	spopond-ī	spons-us	[sponsor]	*pledge*
tonde-ō	tond-ēre	totond-ī	tons-us	[tonsure]	*shear*

219   (*d*) From a stem ending in *v*; always without a suffix [Rule 2, § 171]:

cave-ō   cav-ēre   cāv-ī   caut-um [caution]   *beware*

So faveō, *be favourable.*

move-ō mov-ēre mōv-ī   mōt-us   [motion]   *move* (tr.)

So foveō, *warm*; voveō, *vow.*

---

[1] Other (less important) verbs of the 2nd Conj. to which this rule applies are given in the alphabetical list (Appendix): e. g. *algeō, mulceō, tergeō.*

[2] In transitive compounds there is the form *-rīsus*, e. g. *dērīsus, irrīsus.*

20   (e) From stems ending in other consonants :

iube-ō   iub-ēre   iuss-ī   iuss-us   [jussive]   *bid*
mane-ō   man-ēre   mans-ī   mans-um   [mansion]   *remain*
haere-ō   haer-ēre   haes-ī   haes-ūrus   *cling*

[adhesion : *note difference of spelling*]

221   2. **Five verbs of the 2nd Conj. form the Perf. Act. from the stem of the Present** (ending in *e*) with the suffix *v* [Rule 1, § 171] :

com-ple-ō -plē-re   -plēv-ī   -plēt-us   [completion] *fill up*

So dēleō, *destroy*; fleō, *weep*.

abole-ō   abolē-re   abolēv-ī abolit-us   [abolition] *get rid of*
cie-ō[1]   ciē-re   cīv-ī   cit-us   [excite]   *rouse*

222   3. **The following have some peculiarity in the Perf. Part. Pass.** :

doce-ō   docē-re   docu-ī   doct-us   [doctor]   *teach*
tene-ō   tenē-re   tenu-ī   -tent-us   [retention] *hold*
misce-ō   miscē-re   miscu-ī   mixt-us   [mixture]   *mix*
torre-ō   torrē-re   torru-ī   tost-us   *parch*
cense-ō   censē-re   censu-ī   cens-us   [censure]   *decide*

FOURTH CONJUGATION

223   1. **About ten verbs of the 4th Conjugation form the Perf. Act. from a stem ending in a consonant** (= the part of the Infinitive which comes before the ending *īre*), like verbs of the 3rd Conjugation. In this list the Infinitive is divided so as to show this stem.

224   (a) From a stem ending in a guttural, with the suffix *s* :

sanci-ō   sanc-īre   sanx-ī   sanct-us   [sanction]   *ratify*
vinci-ō   vinc-īre   vinx-ī   vinct-us   *bind*

225   The guttural is dropped after a liquid [Rule 3, § 171] :

fulci-ō   fulc-īre   fuls-ī   fult-us   *prop*

So re-fercio, *cram*; sarcio, *patch*.

---

[1] The compounds of *cieō* are of the 4th Conj., e. g. *ex-ciō, -cīre, -cīvī* (or *-ciī*), *-cītus* (or *-citus*).

226 (*b*) From stems ending in other consonants :

saepi-ō	saep-īre	saeps-ī	saept-us		*fence in*
senti-ō	sent-īre	sens-ī	sens-us	[sense]	*feel*
hauri-ō	haur-īre	haus-ī	haust-us	[exhaustion]	*drain*
veni-ō	ven-īre	vēn-ī	vent-um	[advent]	*come*
comperi-ō	comper-īre	comper-ī	compert-us		*learn*
reperi-ō	reper-īre	repper-ī	repert-us	[repertory]	*find*

227 2. The following form the Perf. Act. like *habeō* (2nd Conjugation) :

sali-ō	salī-re	salu-ī	——		*leap*
aperi-ō	aperī-re	aperu-ī	apert-us	[aperture]	*open*

So operiō, *cover*.

228 3. **Sepeliō** forms the Perf. Part. Pass. from the stem *sepel-* :

sepeli-ō	sepelī-re	sepelīv-ī	sepult-us	[sepulture]	*bury*

229 4. **Feriō** forms two Perfects Active, from entirely different stems :

feri-ō	ferī-re	percuss-ī [1]	percuss-us	[percussion]	*strike*
		īc-ī [2]	ict-us		

DEPONENT VERBS

230 Deponent Verbs have only three Principal Parts :

   1. The Present Indicative, 1st pers. sing.
   2. The Present Infinitive.
   3. The Perfect Participle.

3rd Conjugation.

231

fung-or	fung-ī	funct-us	[function]	*discharge*
loqu-or	loqu-ī	locūt-us	[elocution]	*talk*
sequ-or	sequ-ī	secūt-us	[consecutive]	*follow*
fru-or	fru-ī	ūs-us [3]		*enjoy*

[1] From *per-cutiō*, a compound of *quatiō*, like *con-cutiō*, § 205. Used in the literal sense with the abl. *secūrī* ('with an axe') : *secūrī percussī*. 'I have beheaded.'

[2] Used in a figurative sense with the acc. *foedus* ('a treaty') : *foedus ferīre*, 'to make a treaty.'

[3] Borrowed from *ūtor* (see below); *fruct-us* and *fruit-us* [whence English 'fructify' and 'fruition'] are not usual.

nasc-or [1]	nasc-ī	nāt-us	[native]	*be born*
īrasc-or [1]	īrasc-ī	suscensu-ī [2]		*get angry*
vesc-or [1]	vesc-ī	ēd-ī [3]		*feed* (intr.)
adipisc-or [1]	adipisc-ī	adept-us	[adept]	*acquire*
comminisc-or[1]	comminisc-ī	comment-us	[comment]	*devise*
expergisc-or [1]	expergisc-ī	experrect-us		*awake* (intr.)
nancisc-or [1]	nancisc-ī	nact-us *or* nanct-us		*get*
oblīvisc-or [1]	oblīvisc-ī ·	oblīt-us		*forget*
pacisc-or [1]	pacisc-ī	pact-us	[compact]	*make a bargain*
proficisc-or [1]	proficisc-ī	profect-us		*set out*
ulcisc-or [1]	ulcisc-ī	ult-us		*avenge, punish*
nīt-or	nīt-ī	(i) nīs-us		(i) *strive*
		(ii) nix-us		(ii) *rest on*
ūt-or	ūt-ī	ūs-us	[usage]	*use, enjoy*
am-plect-or } com-plect-or }	-plect-ī	-plex-us	[complex]	*embrace*
lāb-or	lāb-ī	laps-us	[relapse]	*slip*
quer-or	quer-ī	quest-us		*complain*

Mixed Conjugation.

32

pati-or	pat-ī	pass-us	[passion]	*suffer*
con-gredi-or	-gred-ī	-gress-us	[congress]	*meet*

So ag-gredior, ē-gredior, trans-gredior, and other compounds of gradior.

mori-or	mor-ī	mortu-us	[mortuary]	*die*
	Fut. Part. morit-ūrus			

1st Conjugation.

33   All the Deponents of the 1st Conj. form their Perf. Part. like *vocō*: e. g. *hort-or, hortā-rī, hortāt-us*, exhort (§ 169).

2nd Conjugation.

34   Most of the Deponents of the 2nd Conj. form their Perf. Part. like *habeō*: e. g. *vere-or, verē-rī, verit-us*, fear; *misere-or, miserē-rī, miserit-us*, pity; *tue-or, tuē-rī, tuit-us*, protect. Note *re-or, rē-rī, rat-us* [rate], think.

[1] The stem of the tenses of incomplete action is extended by the addition of *sc*; cf. *pasc-, cresc-*, &c., § 178.

[2] Borrowed from *suscenseō*, 2nd Conj.; the form *īrātus* is an adjective meaning 'angry'; thus *īrātus sum* means 'I am angry', not 'I got angry'.

[3] Supplied by *edō*, § 184.

The following forms its Perf. Part. like a verb of the 3rd Conj. :

fate-or	fat-ērī	fass-us	*confess*
con-fite-or	-fit-ērī	-fess-us [confession]	

4th Conjugation.

235   Most of the Deponents of the 4th Conj. form their Perf. Part. like *audiō*: e. g. *poti-or, potī-rī, potīt-us,* get possession of; *largi-or, largī-rī, largīt-us,* give bountifully; *menti-or, mentī-rī, mentīt-us,* speak falsely; *mōli-or, mōlī-rī, mōlīt-us,* set in motion; *sorti-or, sortī-rī, sortīt-us,* obtain by lot.

The following form the Perfect Participle like verbs of the 3rd Conj. :

mēti-or	mēt-īrī	mens-us [mensuration]	*measure*
ordi-or	ord-īrī	ors-us[1]	*begin*
ori-or	or-īrī	ort-us[1]	*arise*
(§ 167)		Fut. Part. orit-ūrus	
ex-peri-or	-per-īrī	-pert-us [expert]	*make trial of*
ad-senti-or	-sent-īrī	-sens-us [consensus]	*assent*

SEMI-DEPONENT VERBS

Semi-deponent verbs are verbs which have passive forms with active meaning in only some groups of tenses.

2nd Conjugation.

236 aude-ō	aud-ēre	aus-us	*dare*
gaude-ō	gaud-ēre	gāvīs-us	*rejoice*

sole-ō, solē-re, solit-us, be accustomed, is like *habeō.*

3rd Conjugation.

237 fī-ō	fierī	fact-us	*become* (§ 246)
fīd-ō	fīd-ere	fīs-us	*trust*
re-vert-or	-vert-ī	-versus[2]	*return, turn back* (intr.)

---

[1] *Ors-us* (having begun) from a stem in *d*, but *ortus* (having arisen) from a stem in *r*: see Rule, § 172.

[2] The Perfect Indic. is active in form borrowed from *vertō,* § 188): *revertī.*

IRREGULAR VERBS

238   The verbs whose principal parts are given above (§§ 173–237) are not properly described as irregular, though they form their perfect active and perfect participle passive differently from verbs like *vocō, habeō, regō, audiō,* which are taken as models for the four conjugations. The latter, it is true, form the large majority of verbs in the 1st, 2nd, and 4th conjugations. But *regō* is not really more typical of the 3rd conjugation than verbs which form their perf. act. without *s,* like *legō* (§ 175) or *dēfendō* (§ 186). Nor can perfects like *iūvī* (1st conj., § 209), *vēnī* (4th conj., § 226), or like *auxī* (2nd conj., § 214), *vinxī* (4th conj., § 224) be properly described as irregular. They are merely examples of two of the ways of forming the perfect which are given in § 171.

The term 'irregular' is more fitly used of a small number of verbs which stand apart from all other verbs in the formation of the **tenses of incomplete action,** and of verbs which are defective in some of their tenses, as shown in the sections which follow.[1]

Compounds of sum.

239   Most compounds of *sum,* such as *ad-sum, dē-sum, in-sum, prae-sum,* &c., are conjugated exactly like *sum*; but *prō-sum* and *pos-sum* are peculiar.

In **prō-sum,** *I am helpful,* the preposition *prō* assumes its older form *prōd* when the verbal part begins with a vowel:

Pres. Indic.: prō-sum,   **prōd-es, prōd-est**;
            prō-sumus, **prōd-estis,** prō-sunt.
Fut. Indic. : **prōd-erō,** -eris, -erit, &c.
Past Imperf. Indic. : **prōd-eram,** -erās, -erat, &c.
Past Subj. : **prōd-essem,** -essēs, -esset, &c.
Imperative : **prōd-es,** -estō, -este, -estōte.
Infinitive : **prōd-esse.**

---

[1] Only the forms printed in heavy type in §§ 239–47 need to be learned.

240 **possum,** *I can*, is compounded of *sum* and an indeclinable adjective *potis* or *pote* meaning 'able' : *pos-sum*, ' I am able.' This adjective, which assumes the form *pos-* before *s*, resumes the form *pot-* before a vowel. In the pres. infin. and the past subj. the syllable *es-* of *esse* and *essem* disappears. This verb is also peculiar in the formation of its perf. active stem : *potu-*.

Possum forms no imperative, and the only verb-noun which it has is the infin. (pres. and perf.).

Pres. Indic. : pos-sum, **pot-es, pot-est** ;
                 pos-sumus, **pot-estis**, pos-sunt.

Fut. Indic. : pot-erō, -eris, -erit, *&c.*

Past Imperf. Indic. : pot-eram, -erās, -erat, *&c.*

Pres. Subj. : pos-sim, -sīs, -sit, *&c.*

Past Subj. : **pos-sem, -sēs, -set ; pos-sēmus, -sētis, -sent.**

Pres. Infin. : **pos-se.**

Principal Parts : **possum, posse, potu-ī, ——.**

241 **ferō,** *I bear* ; **ferre, tul-ī, lāt-us**

             drops $\begin{cases} i \text{ before } s \text{ and } t, \\ \text{a short } e \text{ between two } r\text{'s.} \end{cases}$

The Imperative 2nd sing. is *fer*; cf. *dīc, dūc* (§ 176), *fac* (§ 159).

[*See table next page.*

Tenses of incomplete action.

ACTIVE	
INDICATIVE	*IMPERATIVE*

PRESENT

S. ferō	*P.* ferimus		
fers	fertis	*S.* fer, fertō	*P.* ferte, fertōte
fert	ferunt	fertō	feruntō

	SUBJUNCTIVE
FUTURE	PRESENT
feram, ferēs, feret, &c.	feram, ferās, ferat, &c.
PAST IMPERFECT	PAST
ferēbam, ferēbās, ferēbat, &c.	ferrem, ferrēs, ferret, &c.

VERB-ADJS	PRES. PART. ferens (-nt-)	FUT. PART. lātūrus, a, um FUT. INFIN. lātūrus (a, um) esse
VERB-NOUNS	PRES. INFIN. **ferre** GERUND ferendum	SUPINE lātum

PASSIVE	
INDICATIVE	*IMPERATIVE*

PRESENT

S. feror	*P.* ferimur		
ferris	feriminī	*S.* **ferre, fertor**	*P.* feriminī
fertur	feruntur	**fertor**	feruntor

	SUBJUNCTIVE
FUTURE	PRESENT
ferar, ferēris, ferētur, &c.	ferar, ferāris, ferātur, &c.
PAST IMPERFECT	PAST
ferēbar, ferēbāris, ferēbātur, &c.	ferrer, ferrēris, ferrētur, &c.

VERB-ADJ.	GERUND ADJ. ferendus, a um
VERB-NOUNS	PRES. INFIN. **ferrī** FUT. INFIN. lātum īrī

242 volō, *I will*, velle, volu-ī, and its compounds nōlō, *I will not* [from *ně-volō*], nolle, nōluī, and mālō, *I prefer* [from *magis* and *volō*], malle, māluī.

Tenses of incomplete action.

INDICATIVE			IMPERATIVE		
PRESENT					
volō	nōlō	mālō			
vīs	nōn vīs	māvīs	——	nōlī, nōlītō	——
vult	nōn vult	māvult	——	nōlītō	——
volumus	nōlumus	mālumus			
vultis	nōn vultis	māvultis	——	nōlīte, nōlītōte	——
volunt	nōlunt	mālunt	——	nōluntō	——

			SUBJUNCTIVE		
FUTURE			**PRESENT**		
volam	nōlam	mālam	velim	nōlim	mālim
volēs	nōlēs	mālēs	velīs	nōlīs	mālīs
volet	nōlet	mālet	velit	nōlit	mālit
volēmus	nōlēmus	mālēmus	velīmus	nōlīmus	mālīmus
volētis	nōlētis	mālētis	velītis	nōlītis	mālītis
volent	nōlent	mālent	velint	nōlint	mālint
PAST IMPERFECT			**PAST**		
volēbam	nōlēbam	mālēbam	vellem	nollem	mallem
volēbās	nōlēbās	mālēbās	vellēs	nollēs	mallēs
volēbat	nōlēbat	mālēbat	vellet	nollet	mallet
&c.	&c.	&c.	&c.	&c.	&c.

VERB-ADJ.	PRES. PART.			
	volens nōlens ——		[No Fut. Part.]	

VERB-NOUN	PRES. INFIN.	[No Supine]
	velle nolle malle	
	[Gerund only in late Latin]	

243 eō, *I go*, īre, i-ī, it-um

belongs to the 4th conjugation ; but it forms an old-fashioned fut. and past imperf. indic. by adding -bō and -bam to the stem ī-, just like a verb of the 1st or 2nd conjugation (vocābō, habēbō ; vocābam, habēbam). Note the short *i* in *itum*.

Tenses of incomplete action			
INDICATIVE		*IMPERATIVE*	
PRESENT			
S. eō	*P.* īmus		
īs	ītis	*S.* ī, ītō	*P.* īte, ītōte
it	eunt	ītō	euntō

		SUBJUNCTIVE	
FUTURE		PRESENT	
S. ībō	*P.* ībimus	*S.* eam	*P.* eāmus
ībis	ībitis	eās	eātis
ībit	ībunt	eat	eant
PAST IMPERFECT		PAST	
S. ībam	*P.* ībāmus	*S.* īrem	*P.* īrēmus
ības	ībātis	īrēs	īrētis
ībat	ībant	īret	īrent

VERB-ADJS.	PRES. PART. iens (stem **eunt-**)	FUT. PART. itūrus, a, um
VERB-NOUNS	PRES. INFIN. īre / GERUND **eundum**	FUT. INFIN. itūrus (a, um) esse / SUPINE itum

The passive is formed in the same way, but is only used impersonally, e. g. ītur, *there is a going*; but those compounds which are used transitively in the active voice have a fully conjugated passive voice (ad-īrī, *to be approached*, in-īrī, *to be entered*, sub-īrī, *to be undergone*, &c.).

44 Peculiarities in the tenses of completed action :—

The perfect active is *iī* (not *īvī*), and these two vowels are contracted into one long *i* before *s* :

Perf. Indic. : iī, īstī, iit ; iimus, īstis, iērunt.
Past Perf. Subj. : īssem, īssēs, īsset, *&c.*
Perf. Infin. : īsse.

245   queō, *I can*, quīre, quīvī, quitum

nequeō, *I cannot*, nequīre, nequīvī, nequitum

are conjugated like *eō* (§ 243), but are used only in a few forms.

246   fīō (i) *I become*
(ii) *I am made*} fierī, fact·us sum.

In its second meaning *fīō* serves as a passive to *faciō*, which does not itself form a passive of the tenses of incomplete action, except in those compounds which are used transitively in the active voice (afficī, *to be affected*, interficī, *to be killed*, &c.).

Tenses of incomplete action.

. *INDICATIVE*		*IMPERATIVE*
PRESENT		
S. fīō	*P.* ——	[Only in Old Latin and Late Latin]
fīs	——	
fit	fīunt	

SUBJUNCTIVE

FUTURE	PRESENT
fīam, fīēs, fīet, *&c.*	fīam, fīās, fīat, *&c.*
PAST IMPERFECT	PAST
fīēbam, fīēbās, fīēbat, *&c.*	**fierem, fierēs, fieret**, *&c.*

VERB-ADJECTIVES AND VERB-NOUNS

[Pres. Part. and Gerund only in Late Latin.]

PRES. INFIN. **fierī**,
(i) *to become*
(ii) *to be made*

FUT. PART. **futūrus**, *about to become*

FUT. INFIN. **fore**, *or* futūrus esse, *to be about to become*
[factum īrī, *to be about to be made*, belongs to *faciō*]

47 edō, *I eat*, esse, ēd·ī, ·ēs·us (only in compounds, *e.g.* ex-ēsus, *eaten out*, amb-ēsus, *gnawed around*).

Tenses of incomplete action		
INDICATIVE	*IMPERATIVE*	
PRESENT		
S. edō *P.* edimus		
es estis	*S.* es, estō *P.* este, estōte	
est edunt	estō eduntō	
	SUBJUNCTIVE	
FUTURE	**PRESENT**	
S. edam *P.* edēmus	*S.* edim *P.* edīmus	
edēs edētis	edīs edītis	
edet edent	edit edint	
PAST IMPERFECT	**PAST**	
edēbam, edēbās, edēbat &c.	essem, essēs, esset, &c.	
VERB-ADJS.	PRES. PART. edens (-nt-)	FUT. PART. ēsūrus, a, um
VERB-NOUNS	PRES. INFIN. esse	FUT. INFIN. ēsūrus (a, um) esse
	GERUND edendum	SUPINE ēsum

48   The following verbs of 'saying' are used chiefly in the tenses of incomplete action, and in these they are defective :

(1) **inquam**, *say I* (used parenthetically), forms :—
   Pres. Indic. : inquis, inquit ; inquiunt.
   Fut. Indic. : inquiēs, inquiet.
   Past Imperf. Indic. : inquiēbat.

(2) **aiō**, *I say*, forms :—
   Pres. Indic. : ais, ait (two syllables : *a-is, a-it*) ; aiunt.
   Past Imperf. Indic. : aiēbam, aiēbās, aiēbat, &c.
   Pres. Subj. : aiat.

(3) **fārī**, *to speak*, forms chiefly :—
   Pres. Indic. : fātur, *he speaks.*   *Fut. Indic.* : fābitur, *he will speak.*   *Imperat.* : fāre, *speak.*
   Gerund : fandī, fandō, *of speaking, by speaking.*
   Perf. Part. : fātus, a, um, *having spoken.*

249   The following verbs have **no tenses of incomplete action.**

(1) The Perfect **coep-ī**, *I have begun, I began,* **coep-isse,**
coept-us:

ACTIVE

Perf. Indic. : coepī, coepistī, coepit, *&c.*

Fut. Perf. Indic. : coeperō, *I shall have begun,* coeperis,[1]
    coeperit, *&c.*

Past Perf. Indic. : coeperam, *I had begun,* coeperās, coep-
    erat, *&c.*

Perf. Subj. : coeperim, coeperīs,[1] coeperit, *&c.*

Past. Perf. Subj. : coepissem, coepissēs, coepisset, *&c.*

Fut. Part. : coeptūrus, a, um, *about to begin.*

PASSIVE

Perf. Part. : coeptus, a, um, *begun.*

Perf. Indic. : coeptus (a, um) sum, *I have been begun.*

The tenses of incomplete action are supplied by *incipiō,*
incipiam, incipiēbam.

The chief use of both *coepī* and *incipiō* is with an infinitive
as object :

$$\text{aedificāre} \begin{cases} \text{coepī, } \textit{I have begun} \\ \text{incipiō, } \textit{I am beginning} \end{cases} \textit{to build.}$$

Sometimes, however, with other objects or without any object :
ōrātiōnem coepisse (incipere), *to begin a speech.*

The Passive forms are mostly used with a Passive Infinitive,
and are translated by active forms in English : urbs aedificārī
coepta est, *the city began to be built.*

Sometimes, however, in other constructions : amīcitia coepta est,
friendship was begun.

(2) The Perfect **memin-ī**, *I remember,* **memin-isse** (unlike
coepī) has the meaning of a Present tense :

Perf. Indic. : meminī, meministī, meminit, *&c.*

Fut. Perf. Indic. : meminerō, *I shall remember,* memineris,[1]
    meminerit, *&c.*

Past Perf. Indic. : memineram, *I remembered,* meminerās,
    meminerat, *&c.*

Perf. Subj. : meminerim, meminerīs,[1] meminerit, *&c.*

Past Perf. Subj.: meminissem, meminissēs, meminisset, *&c.*

Imperative : S. 2 mementō $\Big\}$ *remember.*
    P. 2 mementōte

---

[1] See notes on pp. 61, 68.

(3) The Perfect ōd-ī, *I hate,* ōd-isse, ōs-us has (like *meminī*) the meaning of a Present tense :

Perf. Indic. : ōdī, ōdistī, ōdit, *&c.*
Fut. Perf. Indic. : ōderō, *I shall hate,* ōderis,[1] ōderit, *&c.*
Past Perf. Indic. : ōderam, *I hated,* ōderās, ōderat, *&c.*
Perf. Subj. : ōderim, ōderīs,[1] ōderit, *&c.*
Past Perf. Subj. : ōdissem, ōdissēs, ōdisset, *&c.*
Fut. Part. : ōsūrus, a, um, *about to hate.*
Perf. Part. : ōsus, a, um, *hating.*

The meaning of the Perf. Part. is neither passive (in spite of its passive form, cf. in French *allé* 'gone ') nor perfect.

---

[1] See notes on pp. 61, 68.

APPENDIX TO PART I

PECULIARITIES OF NOUNS AND ADJECTIVES

Second Declension.

i   *Locus*, m. 'place' generally forms a neuter nom. and acc. plural *loca*. The masc. forms *locī*, *locōs* mostly mean 'passages in books'.

ii   A few nouns in *us* are neuter, with acc. sing. the same as nom. sing.; so *vulgus* 'the rabble' (rarely masc.).

iii   Some adjectives in *us, a, um,* form gen. sing. in *īus*, and dat. sing. in *ī*, see §§ 86, 88.

iv   Some nouns retain an old form of the gen. plur. in *um* (generally side by side with the later form in *ōrum*):

     (*a*) nouns denoting coins and measures; e. g. *nummus*, m. 'coin'; *sēstertius*, m. 'sesterce' (a small silver coin); *talentum*, n. 'talent' (a Greek word denoting a sum of money—about £200).

     (*b*) some nouns denoting persons: e. g. *deus* 'god', gen. plur. often *deum* in poets (§ 22. 3); *līberī* 'children' (§ 21); *socius* 'ally'. *Vir* 'man' (§ 17, p. 21) often forms gen. plur. *virum* in poets.

     (*c*) some nouns denoting nationalities, especially in poets: *Achīvī* 'Achaeans', *Teucrī* 'Teucrians'.

     Similarly some numeral adjectives: *duo* (§ 89), compounds of *centum* (§ 80), and distributive adjectives like *bīnī* (§ 84); thus *pedum quadrāgēnum intervallō* 'at an interval of 40 feet in each case' (Caesar, B. G. iv. 17. 5).

Third Declension.

     (i) Forms with *i* instead of *e*.

v   (*a*) The accusative singular of a few nouns in *is* (Class B, § 28) ends in *im* instead of *em*: thus *vīs*, f. 'violence' forms *vim*; *sitis*, f. 'thirst', *sitim*; *puppis*, f. 'stern of a vessel', *puppim*; so too proper names of rivers and towns, e.g. *Tiberis*, m. 'the Tiber', *Neāpolis*, f. 'Naples'.

     A few nouns have both the form in *im* and that in *em*, e. g. *secūris*, f. 'axe', *secūrim* or *secūrem*.

       Tiberim, vim, Neāpolim; secūrim, sitim, puppim.

(*b*) The ablative singular of the nouns that form the acc. sing. in *im* ends in *ī* instead of *e*: thus *vī* 'by violence', *sitī* 'by thirst'. So too the ablative singular of some nouns which are properly adjectives, such as *nātālis* (originally *diēs nātālis*), m. 'birthday'.

(*c*) *ignis*, m. 'fire' forms abl. *ignī* in certain phrases, e.g. *ferrō ignīque* 'with fire and sword'.

(ii) Genitive plural in *um* instead of *ium*.

(*a*) The nouns *pater*, m. 'father', *māter*, f. 'mother', *frāter*, m. 'brother' have lost an *e* in the acc., gen., dat. and abl. cases: *pater, patr-em, patr-is, patr-ī, patr-e*; plur. *patr-ēs, patr-um patr-ibus*. Thus the genitive plural comes to be contrary to the rule given in § 27.

(*b*) The words *canis*, m. or f. 'dog', *mensis*, m. 'month', *iuve-nis*, m. or f. 'young man' or 'young woman', and *senex* (gen. *senis*), m. 'old man' form the genitive plural irregularly in *um*: *canum, mensum,*[1] *iuvenum* and *senum*.

(*c*) *Parens* (gen. *parentis*), m. or f. 'parent' forms both *paren-tum* and *parentium*.

(iii) Genitive plural in *ium* instead of *um*.

(*a*) The following nouns form the genitive plural in *ium*, con-trary to the rule given in § 23: *vīs*, f. 'violence' (plur. *vīrēs*, 'strength'); *līs* (gen. *lītis*), f. 'dispute'; *faux* (plur. *faucēs*), f. 'throat', 'jaws'; *imber* (gen. *imbris*), m. 'rain'; *nix* (gen. *nivis*), f. 'snow'; *Penātēs* (plur.), m. 'household gods'; *optimātēs* (plur.), m. 'aristocrats'; and proper names of tribes ending in *is* (gen. *ītis*) or as (gen. *ātis*):

> *vīrium, lītium, faucium, Penātium* ;
> *imbrium* and *nivium, Samnītium, optimātium.*

(*b*) Many feminine nouns in *tās* (gen. *tātis*) have a by-form of the gen. plur. in *tātium*, as well as the more usual form in *tātum* ; e. g. *cīvitās*, f. 'state', *cīvitātum* or *cīvitātium*.

(iv) The following nouns are irregular in respect of their stems or their endings. English derivatives showing the stem are given in square brackets.

---

[1] *Mensum* is the ordinary form in classical times; *mensium* and *mensuum* are later (as has been shown by Wagener, *Beiträge zur lateinischen Gram-matik,* 1905).

bōs, m. or f. 'ox' [bov-ine]: *bov-em, bov-is, bov-ī, bov-e*; plur. *bov-ēs, bo-um, būbus* or *bōbus*.

carō, f. 'flesh' [carn-al]: *carn-em, carn-is, carn-ī, carn-e*; plur. = 'pieces of flesh' rare.

cor, n. 'heart' [cord-ial]: *cor* (acc.), *cord-is, cord-ī, cord-e*; plur. *cord-a* (*cord-ium, cord-ibus*, rare).

iter, n. 'journey' [itiner-ary]: *iter* (acc.), *itiner-is, -ī, -e*, plur. *itiner-a, -um, -ibus*.

Iuppiter, m. 'Jupiter', lit. 'Father Jove' [jov-ial]: *Iov-em, Iov-is, Iov-ī, Iov-e*.

iūsiūrandum. n. 'oath', should be written as two words, *iūs* a noun of the 3rd decl. (§ 37), *iūrandum* an adj. of the 2nd decl.: thus *iūs iūrandum, iūris iūrandī, iūrī iūrandō, iūre iūrandō*; no plur. in use.

os, n. 'bone' [oss-ify]: *os* (acc.), *oss-is, oss-ī, oss-e*; plur. *oss-a, oss-ium, oss-ibus*.

senex, m. 'old man' [sen-ior]: *sen-em, sen-is, sen-ī, sen-e*; plur. *sen-ēs, sen-um, sen-ibus*.

sūs, m. or f. 'pig', *su-em, su-is, su-ī, su-e*; plur. *su-ēs, su-um, su-bus* or *su-ibus*.

vīs, f. 'violence', acc. *vim*, no gen. or dat., abl. *vī*; plur. = 'strength', *vīr-ēs, vīr-ium, vīr-ibus*. [Compare above **xi.**]

xiv (v) Some adjectives, with no separate form for the feminine or neuter in the nom. sing., are declined like nouns of the 3rd decl. (Class A, §§ 23-6), i. e. they have the abl. sing. in *e* and the gen. plur. in *um*, or one of these two forms. Contrast *ingens*, § 33.

xv (a) Verb-adjectives in *ns*, gen. *ntis* (Present Participles) form the abl. sing. in *e*, when they are used either as nouns or predicatively in the abl. absolute; thus *ab amante* 'by a lover', *flūmine currente* 'as the river is flowing'. But when they are used as attributes of a noun they have the form in *ī* (like *ingens*, § 33); thus *in flūmine currentī* 'in a flowing river'. In poets they sometimes form the gen. plur. in *um*; thus *amantum* (for *amantium*).

xvi (b) The following adjectives form the abl. sing. in *-e* and the gen. plur. in *-um*:

vetus 'old' (stem *veter-*, whence English 'veter-an').
dīves 'rich' (stem *dīvit-*).
pauper 'poor' (stem *pauper-*).
princeps 'chief' (stem *princip-*, whence English 'princip-al').

Abl. sing. *vetere, dīvite, paupere, principe.*

Gen. Plur. *veterum, dīvitum, pauperum, principum.*

Such adjectives generally have no neuter plur. (nom. or acc.); but *vetus* forms *vetera*, and *dīves* forms *dītia* (contracted).

(vi) *celer* m., *celeris* f., *celere* n. 'swift' is declined like *ācer, ācris, ācre* (§ 32), excepting that it does not drop the *e* of the stem. The genitive plural in the form *celerum* is used only as a noun = 'of the cavalry'.

(vii) A few adjectives are indeclinable, as *tot* 'so many', *nēquam* 'good for nothing' (lit. 'no-how'), *frūgī* 'good for something' (lit. 'for use', dat. of *frux*).

Fourth Declension.

A few masc. and fem. nouns form the dat. and abl. plur. in *ubus*: e.g. *tribus*, f. 'tribe'.

ALTERNATIVE SPELLINGS IN ADJECTIVES AND ADVERBS.

(i) Instead of *imus* in superlatives and ordinal numerals an older form in *umus* is sometimes used: e.g. *pessumus, decumus* (whence *porta decumāna* 'the decuman gate', *decumae* 'tithes'); also in some other adjectives, e.g. *fīnitumus.*

(ii) Instead of *-ensimus* and *-iens* in numeral adjectives and adverbs (§ 80 f.) the spellings *-ēsimus* and *-iēs* are found.

(iii) Instead of *-endus* in gerund adjectives belonging to verbs of the 3rd and 4th conjugation an older form in *-undus* is found: e.g. *repetundus* (whence *pecūniae repetundae* 'moneys to be recovered' = money illegally extorted); *oriundus*, which has come to be used with the meaning of a present participle active, 'arising.'

CHIEF EXCEPTIONS TO RULES OF GENDER (§§ 56–65)

EXCEPTIONS TO RULE FOR 2ND DECL. (§ 60).—Proper names of towns and countries in *us*, and nouns in *us* denoting kinds of trees, are fem.: e.g. *Corinthus* 'Corinth' (*captīva Corinthus*), *Aegyptus* 'Egypt'; *ulmus* 'elm' (*ulmus antīqua* 'an immemorial elm') ; also the word *humus* 'earth' (*humus ātra* 'the black soil'). A few in US are neuter: note *VULGUS* 'the rabble' (*PROFĀNUM VULGUS* 'the profane rabble'), *PELAGUS* 'the sea' (a Greek word, used by poets: *PELAGUS APERTUM* 'the open sea').

Exceptions to Rules for 3rd Decl. (§§ 61, 62).

xxiv 1. The following, which form the nom. sing. by adding the suffix *s* to the stem, are masc. :

(*a*) Nouns ending in **es**, gen. **itis**, and **ex**, gen. **icis**: thus caespes 'turf' (in caespite vīvō 'on the live turf'), gurges 'whirl-pool' (in gurgite vastō 'in the wild whirlpool'), vertex 'summit' (in summō vertice 'on the topmost summit ').

(*b*)

| lapis, sanguis, mons and fons | stone, blood, mountain, fount |
| pēs, grex (greg-is), dens and pons | foot, flock, tooth, bridge |

(*c*) Nouns ending in **nis**, with the same number of syllables in the gen. sing. as in the nom. sing.: **amnis** 'river', **crīnis** 'hair', **fīnis** 'end' (sometimes fem. in the singular), **fūnis** 'rope', **ignis** 'fire', **pānis** 'bread'. Also the following, with some others less important :

| axis, orbis, collis, ensis | axle, orb, hill, sword |
| fascis, piscis, unguis, mensis | bundle, fish, nail, month |

xxv 2. The following, which form the nom. sing. without the addition of the suffix *s*, are exceptional :

Masculina—ordō, cardō	rank, hinge; cf. 'ordin-al', 'cardin-al
pūgiō[1] and scīpiō	dagger, staff
Neutra[2]—*CORD-A, CAPIT-A*	heart (*COR*), head (*CAPUT*)
LĀC MEL, VĒR, ITINER-A	milk, honey, spring, journey (*ITER*)
VERBER-A, CADAVER-A	lash, corpse
ŌR-A, OSS-A, AEQUOR-A	mouth (*ŌS*), bone (*OS*), sea
AER-A, VĀS-A, MARMOR-A	bronze (*AES*), vessel, marble
Feminina—*arbor* nūd*a*	bare tree
vīs et tellūs, carō crūd*a*	violence, earth, raw flesh

xxvi   Feminines of the 4th Decl. (cf. § 63)

The following in *us* are fem. :

| *domus, manus, Īdūs, tribus;* | house, hand, the Ides, tribe ; |
| also *porticus* and *quercus* | colonnade, oak |

xxvii Exception to rule for 5th Decl.—The word **diēs** 'day' is generally masc., but sometimes fem. in the singular number, when it denotes 'lapse of time', e.g. *longa diēs*, or an appointed date, e.g. *diēs dicta, ante eam diem, ad hanc diem.*

---

[1] The quantity of the *u* in *pūgiō* is shown by an epigram of Martial (xiv. 33).

[2] The *plural* of the neuters is given, where it exists, to show the stem.

NOTES ON VERBS

(i) The ending *-ēre* for *-ērunt* in the 3rd person plural of the Perfect Indicative (§§ 140, 142, 151) is especially common in poets and historians.

(ii) The ending *-re* for *-ris* in the 2nd person singular of the passive forms of verbs (§§ 152, 154, 156, 157, 161, 168) is found in prose as well as verse of all periods. Cicero generally used *-ris* in the Pres. Indic., but in the Fut. Indic. and Pres. Subj. and in the Past Imperf. Indic. and Past Subj. he more commonly used *-re*. Virgil and Horace used both *-ris* and *-re*.

(iii) Some forms of the Perfect Active are occasionally contracted: e. g. *amāstī* (for *amāv-istī*), *audīsse* (for *audīv-isse*).

Perfect stems in *īv* sometimes drop the *v* and shorten the *i*: e. g. *audi-erat, peti-erat* (for *audīv-erat, petīv-erat*).

(iv) The verbs *dīcō* 'I say', *dūcō* 'I lead', *faciō* 'I make', *ferō* 'I bear' drop the final *e* of the 2nd pers. sing. imperative active: *dīc, dūc, fac, fer*.

(v) In some verbs the Future Participle cannot be found from the Perfect Participle Passive: e. g. *moritūrus* (§ 166), *oritūrus* (§ 167), *ruitūrus* (§ 181).

(vi) The quantity of the *i* in the endings of the 2nd pers. sing. and plur. and the 1st plur. of the Fut. Perf. Indic. of all conjugations (*-eris, -eritis, -erimus*) is properly short (representing, as it does, what is called a short 'thematic vowel' in Greek); the quantity of the *i* in the corresponding forms of the Perf. Subj. is properly long (representing an optative *ī* in Greek). But, owing to the similarity of these two tenses both in form and in meaning, they were confused at an early date; and poets treated the quantity of the *i* in both tenses as either long or short according to metrical convenience: cf. *plācārīs* (= *plācāveris*, Fut. Perf., Hor. Od. iii. 23. 3), *fēcerĭmus* (Fut. Perf., Catullus 5. 10), *ēgerĭmus* (Perf. Subj., Virg. Aen. vi. 514).

(vii) The quantity of the *e* in *edō* (1st pers. sing. Pres. Indic., § 247) and in all forms of the Future and Past Imperfect Indic. and of the Pres. Subj. is short; so too in the forms *eduntō, edens* (st. *edent-*), *edendum*. The quantity of the *e* in *es* (2nd pers. sing. Pres. Indic.), and before *ss* (as in *essem*) or *st* (as in *est, estō*) is uncertain; till recently it was supposed to be long; but some recent authorities maintain that it was short, as in the corresponding forms of the verb *sum*. [Vollmer, *Glotta* i. 1, pp. 113–16, 1907; Niedermann, *Berl. Phil. Wochenschrift*, 1908, p. 664; *Classical Review*, vol. xxvi (1912), pp. 78–80.]

xxxv   (viii) **Old Latin forms in -sō and -sim.**—Old Latin had many forms in *-sō* and *-sim* which do not belong to any of the ordinary tenses of the verb, and a few of these were still used in the classical period:

> *faxō*, e. g. Virg. Aen. ix. 154, xii. 316, Livy vi. 35. 9.
> *faxis, faxit, faxitis, faxint*, e. g. Hor. Sat. ii. 3. 38, ii. 6. 5, Livy xxii. 10. 4, xxix. 27. 3, xxxvi. 2. 5, Cic. Sen. 73.
> *iussō*, e. g. Virg. Aen. xi. 467.
> *recepsō*, e. g. Catullus 44. 19.
> *ausim, ausis, ausit, ausint*, e. g. Cic. Brutus v. 18, Virg. Ecl. iii. 32, Georg. ii. 289, Hor. Sat. i. 10. 48, Ovid, Met. vi. 466.

The stem from which these forms come is a Perf. Act. stem formed with *s*: *fax-* (= *fac-s-*; contrast the ordinary Perf. Act. stem without *s*, *fēc-* § 204); *iuss-* like the ordinary Perf. Act. stem of *iubeō*, § 220; *aus-* (= *aud-s-*, cf. the Perf. Part. *aus-us*, § 236).

The ending *im* is the same as that in *sim, velim, nōlim, mālim, edim*. The above forms in *im* may, then, be described as old-fashioned Perfect Subjunctives (often with future meaning, like other Perf. Subjunctives).

The ending *ō* is the same as that in the Fut. Perf. Indic. of other verbs: *faxō* and *iussō* may, then, be called old-fashioned Fut. Perf. Indicatives (sometimes without the sense of completion, see § 309. i)

The forms in *is, it, itis, int* may belong either to the forms in *ō* or to those in *im*.

xxxvi   (ix) Some **old-fashioned Present Infinitives Passive in -ier** are found in poets of the classical period, and in some old laws quoted by Cicero:

> e. g. (1st conj.) *dominārier*, Virg. Aen. vii. 70; *laudārier*, Hor. Sat. i. 2. 35.
> (2nd conj.) *fatērier*, Hor. Epist. ii. 2. 148; *torquērier*, Propertius iii. 6. 39.
> (3rd conj.) *accingier* Virg. Aen. iv. 493; *spargier*, Hor. Od. iv. 11. 8.

vii   (x) The gerund adjective (§ 133) is not to be regarded as an adjectival form of the gerund (verb-noun, § 135). On the contrary the gerund grew out of certain uses of the gerund adjective (see Syntax, § 503, note). That this is the true account of the relation of these forms was shown by Weisweiler in his book on the *Participium Futuri Passivi* (Future Participle Passive, the name by which the gerund adjective was always described by the Roman grammarians), published in 1890. The gerund is a declined form of the neuter of the gerund adjective, used as a noun. [From a construction like *eundum est nōbīs* (§ 501) the form *eundum* was detached in the sense of *iter*; cf. *iter est nōbīs* ' our way is ', Virg. Aen. xi. 17 : and from this was formed a genitive *eundī* ' of the going ' and an ablative *eundō* ' by the going '.]

THE CALENDAR

iii   Names of the months :—*Iānuārius, Februārius, Martius, Aprīlis, Māius, Iūnius, Quinctīlis* (or *Iūlius*, after Iūlius Caesar), *Sextīlis* (or *Augustus*, after Augustus), *September, October, November, December.* These words were originally adjectives: *Iānuārius mensis* ' the January month '.—The number of days in each month subsequent to the reform of the calendar by Caesar in B.C. 46 was the same as at the present day.

The 1st day of each month was called *Kalendae* (1st Decl., fem.).

,, 5th ,, most months ,, *Nōnae* ,,

,, 13th ,, ,, ,, ,, *Īdūs* (4th Decl., fem.).

But :—   In March, July, October, May,
             The Ides were on the 15th day,
                  (and the Nones on the 7th).

The intervening dates were expressed as so many days *before* the Nones, Ides, or Calends. In reckoning backwards the Romans were accustomed to count the 'terminus ā quō' as well as the 'terminus ad quem.' Thus *Nōnae* means the 9th (= 8th) day before the Ides. (A good practical rule is to add one in subtracting from Nones or Ides, and two in subtracting from the number of days in the month, for dates before the Calends of the next month.)

Examples.

'On the 1st of January,' *Kalendīs Iānuāriīs* (abl. ; § 444).

„ 2nd   „   *ante diem quartum Nōnās Iānuāriās* (a.d. IV. Nōn. Iān.).

„ 3rd   „   *ante diem tertium Nōnās Iānuāriās* (a. d. III. Nōn. Iān.).

„ 4th   „   *prīdiē Nōnās Iānuāriās* (prīd. Nōn. Iān.).

„ 5th   „   *Nōnīs Iānuāriīs* (Nōn. Iān.).

„ 14th   „   *ante diem ūndēvīcensimum Kal. Februāriās* (a. d. XIX. Kal. Febr.).

The accusative after *ante* in these expressions is due to the position of the word in the sentence : *ante diem quartum Nōnās Iānuāriās* for *diē quartō ante Nōnās Iānuāriās*; compare the expression *ante tertium annum* for *tertiō annō ante.*

ROMAN MONEY

xxxix   Amounts of money were reckoned as so many sesterces. *Sēstertius* was the name given to a small silver coin, of the value of two and a half *assēs*. The word is a compound of *sēmis* 'half an *ās*' [from *sēmi* and *ās*] and *tertius* 'third' : thus it means literally 'the third (*ās*) half an *ās*', and was used in the sense of 'two and a half *assēs*' (two *assēs* and half of the third).

Note the following expressions :

(i) duo sēstertiī, *2 sesterces* ; centum sēstertiī, *100 sesterces.*

(ii) duo mīlia sēstertiōrum *or* sestertium, *2,000 sesterces*, lit. *two thousands of sesterces* (§ 83). *Sēstertium* is an old form of the gen. plur., which is found also in the gen. plur. of some other words of the 2nd decl. ; see above **iv**, p. 104.

(iii) duo sēstertia, *2000 sesterces.* In this expression the genitive *sestertium* has been detached from its governing word in expressions like *duo mīlia sestertium* (ii), and treated as a neuter singular; hence plur. *sēstertia.*

(iv) deciens centēna mīlia sēstertium, lit. *ten times a hundred thousands of sesterces* = *1,000,000 sesterces* ; vīciens centēna mīlia sēstertium, *2,000,000 sesterces*, &c.

These long expressions were generally shortened by omitting the words *centēna mīlia* :

deciens sēstertium, 1,000,000 *sesterces,*

and sometimes the gen. *sēstertium* was detached from these expressions and used as a neuter singular in the sense of 100,000 sesterces : e.g. *ēmī fundum sēstertiō ūndeciens,* 'I purchased an estate *at the price of 1,100,000 sesterces*' (abl. § 438).

Centum sēstertiī may be roughly valued at £1 (reckoning the *ās* as 1*d.*) ; thus *septem mīlia sēstertium* or *septem sēstertia* = £70. The abbreviation *HS* or (better) *IIS* stands for *iis(emis).*

ABBREVIATIONS
Praenōmina.

xl

A.	= Aulus	N. *or* Num.	= Numerius	
C.	= Gāius	P.	= Pūblius	
Cn.	= Gnaeus	Q.	= Quintus	
D.	= Decimus	S. *or* Sex.	= Sextus	
K.	= Kaesō	Ser.	= Servius	
L.	= Lūcius	Sp.	= Spurius	
M. ·	= Marcus	T.	= Titus	
M'.	= Mānius	Ti.	= Tiberius	
Mam.	= Mamercus			

Other Abbreviations.

A.U.C.	= annō urbis conditae	Pr.	= praetor (*or* -ēs)
Aed.	= aedīlis	Pro C.	= prō consule *or* prōconsul
Cos.	= consul *or* consule		
Coss.	= consulēs *or* consulibus	Pro Pr.	= prō praetōre
D.	= dīvus	Pro Q.	= prō quaestōre
D.D.	= dōnō dedit	Q.	= quaestor
D.D.D.	= dat, dicat, dēdicat	S.	= salūtem
D.M.	= dīs mānibus	S.C.	= senātūs consultum
Des.	= dēsignātus		
F.	= fīlius	S.P.D.	= salūtem plūrimam dīcit
HS. (*or* IIS)	= sēstertius (*or plur.*)		
Imp.	= imperātor	S.P.Q.R.	= senātus populusque Rōmānus
N.L.	= nōn liquet	S.V.B.E.E.V.	= sī valēs bene est, ego valeō
O.M.	= optimus maximus		
P.C.	= patrēs conscriptī	V.R.	= utī rogās

PRINCIPAL PARTS OF VERBS IN ALPHABETICAL ORDER

xli   In this list compound verbs are inserted under the uncompounded form, e.g. *abdō* under *dō*.   When a verb has several compounds formed exactly in the same way, only one or two of them are given as examples.

Rules for the formation of the Perfect Active of compounds.
1. The Perf. Act. of the compound has generally the same vowel as the Perf. Act. of the uncompounded verb, even when the vowel of the compound is weakened to a short *i* in the Present; see *agō*, *premō*.

But compounds of *habeō, teneō, rapiō, saliō*, and *statuō* retain the short *i* of the Present in the Perf. Act.

2. Compounds which have a weakened vowel other than a short *i* in the Present retain that vowel in the Perf. Act. and Perf. Part. Pass.; e.g. *claudō, quaerō, quatiō*.

3. Reduplication is generally dropped in the Perf. Act. of compounds, except in those of *discō, dō, poscō, sistō, stō*; see *cadō, pellō*.

Traces of reduplication are preserved in some compounds with *re-*: see *recidō, repellō*.

xlii					
aboleō	abolēre	abolēvī	abolitus	*get rid of*	§ 221
acuō	acuere	acuī	——	*sharpen*	§ 181
adolescō	adolescere	adolēvī	adultus	*grow up*	§ 178
agō	agere	ēgī	actus	*drive, do*	§ 175
per-agō	-agere	-ēgī	-actus	*accomplish*	
ex-igō	-igere	-ēgī	-actus	*demand*	
cōgō	, cōgere	coēgī	coactus	*compel*	
algeō	algēre	alsī	—— ·	*be cold*	§ 215
alō	alere	aluī	altus	*nourish*	§ 194
apiscor	apiscī	aptus sum		*get*	
ad-ipiscor	ad-ipiscī	ad-eptus sum		*acquire*	§ 231
arcessō	arcessere	arcessīvī	arcessītus	*summon*	§ 201
ardeō	ardēre	arsī	arsūrus	*be on fire*	§ 216
arguō	arguere	arguī	——	*accuse*	§ 181
audeō	audēre	ausus sum		*dare*	§ 236
augeō	augēre	auxī	auctus	*increase*	§ 214
bibō	bibere	bibī	{ pōtātus / pōtus	*drink*	§ 191
cadō	cadere	cecidī	cāsūrus	*fall*	§ 184
oc-cidō	-cidere	-cidī	-cāsūrus	*sink*	
re-cidō	recidere	reccidī	recāsūrus	*fall back*	
caedō	caedere	cecīdī	caesus	*fell, slay*	§ 184
oc-cīdo	-cīdere	-cīdi	-cīsus	*kill*	
canō	canere	cecinī	cantātus	*sing*	§ 196
capessō	capessere	capessīvī	——	*catch at*	§ 201

capiō	capere	cēpī	captus	*take*	§ 204
ac-cipiō	-cipere	-cēpī	-ceptus	*receive*	
carpō	carpere	carpsī	carptus	*pluck*	§ 190
dē-cerpō	-cerpere	-cerpsī	-cerptus	*pluck off*	
caveō	cavēre	cāvī	cautum	*beware*	§ 219
cēdō	cēdere	cessī	cessum	*yield*	§ 183
-cendō *not in use*			.		
ac-cendō	-cendere	-cendī	-census	*kindle*	§ 186
censeō	censēre	censuī	census	*decide*	§ 222
cernō	cernere	crēvī	——	*distinguish*	§ 198
dē-cernō	-cernere	-crēvī	-crētus	*decree*	
cieō	ciēre	cīvī	citus	*rouse*	§ 221
ex-ciō	-cīre	-cīvī (*or* -ciī) -citus		*call forth*	§ 221
cingō	cingere	cinxī	cinctus	*surround*	§ 173
claudō	claudere	clausī	clausus	*shut*	·§ 183
in-clūdō	-clūdere	-clūsī	-clūsus	*shut in*	
colō	colere	coluī	cultus	*cultivate*	§ 194
comminiscor	comminiscī	commentus sum		*devise*	§ 231
congruō	congruere	congruī	——	*agree*	§ 181
consulō	consulere	consuluī	consultus	*consult*	§ 194
coquō	coquere	coxī	coctus	*cook*	§ 176
crēdō *see under* dō					
crepō	crepāre	crepuī	crepitum	*creak*	§ 212
crescō	crescere	crēvī	crētus	*grow* (intran.)	§ 178
cubō	cubāre	cubuī	cubitum	*lie down*	§ 212
-cumbō *not in use*					
prō-cumbō	-cumbere	-cubuī	-cubitum	*fall forward*	§ 192
cupiō	cupere	cupīvī	cupītus	*desire*	§ 207
currō	currere	cucurrī	cursum	*run*	§ 200
prō-currō	-currere	-currī } -cucurrī }	-cursum	*run forward*	
dēleō	dēlēre	dēlēvī	dēlētus	*destroy*	§ 221
dīcō	dīcere	dixī	dictus	*say*	176
discō	discere	didicī	——	*learn*	179
dē-discō	-discere	-didicī	——	*unlearn*	
dīvidō	dīvidere	dīvīsī	dīvīsus	*divide*	§ 183
dō	dare	dedī	datus	*give*	210
circum-dō	-dare	-dedī	-datus	*surround*	210
ab-dō	-dere	-didī	-ditus	*hide*	185
crēd-ō	-dere	-didī	-ditus	*trust*	184
vēn-dō	-dere	-didī	-ditus	*sell*	185
doceō	docēre	docuī	doctus	·*teach*	222
domō	domāre	domuī	domitus	*tame*	212
dūcō	dūcere	duxī	ductus	*lead*	176
edō	esse	ēdī	ēsus	*eat*	184
emō	emere	-ēmī	emptus	*buy, take*	196
ad-imō	-imere	-ēmī	-emptus	*take away*	
prōmō	prōmere	prompsī	promptus	*take forth*	197
sūmō	sūmere	sumpsī	sumptus	*take up*	197
eō	īre	iī	itum	*go*	§ 243
red-eō	-īre	-iī	-itum	*return*	
vēn-eō	-īre	-iī	——	*be sold*	

expergiscor	expergiscī	experrectus sum		*awake* (intr.)	§231
exuō	·exuere	exuī	exūtus	*take off*	§181
facessō	facessere	facessīvī	——	*do eagerly*	§201
faciō	facere	fēcī	factus	*make*	§204
pate-faciō	-facere	-fēcī	-factus	*throw open*	
ad-ficiō	-ficere	-fēcī	-fectus	*affect*	.
fallō	fallere	fefellī	falsus	*deceive*	§193
re-fellō	-fellere	-fellī	——	*refute*	
farciō	farcīre	farsī	fartus	*cram*	
re-ferciō	-fercīre	-fersī	-fertus	*cram*	§225
fateōr	fatērī	fassus sum		*confess*	§234
confiteor	-fitērī	-fessus sum		*confess*	
faveō	favēre	fāvī	fautum	*be favourable*	§219
-fendō *not in use*					
dē-fendō	-fendere	-fendī	-fensus	*ward off*	§186
feriō	ferīre	{ percussī / īcī	percussus ictus	*strike*	§229
ferō	ferre	tulī	lātus	*bear*	§200
ad-ferō	adferre	attulī	allātus	*bring to*	
au-ferō	auferre	abstulī	ablātus	*take away*	
con-ferō	conferre	contulī	collātus	*bring together*	
dif-ferō	differre	distulī	dilātus	*defer*	
ef-ferō	efferre	extulī	ēlātus	*carry forth*	
in-ferō	inferre	intulī	illātus	*carry in*	
of-ferō	offerre	obtulī	oblātus	*offer*	
referō	referre	rettulī	relātus	*bring back*	
suf-ferō	sufferre	sustulī	——	*endure*	
fīdō	fīdere	fīsus sum		*trust*	§237
fīgō	fīgere	fixī	fixus	*fix*	§173
findō	findere	fidī	fissus	*split*	§186
fingō	fingere	finxī	fictus	*fashion*	§173
fīō	fierī	factus sum		*become* .	§237
flectō	flectere	flexī	flexus	*bend*	§187
fleō	flēre	flēvī	flētus	*weep*	§221
flīgō *not in use*					
ad-flīgō	-flīgere	-flixī	-flictus	*dash down*	§173
prō-flīgō	-flīgāre	-flīgāvī	-flīgātus	*overthrow*	
fluō	fluere	fluxī	fluxus	*flow*	§182
fodiō	fodere	fōdī	fossus	*dig*	§204
foveō	fovēre	fōvī	fōtus	*warm*	§219
frangō	frangere	frēgī	fractus	*break*	§175
per-fringō	-fringere	-frēgī	-fractus	*shatter*	
fremō	fremere	fremuī	——	*make a noise*	§195
fruor	fruī	ūsus sum		*enjoy*	§231
fugiō	fugere	fūgī	fugitūrus	*flee*	§204
fulciō	fulcīre	fulsī	fultus	*prop*	§225
fulgeō	fulgēre	fulsī	——	*flash*	§215
fundō	fundere	fūdī	fūsus	*pour*	§186
fungor	fungī	functus sum		*discharge*	§231
gaudeō	gaudēre	gāvīsus sum		*rejoice*	§236

gemō	gemere	gemuī	——	*groan*	§ 195
gerō	gerere	gessī	gestus	*carry*	§ 200
gignō	gignere	genuī	genitus	*beget*	§ 195
gradior	gradī	.gressus sum		*step*	
con-gredior	-gredī	-gressus sum		*meet*	§ 232
haereō	haerēre	haesī	haesūrus	*cling*	§ 220
hauriō	haurīre	hausī	haustus	*drain*	226
imbuō	imbuere	imbuī	imbūtus	*tinge*	§ 181
incessō	incessere	incessīvī	——	*assail*	§ 201
indulgeō	indulgēre	indulsī	——	*indulge*	§ 215
induō	induere	induī	indūtus	*put on*	§ 181
īrascor	īrascī	suscensuī		*get angry*	§ 231
iaciō	iacere	iēcī	iactus	*throw*	§ 204
dē-iciō	dēicere	dēiēcī	dēiectus	*cast down*	
iubeō	iubēre	iussī	iussus	*bid*	§ 220
iungō	iungere	iunxī	iunctus	*join*	§ 173
iuvō	iuvāre	iūvī	iūtus	*aid*	§ 209
lābor	lābī	lapsus sum		*slip*	§ 231
lacessō	lacessere	lacessīvī	lacessītus	*provoke*	§ 201
laciō *not in use*					
ē-liciō	-licere	-licuī	-licitus	*lure out*	§ 205
in-liciō	-licere	-lexī	-lectus	*lure on*	§ 205
laedō	laedere	laesī	laesus	*hurt*	§ 183
ē-līdō	-līdere	-līsī	-līsus	*shatter*	
languescō	languescere	languī		*grow weak*	§ 180
lavō	lavāre	lāvī	lautus	*wash*	§ 209
legō	legere	lēgī	lectus	*gather*	§ 175
col-ligō	-ligere	-lēgī	-lectus	*collect* [so ē-(dē-)ligō]	
dī-ligō	-ligere	-lexī	-lectus	*love*	§ 173
intel-legō	-legere	-lexī	-lectus	*understand*	173
neg-legō	-legere	-lexī	-lectus	*disregard*	173
linō	linere	lēvī	litus	*smear*	§ 199
linquō	linquere	līquī	——	*leave*	
re-linquō	-linquere	-līquī	-lictus	*leave*	§ 177
loquor	loquī	locūtus sum		*talk*	§ 231
lūceō	lūcēre	luxī	——	*shine*	§ 214
lūdō	lūdere	lūsī	lūsum	*play*	§ 183
lūgeō	lūgēre	luxī	——	*mourn*	§ 214
luō	luere	luī	——	(i) *loose* (ii) *wash*	§ 181
ab-luō	-luere	-luī	-lūtus	*wash off*	
mālō	malle	māluī	——	*prefer*	§ 194
maneō	manēre	mansī	mansum	*remain*	§ 220
mergō	mergere	mersī	mersus	*dip*	§ 174
mētior	mētīrī	mensus sum		*measure*	§ 235
metō	metere	messem fēcī	messus	*mow*	
metuō	metuere	metuī	——	*fear*	§ 181
micō	micāre	micuī	——	*glitter*	§ 212
minuō	minuere	minuī	minūtus	*lessen*	§ 181
misceō	miscēre	miscuī	mixtus	*mix*	§ 222
mittō	mittere	mīsī	missus	*send*	§ 187

mordeō	mordēre	momordī	morsus	*bite*	§ 217
morior	morī	mortuus sum		*die*	§ 232
moveō	movēre	mōvī	mōtus	*move* (trans.)	§ 219
mulceō	mulcēre	mulsī	mulsus	*soothe*	§ 215
nanciscor	nanciscī	{ nactus sum { nanctus sum		*get*	§ 231
nascor	nascī	nātus sum		*be born*	§ 231
nectō	nectere	nexuī	nexus	*bind*	§ 187
neglegō *see under* legō					
nītor	nītī	{ nīsus sum { nixus sum		*strive* } *rest on* }	§ 231
nōlō	nolle	nōluī	——	*be unwilling*	§ 194
noscō	noscere	nōvī	nōtus	*get to know*	§ 178
ignoscō	ignoscere	ignōvī	ignōtum	*pardon*	
agnoscō	agnoscere	agnōvī	agnitus	*recognize*	
cognoscō	cognoscere	cognōvī	cognitus	*ascertain*	§ 178
nūbō	nūbere	nupsī	nupta	*marry*	§ 190
-nuō *not in use*					
ab-nuō	-nuere	-nuī	——	*deny*	§ 181
oblīviscor	oblīviscī	oblītus sum		*forget*	§ 231
occulō	occulere	occuluī	occultus	*hide*	§ 194
ordior	ordīrī	orsus sum		*begin*	§ 235
orior	orīrī	ortus sum		*arise*	§ 235
paciscor	paciscī	pactus sum		*make a bargain*	§ 231
pandō	pandere	pandī	passus	*spread out*	§ 186
pangō	pangere	pepigī	pactus	*fix*	§ 175
com-pingō	-pingere	-pēgī	-pactus	*join together*	
parcō	parcere	pepercī	parsūrus	*spare*	§ 177
pariō	parcere	peperī	partus	*get*	§ 204
aperiō	aperīre	aperuī	apertus	*open*	§ 227
operiō	operīre	operuī	opertus	*cover*	§ 227
com-periō	-perīre	-perī	-pertus	*learn*	§ 226
re-periō	reperīre	repperī	repertus	*find*	§ 226
ex-perior	-perīrī	-pertus sum		*make trial of*	§ 235
pascō	pascere	pāvī	pastus	*feed* (trans.)	§ 178
patior	patī	passus sum		*suffer*	§ 232
per-petior	-petī	-pessus sum		*endure*	
pellō	pellere	pepulī	pulsus	*push*	§ 193
im-pellō	-pellere	-pulī	-pulsus	*impel*	
repellō	repellere	reppulī	repulsus	*repel*	
pendeō	pendēre	pependī	——	*hang* (intrans.)	§ 218
pendō	pendere	pependī	pensus	*weigh*	§ 186
im-pendō	-pendere	-pendī	-pensus	*weigh, pay*	
percellō	percellere	perculī	perculsus	*cast down*	§ 193
pergō *see under* regō					
petō	petere	petīvī	petītus	*aim at*	§ 189
pingō	pingere	pinxī	pictus	*paint*	§ 173
plaudō	plaudere	plausī	plausum	*clap*	§ 183
ex-plōdō	-plōdere	-plōsī	-plōsus	*hiss off*	
plectō *poetical and rare*					
com-plector	-plectī	-plexus sum		*embrace*	§ 231

-pleō *not in use*

com-pleō	-plēre	-plēvī	-plētus	*fill up*	§ 221

pōnō *see under* sinō

poscō	poscere	poposcī	postulātus	*demand*	§ 179
dē-poscō	-poscere	-poposcī	——	*demand*	

possum *see under* sum

prehendō	prehendere	prehendī	prehensus	*grasp*	§ 186
premō	premere	pressī	pressus	*press*	§ 197
op-primō	-primere	-pressī	-pressus	*surprise*	
proficiscor	proficiscī	profectus sum		*set out*	§ 231

prōmō *see under* emō

pungō	pungere	pupugī	punctus	*prick*	§ 175
quaerō	quaerere	quaesīvī	quaesītus	*seek*	§ 199
re-quīrō	-quīrere	-quīsīvī	-quīsītus	*require*	
quatiō	quatere	——	quassus	*shake*	
con-cutiō	-cutere	-cussī	-cussus	*shatter*	§ 205
queror	querī	questus sum		*complain*	§ 231
queō	quīre	quīvī	quitum	*be able*	§ 245
quiescō	quiescere	quiēvī	quiētus	*go to rest*	§ 178
rādō	rādere	rāsī	rāsus	*scrape*	§ 183
rapiō	rapere	rapuī	raptus	*snatch*	§ 206
dī-ripiō	-ripere	-ripuī	-reptus	*plunder*	
regō	regere	rexī	rectus	*rule*	§ 173
cor-rigō	-rigere	-rexī	-rectus	*correct*	
pergō	pergere	perrexī	perrectum	*go on*	
surgō	surgere	surrexī	surrectum	*arise*	
reor	rērī	ratus sum	.	*think*	§ 234
rīdeō	rīdēre	rīsī	rīsum	*laugh*	§ 216
dē-rīdeō	-rīdēre	-rīsī	-rīsus	*deride*	§ 216
rōdō	rōdere	rōsī	rōsus	*gnaw*	§ 183
rumpō	rumpere	rūpī	ruptus	*burst*	§ 191
ruō	ruere	ruī	ruitūrus	*tumble*	§ 181
ob-ruō	-ruere	-ruī	-rutus	*overwhelm*	§ 181
saepiō	saepīre	saepsī	saeptus	*fence in*	§ 226
saliō	salīre	saluī	——	*leap*	§ 227
dē-siliō	-silīre	-siluī	——	*leap down*	
sanciō	sancīre	sanxī	sanctus	*ratify*	§ 224
sapiō	sapere	sapīvī	——	*be sensible*	§ 207
sarciō	sarcīre	sarsī	sartus	*patch*	§ 225
scandō	scandere	scandī		*climb*	
dē-scendō	-scendere	-scendī	-scensus	*descend*	§ 186
scindō	scindere	scidī	scissus	*tear*	§ 186
sciscō	sciscere	scīvī	scītus	*decree*	§ 178
scrībō	scrībere	scripsī	scriptus	*write*	§ 190
secō	secāre	secuī	sectus	*cut*	§ 212
sedeō	sedēre	sēdī	sessum	*sit*	§ 217
ob-sideō	-sidēre	-sēdī	-sessus	*besiege*	
sentiō	sentīre	sensī	sensus	*feel*	§ 226
con-sentiō	-sentīre	-sensī	-sensum	*agree*	
ad-sentior	-sentīrī	-sensus sum		*assent*	§ 235

sepeliō	sepelīre	sepelīvī	sepultus	*bury*	§ 228
sequor	sequī	secūtus		*follow*	§ 231
serō	serere	——	sertus	*twine*	§ 200
dē-serō	-serere	-seruī	-sertus	*desert*	
serō	serere	sēvī	satus	*sow*	§ 199
con-serō	-serere	-sēvī	-situs	*plant*	
serpō	serpere	serpsī	——	*crawl*	§ 190
sīdō *rare*					
con-sīdō	-sīdere	-sēdī	-sessum	*seat oneself*	l§ 184
sinō	sinere	sīvī	situs	*permit*	§ 198
dē-sinō	-sinere	-siī	-situm	*cease*	
pōnō	pōnere	posuī	positus	*place*	§ 198
sistō	sistere	stitī	status	*stop*	§ 188
con-sistō	-sistere	-stitī	——	*stop*	
soleō	solēre	solitus sum		*be accustomed*	§ 236
solvō	solvere	solvī	solūtus	*loosen*	§ 181
sonō	sonāre	sonuī	sonātūrus	*sound*	§ 212
spargō	spargere	sparsī	sparsus	*scatter*	§ 174
dis-pergō	-spergere	-spersī	-spersus	*scatter abroad*	
speciō *not in use*					
con-spiciō	-spicere	-spexī	-spectus	*look at*	§ 205
spernō	spernere	sprēvī	sprētus	*scorn*	§ 198
spondeō	spondēre	spopondī	sponsus	*pledge*	§ 218
re-spondeō	-spondēre	-spondī	-sponsum	*answer*	
statuō	statuere	statuī	statūtus	*set up*	§ 181
con-stituō	-stituere	-stituī	-stitūtus	*establish*	
sternō	sternere	strāvī	strātus	*strew*	§ 198
stinguō *poetical and rare*					
ex-stinguō	-stinguere	-stinxī	-stinctus	*quench*	§ 173
stō	stāre	stetī	statūrus	*stand*	§ 211
circum-stō	-stāre	-stetī	——	*surround*	§ 211
in-stō	-stāre	-stitī	-statūrus	*pursue*	§ 211
strepō	strepere	strepuī	——	*make a noise*	§ 192
stringō	stringere	strinxī	strictus	*tighten*	§ 173
struō	struere	struxī	structus	*pile up*	§ 182
suādeō	suādēre	suāsī	suāsum	*advise*	§ 216
suescō *poetical*					
ad-suescō	-suescere	-suēvī	-suētus	*be accustomed*	§ 178
sum	esse	fuī	——	*be*	§ 141
prōsum	prōdesse	prōfuī	——	*be serviceable*	§ 239
possum	posse	potuī	——	*be able*	§ 240
sūmō *see under* emō					
surgō *see under* regō					
tangō	tangere	tetigī	tactus	*touch*	§ 175
at-tingō	-tingere	-tigī	-tactus	*touch*	
tegō	tegere	texī	tectus	*cover*	§ 173
temnō	temnere	——	——	*despise*	
con-temnō	-temnere	-tempsī	-temptus	*despise*	§ 197
tendō	tendere	tetendī	tentus	*stretch*	§ 186
con-tendō	-tendere	-tendī	-tentus	*strain*	
os-tendō	-tendere	-tendī	——	*show*	

teneō	tenēre	tenuī	——	*hold*	§ 222
re-tineō	-tinēre	-tinuī	-tentus	*retain*	
tergeō	tergēre	tersī	tersus	*wipe*	§ 215
terō	terere	trīvī	trītus	*rub*	§ 199
texō	texere	texuī	textus	*weave*	§ 202
tingō	tingere	tinxī	tinctus	*dip*	§ 173
tollō	tollere	sustulī	sublātus	*lift*	§ 193
tondeō	tondēre	totondī	tonsus	*shear*	§ 218
at-tondeō	-tondēre	-tondī	-tonsus	*shear*	
tonō	tonāre	tonuī	——	*thunder*	§ 212
torqueō	torquēre	torsī	tortus	*twist*	§ 215
torreō	torrēre	torruī	tostus	*parch*	§ 222
trahō	trahere	traxī	tractus	*draw*	§ 173
tremō	tremere	tremuī	——	*tremble*	§ 195
tribuō	tribuere	tribuī	tribūtus	*assign*	§ 181
trūdō	trūdere	trūsī	trūsus	*thrust*	§ 183
tundō *poetical and rare*					
con-tundō	-tundere	-tudī	-tūsus	*bruise*	§ 184
ulciscor	ulciscī	ultus sum		*avenge, punish*	§ 231
ungō	ungere	unxī	unctus	*anoint*	§ 173
urgeō	urgēre	ursī	——	*urge*	§ 215
ūrō	ūrere	ussī	ustus	*burn*	§ 200
combūrō	combūrere	combussī	-bustus	*burn up*	
ūtor	ūtī	ūsus sum		*use, enjoy*	§ 231
vādō	vādere		——	*go*	
ē-vādō	-vādere	-vāsī	-vāsum	*go out*	§ 183
vehō	vehere	vexī	vectus	*carry*	§ 173
vellō	vellere	vellī	vulsus	*pluck*	§ 193
vendō *see under* dō					
veniō	venīre	vēnī	ventum	*come*	§ 226
vertō	vertere	vertī	versus	*turn*	§ 188
con-vertō	-vertere	-vertī	-versus	*turn*	
re-vertor	-verti	-vertī	-versus	*return*	§ 237
vescor	vescī	ēdī		*feed* (intrans.)	§ 231
vetō	vetāre	vetuī	vetitus	*forbid*	§ 212
videō	vidēre	vīdī	vīsus	*see*	§ 217
vinciō	vincīre	vinxī	vinctus	*bind*	§ 224
vincō	vincere	vīcī	victus	*conquer*	§ 177
vīsō	vīsere	vīsī	——	*visit*	§ 202
vīvō	vīvere	vixī	victūrus	*live*	§ 182
volō	velle	voluī	——	*wish*	§ 194
volvō	volvere	volvī	volūtus	*roll*	§ 181
voveō	vovēre	vōvī	vōtus	*vow*	§ 219

PART II—SYNTAX

I. THE SENTENCE AND ITS PARTS

50 IN Latin, as in English and French, a sentence consists of two parts, the **subject** and the **predicate**. The subject is the word or group of words which denotes the person or thing of which the predicate is said: the predicate is all that is said of the person or thing denoted by the subject:

Subject	Predicate
Exercitus	rediit.
The army	*returned.*
Labiēnus	exercitum reduxit.
Labienus	*brought back the army.*
Exercitus	salvus et incolumis erat.
The army	*was safe and sound.*

51 Subject + predicate may be contained in a single word: redī, *return*. In Latin the subject is often expressed or implied by the inflexion of the verb: redī-s, *you return*; redi-t, *he returns*; redī-mus, *we return*; redī-tis, *you return*; redeu-nt, *they return*.

The parts of the predicate.

52 (1) **The verb.**

A verb may form the whole of the predicate: exercitus rediit, *the army returned*; Trōia **fuit**, *Troy has had its day*. On the other hand predicates may be expressed without a verb: pavidī ducēs, mīlitēs ducibus infensī, *the officers* [*were*] *terrified, the men* [*were*] *enraged with the officers*; nē quid nimis, [*one should do*] *nought to excess*; unde mihi lapidem? *where* [*can I get*] *me a stone?*

53 (2) **The object,** governed by the verb: Labiēnus **exerci·tum** reduxit, *Labienus brought back the army*.

254   (3) **The predicative adjective, predicative noun** or **pre·
dicative pronoun:**

(a) indicating **what** the person or thing denoted by the subject is declared to be, to become, to be made, to be named,
or to seem : exercitus **salvus** et **incolumis** erat, *the army
was safe and sound*; Ubiī **vectīgālēs** Suēbōrum fīunt,
the Ubii become (or *are made*) *tributaries of the Suebi*;
Labiēnus **certior** fit, *Labienus is informed*, lit. *becomes* (or
is made) *more certain*; silva mūnīta **oppidum** ā Britannīs
vocātur, *a fortified wood is called a town by the Britons*;
ascensus minimē **arduus** vidēbātur, *the ascent seemed not
at all steep*; ego is sum, *I am he* (= I am the person in
question).

(b) indicating **what** the person or thing denoted by the
object is declared to be made, or to be named : haec rēs
omnia **tūta** reddidit, *this rendered everything safe*; Suēbī
Ubiōs **vectīgālēs** faciunt, *the Suebi make the Ubii tributaries*; Labiēnum **certiōrem** facit, *he informs Labienus*,
lit. *makes Labienus more certain*; Britannī silvam mūnī-
tam **oppidum** vocant, *the Britons call a fortified wood
a town*.

255   Predicative adjectives and nouns may be used in sentences
which do not contain verbs of ' being ', ' becoming ', ' seeming ',
' making ', or ' naming ': exercitus **salvus** et **incolumis** rediit, *the army returned safe and sound* (this does not mean ' the
safe and sound army returned ', but ' the army was safe and
sound when it returned '); exercitum **salvum** et **incolumem**
reduxit, *he brought back the army safe and sound* (= the army
was safe and sound when he brought it back); nāvēs **humilēs**
factae sunt, *the ships were built low*; nāvēs **actuāriās** fēcit, *he
built the ships as row-barges*; Ubiōs multō **humiliōrēs** redē·
gērunt, *they rendered* (lit. *reduced*) *the Ubii much more humble*,
i. e. *reduced them so that they became more humble* (B. G. iv.
3. 4); nōbilissimōs cīvitātis **lēgātōs** mīsērunt, *they sent the
men of highest position in the state as delegates*; mē **adiūtōre**
ūtere, *use me as a helper*.

Other parts of the sentence.

5   Any noun in the sentence may be qualified by an adjective
or the equivalent of an adjective. An adjective or adjective
equivalent which merely qualifies and is not predicative is
called an **epithet**: exercitus **Rōmānus** rediit, *the Roman
army returned* (epithet adjective). On the ordinary position
of the epithet adjective see § 3.

7   An epithet noun may stand either before or after the noun
to which it belongs. The two nouns often form a kind of
compound noun, of which either the first or the second part
may be regarded as the epithet: urbs Rōma, *the city of Rome*
(i. e. either *the Roman city* or *Rome which was a city*); rex
Galba, *King Galba*; flūmen Rhēnus, *the river Rhine*; Garumna
flūmen, *the river Garonne*; bellātor deus, *a warrior god*.

3   An epithet noun which stands after the noun to which it
belongs and is added as by an afterthought is said to stand
in apposition: Galba, **rex** Suessiōnum, *Galba, the king of the
Suessiones.*

)   The verb, or any adjective or adverb in the sentence, may
be qualified by an adverb or the equivalent of an adverb:
deinde (or **proximā hieme**) Rhēnum transiērunt, *thereupon*
(or *in the next winter*) *they crossed the Rhine*; **longius
annō** | **ūnō in locō** | **incolendī causā** | nōn remanent, *they do
not remain* | *in one place* | *longer than a year* | *for the purpose
of residing there.*

)   A part of a sentence consisting of a group of words equivalent to a noun, an adjective or an adverb, and not having
a subject and a predicate of its own, is called a **phrase**:

> mīlitēs **nāvēs conscendere** iubet, *he bids the soldiers
> embark* (noun phrase, cf. § 461).
> hominēs **capillō prōmissō**, *men with long hair, long-
> haired men* (adjective phrase).
> trans **Alpēs** habitant, *they dwell across the Alps* (**adverb
> phrase**). Other examples in § 259.

261 A part of a sentence consisting of a group of words equivalent to a noun, an adjective, or an adverb and having a subject and a predicate of its own is called a **subordinate clause** :

> causa transeundī fuit **quod bellō premēbantur,** *the cause of their crossing was that they were hard pressed by war,* or *the fact that they were hard pressed by war was the cause of their crossing* (**noun clause**).
>
> eā hieme **quae secūta est** Germānī Rhēnum transiērunt nōn longē ā marī **quō Rhēnus influit,** *in the winter which followed the Germans crossed the Rhine not far from the sea into which* (lit. *whither*) *the Rhine flows* (**adjective clauses**).
>
> Caesar, **cum id nuntiātum esset,** in Galliam Ulteriōrem contendit, *when this was reported, Caesar hastened into Further Gaul* (**adverb clause**).

262 A sentence containing only one predication is called a **simple sentence** :

> longius annō ūnō in locō **incolendī causā remanēre iīs nōn licet,** *it is not permitted to them to remain longer than a year in one place for the purpose of residing there.*[1]

263 A sentence consisting of two or more co-ordinate parts is called a **double sentence** or a **multiple sentence** :

> **prīvātī agrī apud eōs nihil est, neque longius annō remanēre ūnō in locō licet,** *there is no private land among them, nor are they allowed to remain longer than a year in one place* (double sentence); **hī in armīs sunt, illī domī remanent,** *the latter bear arms, the former remain at home* (here the two parts of the double sentence are not connected by any conjunction); **multum sunt in vēnātiōnibus : quae rēs vīrēs alit,** *they are much engaged in hunting : which circumstance increases their strength*

---

[1] The instances in this and the two following sections are taken from Caesar, B. G. iv. 1.

(*quae rēs = et ea rēs*, connecting the two co-ordinate parts of the sentence ; contrast the use of *quae* in §261). Each of the parts of such a sentence may be called a co-ordinate clause.

64   Similarly any member of a sentence may be double or multiple :

hī atque illī in vicem in armīs sunt, *the latter and the former bear arms in turn* (double subject); quae rēs et vīrēs alit et immānī corporum magnitūdine hominēs efficit, *which circumstance both increases their strength and makes them men of vast bodily size* (double predicate) ; sē atque reliquōs alunt, *they support themselves and the rest* (double object); gens est maxima et bellicōsissima, *the tribe is the largest and most warlike* (double predicative adjective); quae rēs et cibī genere et cottīdiānā exercitātiōne et lībertāte vītae vīrēs alit, *which circumstance increases their strength both by the nature of their food and by their daily exercise and by the freedom of their lives* (multiple adverbial qualification); ager prīvātus ac sēparātus, *private and separate land* (double epithet).

65   A sentence containing one main predication and one or more subordinate predications is called a **complex sentence**.

66   All sentences containing a subordinate clause (§ 261) are complex. In most complex sentences the part which is not subordinate has a subject and a predicate of its own, and is called the **main clause** : opportūnissima rēs accidit, quod. Germānī ad Caesarem suī purgandī causā vēnērunt, *a most fortunate thing happened, namely that the Germans came to Caesar for the sake of clearing themselves* (quod . . . *vēnērunt* is a noun-clause in apposition to *rēs*) ; iī quī trans Mōsam ierant nōn redierant, *those who had gone across the Meuse had not returned* (quī . . . *ierant* is an adjective-clause, qualifying *iī*) ; sī gravius quid acciderit, abs tē ratiōnem reposcent, *if anything serious happens they will call you to account* (sī . . . *acciderit* is an adverb-clause, = under certain conditions).

267 But in some complex sentences containing a noun-clause the rest of the sentence is incomplete without the noun-clause : **causa transeundī fuit** quod bellō premēbantur, *the cause of their crossing* (subject) *was* (main verb) *that they were driven by war* (noun clause, used predicatively) ; or *the fact that they were driven by war* (subject) *was* (main verb) *the cause of their crossing* (predicative noun).

268 A complex sentence may form one of the co-ordinate parts of a double or multiple sentence (§ 263): **opportūnissima rēs accidit, quod Germānī ad Caesarem suī purgandī causā vēnērunt** (complex sentence); **quōs Caesar retinērī iussit,** *a most fortunate thing happened, namely that the Germans came to Caesar for the sake of clearing themselves ; and Caesar ordered them to be detained.*

II. AGREEMENT OF THE PARTS OF THE SENTENCE WITH ONE ANOTHER

269 The parts of the sentence are said to ‘agree’ when they are made like one another in certain respects. Agreement binds them together and shows that they form a unity.

1. Agreement of the verb.

270 The verb agrees with the subject in number and person, as in English and French :

> Hostis fugit. *The enemy is running away* (sing.).
> Hostēs fugiunt. *The enemies are running away* (plur.).
> Īte, fīliī, celebrāte exsequiās Scīpiōnis Āfricānī. *Go, my sons, attend the funeral of Scipio Africanus.*
> Quem quaeritis adsum Trōius Aenēās. *I, Aeneas of Troy, whom you are seeking, am here.*

271 A double or multiple subject takes a plural verb :

> Cicerō et Terentia valent. *Cicero and Terentia are well* (3rd person).
> Tūne et uxor tua valētis? *Are you and your wife well?* (2nd person, because the double subject = *vōs*).

Ego et uxor mea līberīque nostrī valēmus. *My wife and I and our children are well.* (1st person, because the multiple subject = *nōs*.)

Constructions according to sense.

72   (1) A singular noun denoting several persons or things may take a plural verb : pars sē recēpērunt, *part* (= some of them) *retired*.

73   (2) When the parts of a double subject are so closely connected that they form one idea, the verb may be singular : senātus populusque Rōmānus dēcrēvit, *the senate and Roman people has resolved.*

74 **2. Agreement of the predicative adjective and predicative noun.**

The predicative adjective and the predicative noun agree as far as possible with the word of which they are predicated (as in French)[1]—the pred. adj. in gender, number, and case ; the pred. noun in case :

Exercitus salvus et incolumis est (*or* rediit, § 255). *The army is* (or *returned*) *safe and sound.*

Rōma erat caput Italiae. *Rome was the head* (*capital*) *of Italy.*

Vīta rustica magistra parsimōniae est. *A country life is the teacher of thrift.* (*magister* happens to have a corresponding feminine *magistra*.)

Cicerōnem populus Rōmānus consulem creāvit. *The Roman people elected Cicero consul.*

Mīlitēs salvōs et incolumēs praestitit. *He secured the safety of the soldiers* (lit. *he secured the soldiers safe and sound*) : cf. Cicero, pro leg. Man. § 55. *Praestō* in this sense is derived from *praes* and *stō*, ' I stand surety.'

---

[1] The predicative adj. or noun is only *part* of what is predicated (see § 250). The agreement of predicative words with the words of which they are predicated is not found in all languages. In German, for example, predicative words (unlike epithets) are uninflected.

Licet iīs incolumibus exīre. *It is allowed to them to depart unharmed*: here *incolumibus* is predicated of *iīs*, which is governed by *licet*.

Administrīs ad ea sacrificia Druidibus ūtuntur. *As agents for those sacrifices they make use of the Druids*: here *administrīs* is predicated of *Druidibus*, which is governed by *ūtuntur*.

275 So too with an infinitive:

Balbus cīvis Rōmānus esse vult. *Balbus desires to be a Roman citizen*: here *cīvis* is predicated of *Balbus*.

Cicerō dixit Balbum cīvem Rōmānum esse. *Cicero declared Balbus to be* (=declared that Balbus was) *a Roman citizen*: here *cīvem* is predicated of *Balbum*.

276 *Double or multiple subject.*

(1) When a double or a multiple subject consists of words denoting persons of different sexes, and the predicate contains a predicative adjective, the plural adjective is put in the masculine gender, as in French:

Pater meus et māter mea salvī sunt. *My father and mother are well.* (The double subject = *duo hominēs*, 'two human beings', and *homō* is always masc.)

(2) When a double or multiple subject consists of words of different genders but not denoting persons, and the predicate contains a predicative adjective, the plural adjective either agrees with the part of the subject which stands nearest to it or is put in the neuter gender:

Bracchia modo eōrum atque ūmerī līberī ab aquā erant. *Only their arms and shoulders were free of the water.*

Mors et somnus similia sunt. *Death and sleep are similar* (similar things).

277 The rules given above for predicative adjectives apply also to verb-adjectives (perfect participles) in compound tenses of verbs: pater meus et māter mea mortuī sunt (captī sunt), *my*

father and my mother are dead (have been taken prisoners);
Cicerō ā populō Rōmānō consul creātus est, *Cicero was elected
consul by the Roman people.*

78 **Peculiarity.** If the subject is a demonstrative, interrogative, or
relative pronoun, and the predicate contains a predicative noun,
the subject is generally made to agree with the predicative noun,
as in French :

Hic vītae Hannibalis exitus fuit. *This was the end of Hannibal's
life.*

Haec est nōbilitās mea, hae imāginēs meae. *This is my title
to nobility, this my gallery of ancestral busts.*

Quae est causa? *What is the reason?*

Rōma, quod caput erat Italiae. *Rome, which was the capital of
Italy.*

Sunt item quae appellantur alcēs. *There are also what (i. e.
animals which) are called elks* (B. G. vi. 27 : *quae* is fem.,
agreeing with *alcēs*).

79 **3. Agreement of epithets.**

The **epithet adjective** agrees in gender, number and case
with the word which it qualifies :

vir bonus, *a good man*; hic vir, *this man* (demonstrative
adj.); quī vir? *which man?* (interrogative adj.); quota
hōra est? *what o'clock is it?* (interrogative numeral adj.);
adulescentēs quīdam, *some young men* (indefinite adj.);
patriam suam relinquit, *he is leaving his native land*
(possessive adj.); duo erant itinera quibus itineribus
exīre possent, *there were two roads by which roads they
would have been able to march out* (relative adj.); castra
mūnīta, *a fortified camp* (verb-adj.).

280 If an epithet adjective qualifies two or more nouns of
different genders, it either (*a*) agrees with the noun that
stands nearest to it, or (*b*) is repeated :

(*a*) signum et manum suam cognōvit, *he recognized his
seal and hand;*

omnēs terrae et maria ⎫
terrae et maria omnia ⎭ *all lands and seas.*

(*b*) māior alacritās studiumque pugnandī māius, *greater keenness and love of fighting*;

omnēs terrae et omnia maria, *all lands and seas.*

281 The **epithet noun** agrees in case with the word to which it belongs :

urbem Rōmam relinquit, *he is leaving the city of Rome*; silva Arduenna ā flūmine Rhēnō ad initium Rēmōrum pertinet, *the forest of the Ardennes stretches from the river Rhine to the frontier of the Remi* (*flūmen* neut., *Rhēnus* masc.).

Nouns in apposition : agrum Helvētiōrum, gentis Gallicae, vastat, *he lays waste the territory of the Helvetii, a Gallic tribe* ; Athēnās, inventrīcēs artium et scientiārum, vīset, *he will visit Athens, the mother of arts and sciences* (*inventor* happens to have a corresponding feminine *inventrix*).

4. Agreement of pronouns.[1]

282 Pronouns agree in gender and number with the noun or noun-equivalent which denotes the person or thing indicated : Silva Hercynia magna est : in **eā** (fem. sing.) sunt multa genera ferārum, **quae** (neut. plur.) reliquīs in locīs vīsa nōn sint : ex **quibus quae** maximē differant ā cēterīs **haec** sunt. Est bōs cervī figūrā, **cūius** (masc. sing.) ā fronte ūnum cornū exsistit : ab **ēius** (neut. sing.) summō sīcut palmae rāmīque diffunduntur. **Eadem** est fēminae marisque nātūra. Sunt item alcēs : **hārum** est consimilis caprīs figūra. . . . **Hīs** sunt arborēs prō cubīlibus : ad **eās** sē applicant (B. G. vi. 25-7). *The Hercynian forest is large : in it there are many kinds of wild beasts, which* (*i. e.* kinds) *have not been seen in other places : of which* (*i. e.* kinds) *those which differ most from the rest are the following. There is an ox with the shape of a stag, from whose forehead springs a single horn : from the top of this*

---

[1] The term 'pronoun', as used here and in the Accidence, does not include indicating adjectives, such as *hic* in *hic vir*, 'this man' (see § 279).

what resembles hands and branches spreads out. The appearance of the male and of the female is the same. There are also elks : their shape is like goats (= that of goats). *Trees serve them as beds : they lean against them* (*i. e.* the trees).

83   The person or thing indicated by a pronoun is not always expressed by a noun or noun-equivalent in the sentence or context ; sometimes the speaker has a person or thing in mind without mentioning it :

> **Eī** quī in statiōne erant interfectī sunt. *Those* (*i. e.* the men) *who were on sentry duty were killed.*
>
> **Ea** quae acciderant nuntiant. *They report the things which had happened.*
>
> Caesarī cum **id** nuntiātum esset, eōs per prōvinciam iter facere cōnārī, mātūrat ab urbe proficiscī. *When that* (*i. e.* that fact) *had been reported to Caesar, namely that they were attempting to march through the province, he hastens to set out from Rome.*

84   The pronoun *ego* indicates the person speaking, who may be male or female ; *nōs* indicates the person speaking and other persons associated with him—*I and you* or *I and he* (*she, they*) : *tū* and *vōs* indicate the person or persons spoken to, who may be male or female. The gender of these pronouns varies accordingly :

> Fuī **ego** (*masc.*) līber ; nunc servus sum.—Ego **tē** (*masc.*) līberum praestābō. *I have been free ; now I am a slave. —I will guarantee you free.*
>
> Fuī **ego** (*fem.*) lībera ; nunc serva sum.—Ego **tē** (*fem.*) līberam praestābō.

85   Predicative pronouns agree not only in gender and number but also in case with the word of which they are predicated :

> Tūne **is** es, quī fēcistī ?—Ego **is** sum. *Are you he who did it ?—I am he.*
>
> Tūne **ea** es, quae fēcistī ?—Ego **ea** sum. *Are you she who did it ?—I am she.*

286 The **relative pronoun** agrees, like any other pronoun, in gender and number with the noun or noun-equivalent which denotes the person or thing indicated. This noun or noun-equivalent is generally found in another clause of the sentence, and is called the **antecedent** of the relative; see some examples in § 282. The case of the relative depends on the construction of the clause in which it stands, just as the case of other pronouns depends on the part which they play as subject, object, &c., in the sentence :

Duās viās occupāvit
He seized the two roads

quae ad portum ferēbant.
which led to the harbour.
quās hostēs sine custōdiīs relīquerant.
which the enemy had left unguarded.
quārum ūna angusta erat.
of which one was narrow.
quibus nullae custōdiae praesidiō relictae erant.
to which no sentries had been left as a protection.
quibus hostēs exierant.
by which the enemy had marched out.
in **quibus** nullae custōdiae erant.
in which there were no sentries.

Haec ā mē beneficia habētis, quem prōditiōnis insimulātis.
These benefits you have from me, whom you accuse of treachery.

287 The relative is always to be regarded as of the same *person* as its antecedent ; the person of the relative is shown by the verb of the relative clause, when the relative is the subject :

Ego, quī tē confirmō, ipse mē nōn possum. *I, who am reassuring you, cannot reassure myself* (Cicero).

Iuppiter, ingentēs quī dās adimisque dolōrēs. *O Jupiter, who dost inflict and take away great sufferings.* Hor. Sat. ii. 3. 288.

Obs. If the antecedent is a predicative noun or predicative pronoun, it is generally treated as of the same person as the subject
of the main clause:

> Sum pius Aeneās, raptōs quī ex hoste penātēs classe vehō
> mēcum. *I am the faithful Aeneas, who carry with me in my
> fleet my household gods rescued from the enemy*: Aen. i. 378.

> Nōn is sum quī mortis perīculō terrear. *I am not one who
> is to be terrified by the danger of death*: in English the
> antecedent ' one ' is treated as of the 3rd person.

See other examples in § 285.

38   If a relative pronoun refers to the whole statement of
another clause, it stands in the neuter singular (often preceded
by *id*, ' that '; so in French *ce qui*), or agrees with *rēs* inserted
in the relative clause:

> Ex litterīs Caesaris diērum quindecim supplicātiō dēcrēta
> est, quod(*or* id quod) ante id tempus acciderat nullī. *As
> a result of the dispatch of Caesar a public thanksgiving
> of fifteen days was decreed— a thing which had not hap-
> pened to any one before that time.*

> Flūmen Axonam exercitum trāduxit: quae rēs omnia
> tūta ab hostibus reddēbat. *He crossed the river Aisne:
> which manœuvre rendered everything safe from the enemy.*

These are double sentences (§ 263).

39   Relative clauses without any antecedent expressed are
common in Latin; *quī = is quī*, 'he who,' French *celui qui*;
quod = id quod, 'that which' or 'what', French *ce qui*; *quīcumque*, 'whoever,' French *quiconque*.   Compare in English
' Who steals my purse steals trash ' (Shakespeare).[1]   In such
cases the relative pronoun agrees in gender and number with
the antecedent which the speaker has in mind:

> Quī ex iīs novissimus convēnit, in conspectū multitūdinis

---

[1] A relative clause of this kind *taken together with its unexprcssed antecedent*
is equivalent to a noun ('*he* who steals my purse' = 'a pickpocket'); but
the relative clause alone should not be spoken of as a noun-clause.

necātur. *He who is the last to present himself, is put to death in the sight of the multitude.*

Ferās, nōn culpēs, quod mūtārī nōn potest.[1] *One should put up with, not find fault with, what cannot be altered* (= 'What can't be cured must be endured').

Habētis quam petīstis facultātem. *You have the chance that you sought* (lit. *what chance you sought*).

Quōs poterat sauciōs sēcum duxit. *He took with him what wounded men he could* (supply *dūcere* : whatever wounded men he could take).

Quibuscumque signīs occurrerant sē adgregābant. *They joined whatever standards they happened to find.*

290 The relative pronoun is never omitted in Latin, as it often is in English : *e. g.* 'This is not the man I saw yesterday', *Latin* Hic nōn is est **quem** herī vīdī.

---

[1] Publilius Syrus, a writer of mimes, contemporary with Julius Caesar (first century B.C.).

III. MOODS AND TENSES

THE INDICATIVE MOOD

91 The Indicative mood relates to a matter of fact (§ 126). Examples of the Indicative in the various kinds of sentence and clause are given in §§ 520–33.

TENSES OF THE INDICATIVE

The Present.[1]

92 In verbs which denote an act as distinct from a state the Present marks the act as either *going on* or *habitual* at the time of speaking:

> librum scrībit, *he is writing a book*; Latīnē loquitur, *he is speaking Latin*; loquiturne Latīnē ?, *is he speaking Latin ?*.
>
> librōs scrībit, *he writes books* (habitually); Latīnē loquitur, *he speaks Latin*; loquiturne Latīnē ?, *does he speak Latin ?*.

In verbs which denote a state as distinct from an act the Present is generally translated by a non-continuous form of the English Present:

> est, *he is*; habet, *he has*; amat, *he loves*; scit, *he knows*; estne ?, *is he ?*; amatne ?, *does he love ?*.

93 **Special uses.**

(i) In connexion with adverbial expressions of 'time how long' the Present denotes what *has been going on* up to the time of speaking:

> multōs annōs librum scrībit, *he has been writing a book for many years*; iam diū Rōmae habitō, *I have been living at Rome for a long time*; French *je demeure à Rome depuis longtemps*.

---

[1] The Latin Present Indicative has the same meanings as the French Present Indicative (French Grammar, §§ 292, 293).

(ii) The Present is sometimes used in vivid narration of past events (as in English and French), to represent the actions picturesquely, as if they were going on at the time of speaking (**Historic Present**):

> Caesar acceptīs litterīs statim nuntium ad Crassum mittit; iubet mediā nocte proficiscī celeriterque ad sē venīre. Exit cum nuntiō Crassus. Scrībit Labiēnō, sī reī publicae commodō facere possit, cum legiōne veniat. *After receiving the dispatch Caesar immediately sends a messenger to Crassus, bids him start at midnight and come to him quickly. Crassus sets out together with the messenger. To Labienus he writes that if he be able to do so to the advantage of the state, he is to come with his legion*: B. G. v. 46. In this example the Historic Present is treated as a tense of present time; but it sometimes takes the sequence of a past tense. Thus Caesar might have written *posset*, 'should be able,' for *possit*, 'shall be able,' and *venīret*, 'he was to come,' instead of *veniat*, 'he is to come.'

The Past Imperfect.[1]

294 The Past Imperfect (or Past Continuous) tense is a Present in the past, *i.e.* it has the meanings of the Present tense transferred to past time. Thus in verbs which denote an act, it marks the act as either *going on* or *habitual* at some time in the past which the speaker has in mind or which is referred to in the context:

> librum scrībēbat, *he was writing a book*; Latīnē loquēbātur, *he was speaking Latin*; loquēbāturne Latīnē?, *was he speaking Latin?*.
>
> librōs scrībēbat, *he wrote* (= used to write) *books*; Latīnē loquēbātur, *he spoke* (= used to speak) *Latin*; loquēbāturne Latīnē?, *did he speak* (= used he to speak) *Latin?*.

---

[1] The Latin Past Imperfect Indicative has in general the same meanings as the French Past Imperfect (French Grammar, §§ 294, 296); but it is not used like the French Past Imperfect in *if*-clauses which refer to present or future time (French Grammar, §§ 295, 315).

In verbs which denote a state the non-continuous form of the English Past is generally used : erat, *he was*; habēbat, *he had*; amābat, *he loved*; sciēbat, *he knew*.

> Hominēs nōmen hōrum amābant. *People loved the name of these men*: Cicero, pro Sestio, § 105; the time at which they loved is expressed in a previous sentence : illīs temporibus, *in those days*.

5   The Past Imperfect sometimes marks an act as attempted or begun :

> Britannī nostrōs intrā mūnītiōnēs ingredī prohibēbant. *The Britons tried to* (or *began to*) *prevent our men from entering within the fortifications.*

Special use.

6   In connexion with adverbial expressions of ' time how long' the Past Imperfect denotes what *had been going on* up to some point of time in the past (cf. § 293 (i)):

> iam diū librum scrībēbat, *he had been writing a book for a long time*; domicilium ibi multōs iam annōs habēbat, *he had had his home there for many years*; French, *il demeurait là depuis plusieurs ans.*

The Future.[1]

17   The Future tense marks the action of the verb as about to take place after the time of speaking :

> librum scrībam (scrībēs, scrībet), *I shall* (*you will, he will*) *write a book*; sciam (sciēs, sciet), *I shall* (*you will, he will*) *know.*

18   A substitute for the Future, sometimes used with special meanings, is formed by *sum* with a Future Participle :

> librum scriptūrus est, *he is about to write* (*likely to write, sure to write, bent on writing*) *a book.*

---

[1] The Latin Future Indicative has the same meanings as the French Future Indicative (French Grammar, §§ 297-9).

The Past tense of *sum* with a Future Participle expresses the meaning of a Future in the past:

> librum scriptūrus erat, *he was about to write* (*likely to write, sure to write, bent on writing*) *a book.*

299　The original meaning of the Future. Most (or all) Latin Futures are derived from Subjunctives,[1] and some of their uses show traces of their Subjunctive origin, *i. e.* express what *is to be done* or *shall be done*, as distinct from what *will be done*; see Subjunctive, § 318 f.

(*a*) in Statements:

> Post nōnam veniēs. *You shall come* (= come *or* you must come) *after the ninth hour*; Hor. Epist. i. 7. 71; so too l. 27 *reddēs.* Compare Subjunctive, § 321, note.
>
> Hunc tū ōlim caelō, spoliīs Orientis onustum, accipiēs sēcūra; vocābitur hic quoque vōtīs. *Him thou shalt one day welcome light of heart to heaven, laden with the spoils of the East*; *he too shall listen to the voice of prayer*: Aen. i. 289 f. (a promise).

(*b*) in Questions:

> Nīl ergō optābunt hominēs? *Shall men then pray for nothing?* Juv. x. 346.

The Perfect.

300　The Perfect tense is used in two ways [2]:—

(1) as a **Present Perfect**, like the English Present Perfect with 'have', *i.e.* as a tense of present time. When used in this way the Perfect describes an action of the past as affecting the doer at the time of speaking: librum scripsit, he *has written* a book = he *is in the position of having written* a book; servus fuī, I *have been* a slave = I *am in the position of having been* a slave.

> Vixī et quem dederat cursum Fortūna perēgī. *I have lived*

---

[1] On this point further information will be found in Lindsay's *Short Historical Latin Grammar*, p. 97.—The English Future Indicative formed with 'shall' is properly an expression of obligation, like the Subjunctive. The French Future Indicative was also originally akin to an expression of obligation: *je donnerai = je donner-ai*, 'I have to give.'

[2] The Latin Perfect has the same two uses as the French Perfect. The main difference between Latin and French is that Latin has no separate Past Historic tense (French Grammar, §§ 301, 302).

and have run the course which my destiny had assigned me:
Aen. iv. 653.—Nē qua cīvitās Rōmānōs suīs fīnibus recipiat
ā mē prōvīsum est. *I have taken steps to secure that no state
shall admit the Romans within their territory*: B. G. vii. 20. 12.
—Mihi quidem Scīpiō, quamquam est subitō ēreptus, vīvit
tamen semperque vīvet; virtūtem enim amāvī illīus virī quae
exstincta nōn est. *Although Scipio has been suddenly taken
from me, yet for me he lives and will always live; for I have
loved his noble qualities, and they have not perished*: Cic. de
Amic. § 102. If the speaker had been referring to some past
time *at which* he loved Scipio, he would have used the Past
Imperfect *amābam* (§ 294).

OBS. In special contexts the Perfect may suggest that the
action of the verb is over and done with : vixī, *I have had my
day* = my life is over; dixī, *I have spoken* = my speech is
ended; fuimus Trōēs, fuit Īlium et ingens glōria Teucrōrum,
we are Trojans no more (*i.e.* our existence as a nation is over),
Ilium is no more and the great glory of the Trojans: Aen. ii. 325.

ɩ (2) more commonly as a **Past Historic**, *i.e.* as a tense of
past time which marks the action of the verb as having taken
place before the time of speaking, without describing it as
affecting the doer at the time of speaking : Hieme annī post
urbem conditam DCCII Caesar commentāriōs suōs dē bellō
Gallicō scripsit, *Caesar wrote his notes of the Gallic war in the
winter of the year 702 after the foundation of Rome*. In this
use the Latin Perfect corresponds to the English Past tense.
Observe that *scripsit* could not here be translated 'has written',
as in § 300 : for that would mean 'Caesar *is* (at the present
time) *in the position of having written*'. He *was* once in that
position ; but that idea would be expressed not by the Perfect
but by the Past Perfect (*scripserat*).

The meaning of the Perfect as a Past Historic differs still
more from the meaning of the Past Imperfect, which marks
the action of the verb as going on or habitual *at* the time
spoken of (§ 294): hieme annī post urbem conditam DCCII

Caesar commentāriōs suōs scrībēbat, *in the winter of the year 702 Caesar was writing his notes*; hieme Caesar commentāriōs suōs scrībēbat, *Caesar used generally to write his notes in the winter* (i. e. after the conclusion of a campaign in the summer).

302 The Perfect as a Past Historic is specially common in narrative, where it is used to recount a number of past actions which took place *in succession* (one after the other). Here the Perfect answers the question What happened next ?, whereas the Past Imperfect is used of actions going on at the time indicated. In the Perfect the narrative advances, in the Past Imperfect it stands still : Ad extrēmum agrīs expulsī Ūsipetēs ad Rhēnum **pervēnērunt,** quās regiōnēs Menapiī **incolēbant.** Hī ad utramque rīpam flūminis agrōs **habēbant;** sed tantae multitūdinis adventū perterritī ex iīs aedificiīs quae trans flūmen habuerant dēmigrāverant, et Germānōs transīre **pro· hibēbant.** Illī omnia expertī, cum transīre nōn **possent,** revertī sē in suās sēdēs **simulāvērunt,** et trīduī viam prō· gressī rursus **revertērunt,** atque inopīnantēs Menapiōs **op· pressērunt.** *At last the Usipetes, driven from their lands, arrived at the Rhine, the territory which the Menapii inhabited* (*i. e.* at that time). *The latter possessed* (at that time) *lands on both banks of the river ; but having been frightened by the arrival of so great a multitude they had removed from the buildings which they had had on the east of the Rhine, and were trying to prevent the Germans* (*i. e.* the Usipetes) *from crossing. The Germans, having tried every device, as they were not able* (Past Subjunctive used like Past Imperfect Indic.) *to cross, thereupon pretended that they were returning to their own homes, and then, after proceeding a three days' journey, came back again and took the unsuspecting Menapii by surprise* : B. G. iv. 4.

303 The **Perfect· Passive** is, according to its form, a Present Perfect : Ūsipetēs expulsī sunt, lit. *the Usipetes are driven out* (= are in the position of having been driven out). But it came to be used also as a Past Historic: expulsī sunt, *they were driven out* (cf. Accidence, § 153).

The Past Perfect.[1]

>4   The Past Perfect tense marks the action of the verb as already completed at some time in the past which the speaker has in mind or which is referred to in the context: librum scripserat antequam Rōmā discessit, *he had written the book before he left Rome.*

> Ex iīs aedificiīs quae trans Rhēnum habuerant dēmigrāverant. *They had removed from the buildings which they had had on the other side of the Rhine* (quoted in § 302).

The Future Perfect.[1]

>5   The Future Perfect tense marks the action of the verb as already completed at some time in the future which the speaker has in mind or which is referred to in the context: librum ante fīnem hiemis scripserit, *he will have written the book before the end of the winter.*

>6   The Fut. Perf. is found chiefly in subordinate clauses:

> Quicquid fēceris, approbābō. *Whatever you do* (lit. *shall have done*), *I shall think right.*
> Dē Carthāgine verērī nōn ante dēsinam quam illam excīsam esse cognōverō. *I shall not cease to be alarmed about Carthage until I have learned* (lit. *shall have learned*) *that it is razed to the ground*: Cic. de Sen. § 18.

07   Often accompanied by a Fut. Perf. in the main clause:

> Praeclārē vixerō, sī quid mihi acciderit priusquam hōc tantum malī vīderō. *I shall have lived gloriously if I die* (lit. *if anything shall have happened to me*) *before I see* (lit. *shall have seen*) *this great disaster happen*: Cic. pro Mil. 99.

---

[1] The Latin Past Perfect has the same meanings as the 1st Past Perfect of French. The Latin Future Perfect has the same meanings as the French Future Perfect.

308   Sometimes the Fut. Perf. denotes the future position which will result from a completed action, or what *will be found to have happened*:

> Adulescens senem vīcerō. *I, a young man, shall be in the position of having overcome* (or *shall be found to have overcome*) *an old man*: Livy xxviii. 44. 18.

309   **Special uses.**

(i) Sometimes the Fut. Perf. expresses no distinct idea of completion, and may then be translated by the English Future; so especially in Plautus and Terence: abierō, *I shall depart*.

(ii) The Fut. Perf. is sometimes used, like the Future (§ 299), with *shall* meaning:

(*a*) in Statements:

> Quam id rectē faciam, vīderint sapientēs. *How far I should be right in doing so, it is for philosophers to consider* (lit. *philosophers shall consider*): Cic. de Amic., § 10.

(*b*) in Questions:

> Coniugiumque domumque patris nātōsque vidēbit? . . . Occiderit ferrō Priamus? Trōia arserit ignī? *Shall Priam have fallen by the sword? Shall Troy have been burned? And shall Helen see her husband and the home of her father and her children?* (*i.e.* shall Helen return home *after* Priam has been slain and Troy burned?): Aen. ii. 579, 581.

But the Romans did not always distinguish between the Fut. Perf. Indic. and the Perfect Subjunctive (cf. § 299), except in the 1st person singular.

COMPARISON OF ENGLISH AND LATIN TENSES IN CERTAIN SUBORDINATE CLAUSES

310   (1) Where English uses the Present tense in subordinate clauses referring to future time, the Future or the Future Perfect is generally used in Latin:[1]

> Quid animī consanguineīs nostrīs erit, sī paene in ipsīs cadāveribus dēcertāre cōgentur? *What will be the*

---

[1] Often, however, the Pres. Indic. after *antequam* and *priusquam* (as in Virg. Aen. iv. 27, and frequently in Cicero).—For the use of a prospective Subjunctive in subordinate clauses see §§ 339, 340.

feelings of our kinsmen if they are forced (lit. *shail be forced*) *to fight over our very corpses?* : B. G. vii. 77.

Sī gravius quid acciderit, abs tē ratiōnem reposcent. *If any disaster occurs* (lit. *shall have occurred*), *they will demand a reckoning at your hands* : B. G. v. 30.

(2) The tense used in subordinate clauses to denote an action which had taken place before some other action of the past depends on the subordinating conjunction employed: *postquam, posteāquam, ubi, ut, simul atque* commonly take the Perfect Indicative; *cum* the Past Perfect Subjunctive (§ 354). The tenses employed in English are the Past and the Past Perfect:

Quod ubi Caesar animadvertit, nāvēs longās rēmīs incitārī iussit. *When Caesar observed this, he ordered the ships of war to be set in motion by means of oars.*

Hostēs, simul atque sē ex fugā recēpērunt, lēgātōs dē pāce mīsērunt. *As soon as the enemy recovered after their flight, they sent envoys to treat about peace.*

Posteāquam equitātus noster in conspectum vēnit (*or* Cum equitātus noster in conspectum vēnisset), hostēs terga vertērunt. *After (When) our cavalry came (had come) in sight, the enemy fled.*

(3) *Dum* 'while' frequently takes the Present Indicative (Historic Present, § 293. ii) in narrative:

Dum haec geruntur, quī erant in agrīs discessērunt. *While this was going on* (lit. *is going on*), *those who were in the fields departed.*

THE IMPERATIVE MOOD

313 The imperative is used (as in English and French) to
denote what is *desired* by the speaker, in commands, requests,
entreaties, and, less commonly, in wishes:[1]

Dā mihi operam. *Pay attention to me* [command].

Dā, pater, augurium. *Give an omen, O Father*: Aen. iii.
89 [request or entreaty].

Valē. *Farewell.*—Salvē. *Hail* [wishes: lit. *be well*].

OBS. Originally the long forms of the imperative referred to a
more remote future than the short forms, which were used to denote that something was to be done in the *immediate* future. This
explains why the long forms had a 3rd person. The long forms,
then, as used in Old Latin, might be called Future imperatives.
But in the classical period the distinction of meaning between the
long and the short forms had to a great extent disappeared.

314 But the imperative has a restricted use in Latin of the
classical period:—

(1) The long forms (in *-tō, -tōte, -ntō*) are not much used
except in legal phraseology and in poets:

Amīcitia rēgī Antiochō cum populō Rōmānō estō. *There
shall be friendship between King Antiochus and the
Roman people*: Livy xxxviii. 38. 1.

Tū nē cēde malīs, sed contrā audentior ītō. *Yield thou not
to misfortunes, but go to meet them all the bolder*: Aen.
vi. 95.

315 (2) The negative used with the imperative is *nē*; but
a negatived imperative is found only in legal documents
and in poets:

Equō nē crēdite, Teucrī. *Trust not to the horse, Trojans*:
Aen. ii. 48.

[1] The name imperative comes from *imperāre*, command; but command, in
the ordinary sense of the term, is not the only meaning of the imperative
mood.

6 Instead of the 3rd person singular and plural of the imperative (long forms) and the imperative with *nē*, the subjunctive mood is commonly employed (§ 320). The following table shows the forms of the imperative and the subjunctive most commonly used in commands, requests, and entreaties (positive and negative).

	POSITIVE	NEGATIVE
2nd pers. sing.	dā, *give*	{ nē dederīs, *don't give* [1] { nōlī dare, *please not to give* [2]
plur.	date, *give*	{ nē dederītis, *don't give* [1] { nōlīte dare, *please not to give* [2]
3rd pers. sing.	det, *let him give*	nē det, *let him not give*
plur.	dent, *let them give*	nē dent, *let them not give*

[1] literally *you shall not give* or *you are not to give*; see § 322.
[2] imperative of *nōlō* with infinitive : literally *will-not to give*.
This is the politer and more usual form of a negative command or request.

17 From the use of the imperative in commands comes a use in which it expresses a supposition ('supposing that'):

Ostendite modo bellum ; pācem habēbitis : videant vōs parātōs ad vim ; iūs ipsī remittent. *Just make a show of war; you shall have peace : let them see you prepared to use force ; they will themselves abandon their claim* : Livy vi. 18. 7.

THE SUBJUNCTIVE MOOD

18 The uses of the subjunctive mood may be divided into three classes :

(*A*) Those in which it denotes what *is to be done*;

(*B*) Those in which it denotes what *would happen* under certain imagined conditions ;

(*C*) Those in which it has been so much weakened that it differs little from an indicative in meaning.

The first two uses have something in common, and it is possible that use *B* grew out of use *A*. Use *C* is clearly of later origin than the other two.

319 ## (*A*) SUBJUNCTIVES DENOTING WHAT
IS TO BE DONE

These subjunctives express the meanings of the English
verb 'shall' (obligation and futurity).[1]

I. In Simple Sentences and Main Clauses.

The Pres. Subj. denotes what *is* to be done :

QUESTION. Quid faciam ? *What am I to do ?* or *What
shall I do ?*

ANSWER. Inveniās argentum. *You are to find the money*
(= you must find the money).

Cēdat, opīnor, forum castrīs. *The forum, I suppose, is to*
(or *must*) *yield to the camp.*

The Past and the Past Perf. Subj. denote what *was* to be
done :

QUESTION. Nōnne argentum redderem ? *Was I not to
pay back the money ?* (= ought I not to have paid back
the money ?)

ANSWER. Nōn redderēs. *You ought not to have paid it
back* (you were not to pay it back).

At tū dictīs, Albāne, manērēs. *But thou, Alban, should'st
have kept to thy word*: Aen. viii. 643.

Eadem mē ad fāta vocassēs. *You should have called me
to share your fate*: Aen. iv. 678.

320 When the thing that is to be done by the person addressed
or spoken of is *desired* by the speaker, the statement becomes
equivalent to a command, request, entreaty, or wish ; and in
these cases the subjunctive, if negatived, is negatived by *nē*,
like the imperative (§ 315).

---

[1] The verb 'shall' originally denoted obligation (*I shall = I owe* or *I am
under an obligation*) ; and in some uses it still expresses this idea, as in *Thou
shalt not steal.* But in other uses it has come to denote merely future
time, especially in the 1st person.

21   The Present Subjunctive in desires refers to future time :

Nē sim salvus, sī aliter scrībō ac sentiō. *May I perish,
if I write otherwise than I think* (Cicero).—Sīs fēlix.
Be prosperous (Catullus).—Dī tibi praemia digna ferant.
God grant thee a fitting reward : Aen. i. 605. These
are wishes ; compare the English and the French
subjunctive in *God save the King, Dieu vous bénisse, Vive
la République.*—*Utinam* (originally = ' how ? ') is sometimes added : Utinam illum diem videam. *O that I
may see that day* : originally ' how, pray, am I to see
that day ? '

Exeant ; nē patiantur Catilīnam tābescere. *Let them
depart ; let them not suffer Catiline to pine away* : Cic.
Cat. ii. 6. This is a command ; compare the French
subjunctive in *qu'ils partent.*[1]

Proinde hōs latrōnēs interficiāmus. *Accordingly let us
kill these robbers* : B. G. vii. 38.—Sequāmur ; plācēmus
ventōs et Gnōsia regna petāmus. *Let us follow ; let us
appease the winds and make for the realms of Crete* :
Aen. iii. 114 f. These are requests addressed to
a group of persons in which the speaker is included.
Compare the English subjunctive in ' Prepare we for
our marriage ' (Shakespeare), and the French imperative, 1st pers. plur., in *tuons* ' let us kill '.

22   The Perfect Subjunctive, 2nd person sing. and plur., is
sometimes used in negative commands (cf. § 316) :

Nē transierīs Hibērum ; nusquam tē vestīgiō mōverīs.
Do not cross (or *You shall not cross*) *the Ebro ; do not
move anywhere from the spot* : Livy xxi. 44. This

---

[1] The 2nd person, sing. and plur., of the Pres. Subj. denoting command
is not much used in classical Latin, except in poets : at rāmum hunc agnoscās,
yet recognize this branch : Aen. vi. 406 f. In old Latin (Plautus and Terence)
this use is very common ; but in Latin of the classical period commands,
requests, and entreaties in the 2nd person are generally expressed by the
imperative.

usage is fairly common in Cicero's letters, in Livy, and in Seneca.

323 The Past and the Past Perfect Subjunctive are used with *utinam* in wishing that something were or had been otherwise than it actually is or was.[1]

> Utinam adesset. *O that he were here*; cf. Aen. i. 575.
> Utinam adfuisset. *O that he had been there.*

2. In Subordinate Clauses.

324 Most of the above uses of the subjunctive in simple sentences and main clauses cannot occur in historical narrative ; hence they are not found in Caesar's Gallic War. But in subordinate clauses subjunctives denoting what *is* (or *was*) *to be done* are exceedingly common in all writers.[2] They may generally be translated by 'shall' or 'should' with the infinitive.

(*a*) In Noun Clauses.

325 The simplest form of subordination is that in which no conjunction is employed :

(i) Complex sentences containing a dependent question as to what *is* (or *was*) *to be done* :

> Quid faciam nesciō. *What I am to do I don't know.*
> This sentence is formed out of two simple sentences:
> quid faciam ? *what am I to do ?* (§ 319); nesciō, *I don't know.*

---

[1] Compare the use of these tenses in § 319 (last two examples). A sentence denoting what *ought to have been* easily passes into an expression of wish that something *had been* : e. g. *manērēs* (Aen. viii. 643) might in another context mean 'would that you had remained', and *vocassēs* (Aen. iv. 678) might mean 'would that you had called'. In some passages it is doubtful which meaning is intended (e. g. Aen. x. 854, xi. 162).—Compare in English the use of 'should' in wishes : 'My poor father should have been here.'

[2] It was from the frequent use of the subjunctive in subordinate clauses that the mood got its name (= *subjoining*).

Quid facerem nesciēbam. *What I was to do, I didn't know ; i.e.* quid facerem? *what was I to do ?* (§ 319); nesciēbam, *I did not know.*

Sortibus consultum est utrum ignī statim necārētur an in aliud tempus reservārētur. *Lots were cast as to whether he should be (was to be) burned immediately or reserved for another occasion* : B. G. i. 53.

(ii) Complex sentences containing a dependent statement of obligation or a dependent desire :

Caesar huic imperat adeat cīvitātēs. *Caesar gives him the order he is to approach the states*: B. G. iv. 21 ; *i.e.* adeat cīvitātēs, *he is to approach the states* (§ 319) or *let him approach the states* (§ 321); Caesar huic imperat, *Caesar gives him the order.* Compare the English subjunctive in ' Mind you come ' = ' Bear in mind, you *are to come* '.

{26 But dependent statements of obligation and dependent desires are generally introduced by the subordinating conjunction *ut* ' that ' :

Caesar huic imperat ut cīvitātēs adeat. *Caesar gives him the order that he is to approach the states.*

Hortātur ut populī Rōmānī fidem sequantur. *He exhorts them to place themselves* (lit. *that they shall place themselves*) *under the protection of the Roman people*: B. G. iv. 21. It is not true to say that in this construction *ut* takes the subjunctive ; the real fact is that the subjunctive clause in this construction takes *ut* ' that '.

327 Noun clauses which express that something is *not* to be done are introduced by *nē* ' not ', which in English is translated by ' that . . . not ' :

Labiēnō praeceptum erat nē proelium committeret. *Instructions had been given to Labienus that he should not (was not to) join battle*: B. G. i. 22. An *ut* is sometimes added (*ut nē* for *nē*).

Litterās mīsit nē eōs frūmentō nēve aliā rē iuvārent. *He*

sent a dispatch that they were not to assist them with corn nor with anything else : B. G. i. 26 (nēve = *and not*).

328 Noun clauses denoting that something is (or is not) to be done depend either on a verb (§§ 329-32), or on a noun or noun-equivalent (§ 333).

329 (i) Depending on verbs of 'asking', 'bidding', 'trying', 'bringing about', and the like. The corresponding English verbs more commonly take an infinitive with 'to' :[1]

Petunt ut Mandubracium dēfendat. *They ask that he shall defend (They ask him to defend) Mandubracius* : B. G. v. 20.—Ōrābant ut sibi auxilium ferret. *They begged that he should bring them aid* : B. G. iv. 16.—Labiēnō imperat (*or* dīcit *or* scrībit) ut quam plūrimās nāvēs instituat. *He gives orders* (or *says* or *writes*) *to Labienus that he is to build as many ships as possible* : B. G. v. 11.— Senātus censuerat ut Caesar Haeduōs dēfenderet. *The Senate had resolved that Caesar was to protect the Haeduans* : B. G. i. 35.—Haec ab Ariovistō postulāvit : prīmum nē Germānōs amplius trans Rhēnum trādū-ceret ; deinde obsidēs Haeduōrum redderet, Sēquanīs-que permitteret ut obsidēs redderent ; nēve Haeduīs bellum inferret. *This is what he demanded of Ariovistus: first, that he should not bring Germans across the Rhine any more ; secondly, he was to send back the hostages of the Haedui and give permission to the Sequani that they should send back hostages ; and that he was not to make war upon the Haedui* : cf. B. G. i. 35.—Dabat operam (*or* Id agēbat) ut in officiō Dumnorīgem continēret. *He was trying to keep Dumnorix to his duty* : B. G. v. 7.—Nullī cīvitātī persuādērī potuit ut Rhēnum transīret. *No state could be persuaded to cross* (lit. *that it should cross*)

---

[1] The only Latin verbs which ordinarily take an infinitive to denote what *is to be done* are verbs of 'willing' (volō, nōlō, mālō, cupiō), iubeō, *I bid*, sinō, patior, *I permit*, cōgō, *I compel*, and the similar verbs of negative meaning—vetō, *I forbid*, and often prohibeō, *I prevent* : see §§ 459, 465. Optō, *I ask, I desire*, takes either construction.

the Rhine : B. G. v. 55.—Dumnorix ā Sēquanīs impetrat ut per fīnēs suōs Helvētiōs īre patiantur. *Dumnorix prevails on the Sequani that they shall allow the Helvetii to pass through their territory* : B. G. i. 9.—Efficiam posthāc nē quemquam vōce lacessās. *I will bring it about that you shall not challenge any one to sing hereafter* : Virg. Ecl. iii. 51.

30   (ii) Noun clauses depending on verbs of 'forbidding', 'preventing', and 'resisting'. These clauses are introduced by *nē*, because they denote what *is not to be done*. In English no negative is required if the clause is translated by a verb-noun : [1]

Interdīcit Cassivellaunō nē Mandubraciō neu Trinobantibus noceat. *He forbids Cassivellaunus to injure Mandubracius or the Trinobantes* ; lit. *He lays an interdict on Cassivellaunus, he shall not* (is not to) *injure*, &c. : B. G. v. 22.—Plūra nē dīcam dolōre impedior. *I am prevented by grief from saying more* : formed out of ' I am not to say more : I am prevented by grief' ; cf. § 325.—Recūsābant nē ūnus omnēs antecēderet. *They protested against one man having precedence over all.*

Compare French : 'la pluie empêche qu'on *ne* sorte' ; and the following sentence from Shakespeare : 'You may as well forbid the mountain pines to make *no* noise.'

OBS. *Quōminus* 'by which the less' is often used instead of *nē* ; in this expression *minus* is a negative :

Nōn recūsābimus quōminus sub diciōne Rōmānōrum sīmus. *We shall not protest against being under the authority of the Romans* : cf. B. G. i. 31.

31   When the main clause is negatived or interrogative the noun clause is usually introduced by *quīn* (derived from *quī-ne*, originally = 'why not?' or 'how not?') :

Germānī retinērī nōn poterant quīn tēla in nostrōs

---

[1] For some Latin verbs of this class which take an infinitive (without a negative) see note to § 329.

conicerent. *The Germans could not be restrained from hurling missiles against our men*: B. G. i. 47.—Nōn recūsāmus quīn armīs contendāmus. *We do not refuse to fight* (originally 'Why should we not fight? we have no objection ').

332 (iii) Noun clauses depending on verbs of 'fearing'. Here too the noun clause expresses (from the Latin point of view) a desire that something *shall not be done*: hence it takes *nē* where the English uses 'that' or 'lest'. Compare the use of *ne* in French: *je crains que je ne meure* = 'I fear that I shall die'. The Latin *nē moriar metuō* meant originally 'may I not die! I have my fears'.

> Veritus nē ab omnibus deserātur, lēgātōs ad Caesarem mittit. *Fearing lest he be deserted by all, he sends envoys to Caesar*: cf. B. G. v. 3.—Veritus nē hostium impetum sustinēre nōn posset litterās Caesarī remīsit. *Fearing lest he should not be able to resist the attack of the enemy he sent a dispatch to Caesar*: B. G. v. 47.

Instead of *nē nōn* 'that not' *ut* is often used:

> Ut rēs frūmentāria supportārētur timēbant. *They feared lest supplies should not be brought up*: cf. B. G. i. 39.

The *ut* was originally interrogative (like *utinam* in wishes, § 321): 'how were the supplies to be brought up? they had their fears.'

333 (iv) Noun clauses depending on a noun or noun-equivalent (pronoun or adjective used as a noun):

> Iūs est bellī ut victōrēs victīs imperent. *It is the law of war that the victors shall give commands to the vanquished*: cf. B. G. i. 36.—Dē senātūs consultō certior factus est ut omnēs iūniōrēs Italiae coniūrārent. *He was informed of the vote of the Senate* [to the effect] *that all the younger men of Italy should* (were to) *take the military oath*: B. G. vii. 1. Similarly in dependence on nouns like *sententia, fātum, mōs, potestās, occāsiō*.

Suum illud, nihil ut adfirmet, tenet ad extrēmum. *He maintains to the last that habit of his of affirming nothing (that he shall affirm nothing)*: Cic. Tusc. i. 99.—Quid melius est quam ut nihil adfirmem? *What is better than that I should affirm nothing?*

Vērum est ut bonī bonōs dīligant. *It is right that good men should love good men*: Cic. de Amic. 50.—An vērīsimile est ut cīvis Rōmānus haec fēcerit? *Is it probable that a Roman citizen should have done this?* Cic. Sest. 78.

(b) In adjective and adverb clauses.

34 Here the *shall*-subjunctive assumes various shades of meaning.

(i) It may denote what is obligatory or proper or necessary or destined:

Circumscrībit nōs terminīs quōs nōn excēdāmus. *He confines us within limits which we are not to* (= must not) *pass over*: Livy xxi. 44. 5.—Quam multī diēs reperīrī possunt quī tālī noctī antepōnantur? *How many days can be found which are to be preferred to such a night* (*i. e.* to the sleep of death)? Cic. Tusc. i. 97.—Accipe quod numquam reddās mihi. *Here is a sum of money which you need never repay me* (lit. *which you are not bound ever to repay me*): Hor. Sat. ii. 3. 66.—Nascētur Trōiānus ... fāmam quī terminet astrīs. *There shall be born a Trojan who shall extend his glory to the stars*: Aen. i. 286 f.

35 (ii) It may denote the necessary or natural effect of an antecedent: English 'such (*or* so) as to' with the infinitive. Compare 'Build me straight a goodly vessel which shall laugh at all disaster' (Longfellow): which shall laugh = such as to laugh. 'There was no reason why I should rejoice' = no reason such as to make me rejoice. Such clauses are often preceded by a word meaning 'so' or 'such' or 'enough',

'worthy', 'fitting', &c., in the main clause; compare the French *tel que* and *de sorte que* with the subjunctive.

Quī-clauses.—Neque ulla tanta vīs reperiētur quae con-iunctiōnem vestram labefactāre possit. *Nor will any force be found so strong as to be able* (lit. *which shall be able*) *to weaken your alliance* : Cic. Cat. iv. 22.—Nōn is sum quī mortis perīculō terrear. *I am not a man of such a character as to be terrified* (*not one who is to be terrified*) *by the danger of death*: B. G. v. 30.—Satis erat causae quārē Caesar in Dumnorīgem adverteret. *There was sufficient reason why Caesar should punish* (*was to punish*) *Dumnorix*: B. G. i. 19.—Dignī sunt quōrum salūtī consulātis. *They deserve* (lit. *they are worthy*) *that you should consider their welfare*: cf. Cic. leg. Man. 13.—Idōnea mihi Laeliī persōna vīsa est quae dē amīcitiā dissereret. *I thought Laelius a suitable character to discuss* (lit. *who should discuss*) *friendship* : Cic. Amic. 4.

Secūtae sunt tempestātēs quae nostrōs in castrīs conti-nērent. *There followed storms which were to keep our men in camp* (= storms so severe as to keep): B. G. iv. 34.—Quid est quod rīdeās ? *What is there that you should* (or *have to*) *laugh at ?*—Nihil habeō quod agam. *I have nothing to do* (= nothing which I am to do): Hor. Sat. i. 9. 19.—Haec habuī dē senectūte quae dīcerem. *I had this much to say about old age* (= this much which I was to say): Cic. Sen. 86.

336 *Ut*-clauses.—Haec omnia sīc agentur, ut bellum intestī-num sēdētur. *All this shall be done in such a manner that the civil war shall be ended* : Cic. Cat. ii. 28.—Ita currūs collocant, ut expedītum ad suōs receptum habeant. *They place their chariots in such a position as to have a ready retreat to their friends* : B. G. iv. 33.—Mihi cūiusquam salūs tantī fuisset, ut meam neglegerem ?

Should anyone's welfare have been (§ 319) *of so great importance to me that I was to* (as to make me) *disregard my own?* Cic. Sulla 45.—Quid in mē admīsī, ut loquī nōn audeam? *What crime have I committed that I should not venture to speak?* Plaut. Men. 712.—Nec tantum maerōrem senātuī mors Clōdiī afferēbat, ut nova quaestiō cōnstituerētur. *Nor did the death of Clodius cause the senate so much grief that a new court of inquiry had to be constituted:* Cic. Mil. 13.—Nēmō erat adeō tardus, quīn (= ut nōn *or* quī nōn) statim castrīs exeundum et occurrendum putāret. *No one was so sluggish as not to think that he must immediately march out of the camp and oppose us:* B. C. i. 69.—Nōn possunt ūnā in cīvitāte multī fortūnās āmittere, ut nōn plūrēs sēcum in eandem trahant calamitātem. *It is not possible for many men in one and the same state to lose their property without dragging* (lit. *in such a way as not to drag*) *a greater number with them into the same misfortune:* Cic. leg. Man. 19).

337 (iii) An adjective or adverb clause with a *shall*-subjunctive may be subordinated to *quam* 'than', preceded by a comparative adjective or adverb in the main clause:

Māior sum quam cui (*or* quam ut mihi) possit Fortūna nocēre. *I am too great for Fortune to be able* (*than that Fortune should be able*) *to injure me:* Ovid, Met. vi. 195.—Longius aberant quam quō tēlum adicī posset. *They were too far off for a javelin to reach them.* Similarly *quasi* 'as if' = *quam sī* (with a postulative subj., § 343: loqueris quasi nesciās.

338 (iv) Many adjective and adverb clauses with a *shall*-subjunctive denote what is *desired*. The subordinate clause (called a clause of purpose) is introduced either by a relative pronoun or by *ut* 'that', *nē* 'that ... not', or *quō* 'whereby' (*quō* being generally followed by a comparative). They may often be translated by an English infinitive.

Explōrātōrēs mittit quī locum idōneum castrīs dēligant. *He sends scouts to choose a suitable place for a camp*; lit. *who shall choose*, or *who are to choose*: B. G. ii. 17.

Labiēnum in continentī relīquit ut portūs tuērētur. *He left Labienus on the continent in order that he should (might) protect the harbours*: B. G. v. 8.

Nē aestātem in Treverīs consūmere cōgerētur, Indutiomārum ad sē venīre iussit. *Lest he should* (or *In order that he might not*) *be compelled to waste the summer in the country of the Treveri, he commanded Indutiomarus to come to him*: B. G. v. 4.

Mīlitēs manipulōs laxāre iussit, quō facilius gladiīs ūtī possent. *He ordered the soldiers to open up their ranks, whereby the more easily they should* (might) *be able to use their swords*: B. G. ii. 25.

339 In some adjective and adverb clauses the *shall*-subjunctive denotes little more than the idea of future time. Such subjunctives may be called 'prospective', because they mark the action as *in prospect* either at the time of speaking or at some point of time in the past which the speaker has in mind.

340 Prospective subjunctives are often found in clauses of time introduced by words meaning 'until' or 'before':

Exspectāre dum hostium cōpiae augeantur summae dēmentiae est. *To wait till the forces of the enemy shall be increased is the height of folly*: B. G. iv. 13.—Nōn prius ducēs ex conciliō dēmittunt quam ab iīs sit concessum ut arma capiant. *They do not let the leaders go out of the council till permission to take up arms has been* (lit. *shall have been*) *granted by them*: B. G. iii. 18. —Dum reliquae nāvēs eō convenīrent in ancorīs exspectāvit. *He waited at anchor till the rest of the ships should assemble there*: B. G. iv. 23.—Priusquam sē hostēs ex terrōre reciperent, exercitum in Suessiōnēs duxit. *He led his army into the country of the Suessiones before the enemy should recover from their alarm*: B. G. ii. 12.

41 Prospective subjunctives are especially common in adjective and adverb clauses which are subordinated to a clause which itself refers to future time :

Fraus fidem in parvīs sibi praestruit, ut, cum ˈoperae pretium sit, cum mercēde magnā fallat. *Fraud contrives for itself credibility in small things, in order that, when it shall be worth while, it may deceive with great profit*: Livy xxviii. 42. 7.—Exspectābat ut, sī forte hostēs ēlicere posset, citrā vallem contenderet. *He was waiting in order that, if perchance he should be able to lure out the enemy, he might fight on this side of the valley*: B. G. v. 50. (Contrast *sī* with the Past Subj. in § 350. 2.)— Imperāvit ut sustinērent quoad ipse propius accessisset. *He ordered them to hold out till he himself should have come nearer*: cf. B. G. iv. 11.—Sabellīs docta ligōnibus versāre glēbās . . . sōl ubi montium mūtāret umbrās, *taught to turn the sod with Samnite mattocks when the sun should lengthen the shadows of the mountains*: Hor. Od. iii. 6. 38–41 (*Sabellus* means ' Samnite ', not ' Sabine ').

42 In some adjective and adverb clauses the *shall*-subjunctive expresses a supposition ('supposing that'). In this use the subjunctive may be called 'postulative', because it denotes what is assumed or demanded for the purpose of argument.

The origin of this use is seen in simple sentences (§§ 317, 321) :

Vendat aedēs vir bonus ; nōrit ipse vitia eārum, cēterī ignōrent: vitia emptōrī dīcere dēbet. *Let an honest man sell a house ; let him know its defects himself, but let all other men be ignorant of them : he ought to point out the defects to a purchaser* (cf. Cic. Off. iii. 13). Here the sentences with the subjunctive are commands ; but they are equivalent to suppositions: *should an honest man sell a house . . . he ought to point out its defects.* Compare in English ' Let two parallel lines be pro-

duced to infinity: they will never meet'; 'Be he alive
or be he dead'; 'will he nill he'; and in French *soit*
= 'supposing it to be so.'

Modo Iuppiter adsit: tertia lux classem Crētaeīs sistet in
ōrīs. *Only let Jupiter stand by us: the third dawn shall
set our fleet on the shores of Crete*: Aen. iii. 116 f.

A postulative subjunctive of the past is seen in instances
like the following:—

Deciens centēna dedissēs huic parcō, quinque diēbus nīl
erat in loculīs. *Supposing that you had given a million
sesterces to this thrifty man, in five days there was nothing
in his money box*: Hor. Sat. i. 3. 15 f.

343 But postulative subjunctives are generally introduced by
a subordinating conjunction—*sī* 'if',[1] *ut* 'supposing that',
dum or *dummodo* 'so long as', *quamvīs* 'even if', 'although'
(literally 'as you will', from *quam* and the 2nd pers. sing.
pres. indic. of *volō*)—or by a relative pronoun:

Sī vendat aedēs vir bonus, &c. *If an honest man should
sell a house*, &c. For the use of the tenses of the subjunctive in such *if*-clauses see § 350.[2]—Ut omnia contrā
opīniōnem acciderent, tamen sē plūrimum nāvibus
posse. [*They reflected that*] *supposing that everything*

---

[1] *Sī* means literally 'so'; the same word is seen with the suffix *c* in *sīc*
(*sī* 'in case', *sī-c* 'in that case'). In Shakespeare's time 'so' was sometimes used in the sense of 'if'; e. g. 'No matter whither, *so* you come not
here' (As You Like It, ii. 3. 30); Latin *Nōn rēfert quō eās, sī nōn hūc veniās.*

[2] But the tenses of the subjunctive may be used without the special
implications which they have in the sentences quoted in § 350: e. g. *Mūrus
oppidī ā plānitiē atque initiō ascensūs rectā regiōne, sī nullus anfractus inter-
cēderet, MCC passūs aberat*, 'The wall of the town was 1,200 paces distant
from the plain and the beginning of the slope in a straight line, supposing
no bend in the road to intervene' (= disregarding bends in the road):
B. G. vii. 46—*Sī in Italiā consistat, erimus ūnā; sīn cēdet, consilī rēs est*,
'Supposing him to make a stand in Italy, we shall meet; but if he yields
(*lit.* shall yield), the matter demands thought': Cic. ad Att. vii. 10: cf. Hor.
Od. ii. 14. 6, ii. 17. 14, iii. 3. 7.

*should happen contrary to their expectation, they were never-
theless very strong in ships*: B. G. iii. 9.—Ōderint dum
metuant. *Let them hate, so long as* (= *provided that*) *they
fear.*—Ea voluptās, quamvīs parva sit, pars tamen est
vītae. *That pleasure, be it ever so small* (lit. *be it small as
you will*) *is nevertheless a part of life.*—Quī reī publicae
sit hostis, fēlix esse nōn potest. *Whoso shall be an
enemy of the state, cannot be a happy man.*

44   Such clauses often have a limiting or restrictive sense.
(*a*) Relative clauses limiting a superlative or negative :
   Omnium ōrātōrum, quōs quidem ego cognōverim, acū-
   tissimus. *The most keen-witted of all orators, at any rate
   of those whom I have known* (all, provided that I have
   known them): Cic. Brutus 180.—Servus est nēmō,
   quī modo tolerābilī condiciōne sit servitūtis, quī nōn
   audāciam hōrum cīvium perhorrescat. *There is no
   slave, provided only that he be in a not unendurable state
   of servitude, who does not* (§ 335) *shudder at the crimi-
   nality of these citizens*: Cic. Cat. iv. 16.—Often in the
   expression *quod sciam* 'so far as I know' (lit. 'supposing
   me to know it ').

45 (*b*) *Ut*-clauses preceded by *ita* = *eā condiciōne* : Equitēs vōbīs
   ita concēdunt ut vōbīscum dē amōre reī publicae cer-
   tent. *The knights yield to you* (*senators*) *only on the
   understanding that they shall vie with you in patriotism*:
   Cic. Cat. iv. 15.—Ita illī audīre poterunt ut vōs quoque
   audiātis. *They will not be able to hear without your
   hearing also*: cf. Cic. Sulla 31.

46   A postulative *quī*-clause (especially with *quippe* or *ut* 'as')
   may assume causal meaning: cf. *siquidem*, originally = 'if
   indeed ', hence 'since ' :
   Insipiens sum, quī quidem contrā eōs tam diū disputem.
   I am foolish to argue so long against them (Cicero) ; lit.
   if I argue, considering that I argue.

(B) SUBJUNCTIVES DENOTING WHAT *WOULD HAPPEN* UNDER CERTAIN IMAGINED CONDITIONS

347 These subjunctives are translated by 'should' in the 1st person and 'would' in the 2nd and 3rd persons.

What *would happen* is what *will happen* (or *is likely to happen*) *under certain imagined conditions*: e.g. 'What would you do?' means 'What are you likely to do in that case (*or* under those circumstances)?' The idea is that of a future action, the occurrence of which depends on a condition which the speaker has in mind.

These subjunctives, then, may be called **subjunctives of conditioned futurity.**[1] They express the meanings which are generally expressed in French by the Futures in the past.

1. In Simple Sentences.

348 The Present and the Perfect Subjunctive denote what *is* likely to happen under certain imagined conditions of the present or future:

> Hoc Ithacus velit et magnō mercentur Atrīdae. *This the Ithacan would desire and the sons of Atreus would purchase at a great price;* 'would desire'='is likely under these circumstances to desire': Aen. ii. 104; cf. ii. 8 *quis tālia fandō temperet ā lacrimīs?*
>
> Dīcere nōn ausim (= audeam). *I should not venture to say.* Similarly *velim* 'I should like', *nōlim* 'I should not like', *mālim* 'I should prefer'.
>
> Hoc nōn facile dixerim. *I should not readily assert this, I am not likely to . . .*: Cic. Verr. iv. 94.

[1] Subjunctives of conditioned futurity may have originally denoted what *ought* (logically) to be the case, marking a statement as a necessary inference from some supposition: sī hoc vērum sit, illud sit falsum, *supposing this to be true, that must be (ought to be) false.* If so, these subjunctives are in origin subjunctives denoting what *is to be* (see §§ 318, 319). Note that in the fourth example above *quis arbitrārētur* might be translated '*who was to think?*'

The Past and the Past Perfect Subjunctive denote what *was* likely to happen under certain imagined conditions of the past:[1]

> Quis arbitrārētur hoc bellum ūnō annō conficī posse? *Who would have thought* [under those circumstances] *that this war could be brought to an end in one year?* Cic. leg. Man. 31.
>
> Crēderēs victōs. *You would have supposed them conquered*: Liv. ii. 43. In such sentences 'you' may mean either the person addressed or any one ('one').
>
> Nulla alia gens tantā clāde nōn obruta esset. *Any other nation would have been overwhelmed by so great a disaster*: Liv. xxii. 54.
>
> Similarly *vellem* 'I should have liked', *nollem*, *mallem*.

2. In the Main Clause of a Complex Sentence.

349   The combination of a clause containing a subjunctive of conditioned futurity with a clause containing a postulative subjunctive (§ 342) forms a conditional sentence of a particular kind, in which there is an implication that the speaker does not vouch for the condition being (or having been) fulfilled. The use of the subjunctive in the *if*-clause marks the condition as a mere assumption (*if it be supposed that*), and in some cases implies that it is contrary to fact.

350   In conditional sentences of this kind[2] the tenses of the subjunctive are used in special senses by writers of the classical period.[3]

1. When the *if*-clause refers to future time, it takes the

---

[1] The same idea is sometimes expressed by the Future Participle with a past tense of *sum*: see § 352.

[2] There is another kind of conditional sentence, in which the *if*-clause is *open*, i. e. in which there is no implication as to the fulfilment of the condition. Such *if*-clauses take the indicative mood: see § 531.

[3] In the Old Latin writers the tenses of the subjunctive are somewhat differently used.

Present Subjunctive, and is accompanied by a Present Subjunctive in the main clause, denoting what *would happen* : [1]

> Sī vir bonus habeat hanc vim, ut digitōrum percussiōne nōmen suum in locuplētium testāmenta inserere possit, hāc vī nōn ūtātur. *If a good man were to have the power of being able by snapping his fingers to introduce his name into the wills of wealthy persons, he would not use the power*: cf. Cic. Off. iii. 75.—*Sī habeat* 'if he were to have' or 'if he should have' or 'should he have' implies ' I do not say that he *will* have '. The speaker (or writer) guards himself against being supposed to mean that the condition will be fulfilled.

> Sī per tē liceat, perendinō diē commūnem cum reliquīs bellī cāsum sustineant. *If you were to permit them, they would the day after to-morrow face the chances of war in common with the others*: B. G. v. 30. 3.

2. When the *if*-clause refers to present time, it takes the Past Subjunctive, and is accompanied by a Past Subjunctive in the main clause, denoting what *would happen* :

> Sī vir bonus hanc vim habēret, eā nōn ūterētur. *If a good man had this power, he would not use it.*—*Sī habēret* 'if he had' implies that he *has not* the power. The condition is contrary to present fact.

> Cūius reī sī exemplum nōn habērēmus, tamen instituī pulcherrimum iūdicārem. *Even if we had no precedent, I should nevertheless regard it as a fine thing that one should be established*: B. G. vii. 77. 13.

3. When the *if*-clause refers to past time, it takes the Past Perfect Subjunctive (or sometimes the Past Subjunctive [2]),

---

[1] The Perfect Subjunctive is occasionally used in this case, but it is very rare.

[2] The use of the Past Subjunctive with reference to past time is the older usage, often found in Plautus, *e. g.* deōs voluisse crēdō ; nam nī vellent, nōn fieret, *I believe that the gods willed it ; for if they had not willed it, it would not have happened* (Aulularia 742). But, as in English and French, a form which originally denoted past time, came to be used with reference to present time : nisi Alexander essem, Diogenēs esse vellem, *if I were not Alexander,*

and is accompanied by a Past Perfect (or sometimes by a Past) Subjunctive in the main clause, denoting what *would have happened*:

> Sī M. Crassus hanc vim habuisset, eā ūsus esset. *If Marcus Crassus* (an unscrupulous man) *had had this power, he would have used it.—Sī habuisset* 'if he had had' implies that he *had not* the power. The condition is contrary to past fact.

> Darēs hanc vim M. Crassō, in forō saltāret. *Had you given (supposing you to have given) this power to Marcus Crassus, he would have danced for joy in the forum* (Cicero, in the continuation of the passage quoted above. Crassus was dead when Cicero wrote).

> Nisi mīlitēs dēfessī essent, omnēs hostium cōpiae dēlērī potuissent. *If the soldiers had not been tired out, all the forces of the enemy might have been destroyed*: B. G. vii. 88. *Nisi* or *nī* means 'if ... not' or 'unless'.

351 An *if*-clause referring to past time may be accompanied by a main clause referring to the time of speaking:

> Sī mens nōn laeva fuisset ... Trōia nunc stārēs. *If our hearts had not been blinded, thou, Troy, would'st now be standing*: Aen. ii. 54 f.

352 Instead of the Past Perfect Subjunctive in the main clause the Future Participle with *eram* or *fuī* is sometimes used:

> Ēmendātūrus, sī licuisset, eram. *I should have corrected the faults, if I had been allowed to do so*: Ovid, Tristia i. 7. 40; lit. *I was likely to* (or *going to*) *correct the faults.*

353 Instead of the subjunctive of a verb denoting 'can', 'must', or 'ought' in the main clause, the indicative may be used:

> Quodsī Pompēius prīvātus esset hōc tempore, tamen ad

I should wish to be Diogenes. The English *were* (Subj. of *was*) originally related to past time, as in 'If it *were* so, it was a grievous fault' (Shakespeare); but it generally expresses a contrary-to-fact supposition of the present. So too the French Past Imperfect Indicative (see French Grammar, § 315).

tantum bellum is erat dēligendus. *But even if Pompey were a private citizen at the present time, nevertheless it is he who ought to be chosen for the conduct of so great a war*: Cic. leg. Man. 50. Similarly *dēligī eum oportēbat* 'he ought to be chosen'; *dēligī poterat* 'he might be chosen'.

Sī prīvātus tum fuisset, dēligendus fuit. *If he had been a private citizen at that time, he ought to have been chosen.* Similarly *dēligī eum oportuit* 'he ought to have been chosen'; *dēligī potuit* 'he might have been chosen'.

Contrast the Past Perfect Subj. *potuissent* in the last example of § 350.

354 In conditional sentences with a subjunctive in the *if*-clause, the subjunctive of conditioned futurity in the main clause generally assumes a negative shade of meaning, *i.e.* denotes some degree of *unlikelihood*. But not necessarily; for when a word meaning 'even' is added in the *if*-clause, or when *sī* alone means 'even if' (as in some of the examples above), the speaker means that the action of the main clause is or was likely to happen in any case. For example, the passage quoted above (§ 350. 1) from Cicero goes on as follows:

Sī vir bonus hanc vim habeat, nōn ūtātur, nē sī explōrātum quidem habeat id omnīnō nēminem umquam suspicātūrum. *If a good man were to have this power, he would not use it, not even if he were to be sure that not a single person would ever suspect him*: 'he would not use it' = his refusal to use it is likely.

3. In Subordinate Clauses.

355 Subjunctives of conditioned futurity may be subordinated to a relative pronoun or a subordinating conjunction:

Nēmō est quī illum nōn ad Manlium quam ad Massiliensēs īre mālit. *There is no one who would not prefer that he should go to Manlius rather than to the people of Marseilles*: Cic. Cat. ii. 16.

Maestī rediērunt, ut victōs eōs crēderēs. *They returned sad at heart, so that one would have supposed them conquered*: cf. § 348.

Honestum tāle est, ut vel sī ignōrārent id hominēs vel sī obmūtuissent, suā tamen pulchritūdine esset laudābile. *Righteousness is of such a nature that even if men were unacquainted with it or had said nothing about it, it would nevertheless be commendable by reason of its own beauty*: Cic. Fin. ii. 49.

Nesciō num sī hanc vim habērem ut digitōrum percussiōne hērēs locuplētium scrībī possem, hāc vī ūterer. *I do not know whether, if I had the power of being able by snapping my fingers to be written down as the heir of wealthy persons, I should use it* (cf. § 350. 2).

Nōn dubitō quīn sī hominēs hanc vim habuissent, saepe ūsurpāta esset. *I do not doubt that if people had had this power, it would often have been used.*[1]

356 But instead of the Past Perfect Subjunctive denoting conditioned futurity in subordination to a conjunction which itself requires the subjunctive,[2] or in a dependent question, the Future Participle with *fuerim, fuerīs, fuerit* is generally employed, if the meaning is active and the verb has a Future Participle :

Nōn dubitō (*or* Nōn dubitābam) quīn sī M. Crassus hanc vim habuisset, eā ūsūrus fuerit. *I do not* (or *did not*) *doubt that if Crassus had had this power, he would have used it*: lit. *was likely to use it.*[1]—Dīc quidnam factūrus fuerīs, sī eō tempore censor fuissēs. *Say what you would have done* (lit. *were likely to do*), *if you had been censor at that time*: Livy ix. 33. 7.[1]—Adeō inopiā coactus est Hannibal, ut, nisi cum fugae speciē abeun-

---

[1] Note that in all these subordinate expressions of conditioned futurity no regard is paid to the rule of sequence of tenses (§ 365).

[2] E. g. *ut* or *quīn* (§ 362) or *cum* (§ 358). By means of the combination of the future participle with *fuerim* Latin is able to express futurity and at the same time to maintain the subjunctive construction required by the conjunction.

dum timuisset, Galliam repetītūrus fuerit. *Hannibal was driven to such straits by want, that if he had not feared that his departure would have involved the appearance of flight, he would have retreated to Gaul*: Livy xxii. 32. 3.[1]

For the way in which conditioned futurity is expressed in dependence on a verb of 'saying' or 'thinking' see § 471 (*Dīcō M. Crassum hāc vī ūsūrum fuisse, sī eam habuisset*).

(C) SUBJUNCTIVES WITH WEAKENED MEANING IN SUBORDINATE CLAUSES

357 In course of time the subjunctive came to be used in some constructions with a weakened meaning, little different from that of an indicative. These weakened subjunctives are, however, found **only in certain subordinate constructions (five in number)**; and the origin of most of them can be traced. In some cases it is the *shall*-meaning, in others the *would*-meaning, that has been weakened. The loss of the *shall*-meaning is similar to the loss of the sense of obligation or necessity in some constructions of the gerund adjective (§ 502).

Note the following features which are common to all these weakened uses of the subjunctive:

(i) The tenses of the subjunctive are translated by the corresponding tenses of the English indicative:

the Present Subj. by a Present Indic.
the Past Subj. by a Past Indic., or by its continuous form.
the Perfect Subj. by a Perfect or a Past Indic.
the Past Perf. Subj. by a Past Perf. Indic.

(ii) Where future time has to be expressed, it is expressed by adding the Future Participle: *e.g.* interrogō num ventūrus sit, *I ask whether he will come*: interrogāvī num ventūrus esset, *I asked whether he would come*.

---

[1] Note that in the subordinate expression of conditioned futurity no regard is paid to the rule of sequence of tenses (§ 365).

(iii) The negative is always *nōn*. Contrast the use of *nē* as the negative of some of the subjunctives which denote what *is* or *was to be done* (§§ 320, 327, 330, 332, 338).

358   1. **Certain clauses of time, cause, and concession take a subjunctive with weakened meaning.**

(*a*) *Cum* meaning 'when' generally takes the subjunctive in past time (*i. e.* when the time of the main clause is past). The tenses of the subjunctive used in such *cum*-clauses are the Past and the Past Perfect.

The *cum*-clause is best translated by a participle without any conjunction : the *cum* does not mean exactly 'at the time when' (in which sense it takes the indicative), but rather 'whereas', denoting the **circumstances under which** the action of the main clause takes place [1] :

> Cum esset Caesar in Galliā Citeriōre, certior fīēbat Belgās coniūrāre. *Being in Hither Gaul, Caesar was informed that the Belgae were leaguing together* : B. G. ii. 1.
>
> Caesar, cum id nuntiātum esset, in Galliam Ulteriōrem contendit. *This having been reported, Caesar hastened into Further Gaul* : B. G. i. 7.

(*b*) *Cum* meaning 'because' or 'although', and *quī, quae,*

---

[1] The word *cum* is in origin an accusative of the relative pronoun (stem *quo-*) ; its root-meaning is, therefore, 'as to which,' or 'whereas'. 'Whereas' is not very different from the meaning which *sī* (originally 'so') acquired when it became a subordinating conjunction ; cf. § 343 note. In English 'when' and 'if' are often interchangeable : 'when it rains (= whenever it rains), I stay at home,' 'if it rains, I stay at home.' Similarly in Latin : *difficile est tacēre cum doleās*, 'it is difficult to hold one's peace when one is hard hit' (*sī doleās*, 'if one is hard hit') : Cic. Sull. 31. It is possible, then, that the subjunctive which is used in circumstantial *cum*-clauses is in origin postulative, like the subjunctive with *sī* : *sī ita esset*, 'supposing that it was so,' *cum ita esset*, 'under whatever circumstances it was so.' The past tense of the postulative subjunctive does not necessarily imply that the supposition is contrary to fact : see § 343, note 2. Cicero uses *sī ita esset* without this implication in Tusc. v. 11. 33 ; cf. Shakespeare's 'If it were so (= supposing that it was so), it was a grievous fault' : Julius Caesar iii. 2. 84. The subjunctive in *cum*-clauses of time, cause, and concession did not become common till the time of Cicero,

quod, meaning 'because he (she, it)', 'although he (she, it)', take the subjunctive in both present and past time.

Here, too, the *cum*-clause and the *quī*-clause are best translated by a participle :—

Quae cum (= Et cum ea) ita sint { ēgredere ex urbe (Cic. Cat. i. 10). tamen pācem faciam (B. G. i. 14).

this being so = (1) *because this is so*, (2) *although this is so.*

Cum nōn amplius octingentōs equitēs habērent, impetum fēcērunt. *Having* (= *Though they had*) *not more than 800 horsemen, they charged* : B. G. iv. 12.

Titūrius, quī nihil ante prōvīdisset, trepidāre. *Titurius, having foreseen nothing, became alarmed* : B. G. v. 33.

359 In translating from English into Latin, *cum* with the subjunctive is a very useful equivalent for the English participle. One reason for this is that Latin has no perfect participle with active meaning, except in deponent verbs, and no present participle passive of any verb : nor has it any present participle of the verb *sum*. The *cum*-clause came to be used as a substitute for these wanting forms.

360 2. **Certain clauses of result introduced by** *ut*, **or by** *quī*, *quae*, *quod*, **take a subjunctive with weakened meaning**[1] :

Tanta tempestās coorta est ut nāvēs cursum tenēre nōn possent. *So great a storm arose that the ships were not able to hold their course* : cf. B. G. iv. 28.

Cicerō nē nocturnum quidem sibi tempus ad quiētem relinquēbat, ut ultrō mīlitum vōcibus sibi parcere cōgerētur. *Cicero did not allow himself even the night*

---

[1] The origin of this construction, which is such a curious feature of the Latin language, is shown in §§ 335 6. The Romans regarded a result as the *necessary effect* of a cause—as something *bound to happen*, something which *is* or *was to come about*. The subjunctive mood was very well fitted to express this idea, which is closely akin to that of the root-meaning of the subjunctive. And the Romans employed this mood in *all* clauses of result— not only those in which English often uses the infinitive with 'as to' and French the subjunctive after *de sorte que* and similar expressions, but also those which are expressed in English and French and other languages as statements of *fact* (by the use of the indicative mood).

for sleep, so that he was actually compelled by the protests of the soldiers to spare himself: B. G. v. 40.

Tam parātus fuit ad dīmicandum animus hostium ut ad galeās induendās tempus dēfuerit. *So eager were the enemy for fighting that time failed our men for putting on their helmets*: B. G. ii. 21.

Habētis eum consulem quī pārēre vestrīs dēcrētīs nōn dubitet. *You have a consul of such a character that he does not hesitate to obey your decrees*: Cic. Cat. iv. 24.

OBS. *Quīn* may be used for *ut nōn* or *quī (quae, quod) nōn*, when the main clause is negative or interrogative:

Numquam tam male est Siculīs quīn aliquid facētē dīcant. *The Sicilians are never in such trouble that they do not say (as not to say) something witty* (lit. *wittily*): Cic. Verr. iv. 95.

361   Out of this construction grew another in which the subordinate clause loses all its sense of result and becomes purely descriptive. When a relative clause (with or without the antecedent *is*) is an essential part of the sentence, which cannot be removed without destroying the sense, it generally takes the subjunctive:

Nulla nāvis quae mīlitēs portāret dēsīderābātur. *No ship that carried soldiers was missed*: B. G. v. 23.

Neque quicquam eōrum quae apud hostēs agerentur eum fallēbat. *Nor did any of the things which were going on among the enemy escape his notice*: Livy xxii. 28. 1.

Sunt quī dīcant... *There are people who say...*[1]

Erant quī cēnsērent ... *There were people who expressed the opinion* ... Livy xxi. 6.[1]

[1] The origin of subjunctives of this type may perhaps be found in sentences like *reperiuntur quī dīcant*, 'people are found to say': e. g. *quī sē ultrō mortī offerant facilius reperiuntur quam quī dolōrem patienter ferant*, people are more readily found to expose themselves (who shall expose themselves) unasked to death than to bear pain with fortitude: B. G. vii. 77. 5.—It should be noticed that the indicative is sometimes used after *sunt quī*, e. g. Caesar, B. G. iv. 10 *sunt quī piscibus et ōvīs avium vīvere existimantur*; Horace, Od. i. 1. 4.

362   3. **Certain noun clauses introduced by** *ut* **or** *quīn* **take a subjunctive with weakened meaning.**[1]

(*a*) *Ut*-clauses depending on verbs of 'happening':

Factum est ut impetum nostrōrum nōn ferrent. *The result was* (lit. *It resulted*) *that they did not stand the attack of our men*: B. G. iii. 19.

Accidit ut lūna plēna esset. *It happened that there was a full moon*: B. G. iv. 29.

(*b*) *Quīn*-clauses depending on negatived or interrogative expressions of 'doubting':

An dubitāmus quīn Rōmānī ad nōs interficiendōs veniant [ventūrī sint, vēnerint]? *Do we doubt that the Romans are coming* [*will come, have come*] *to murder us?* cf. B. G. vii. 38.

Nōn erat dubium quīn Rōmānī ad eōs interficiendōs venīrent [ventūrī essent, vēnissent]. *There was no doubt that the Romans were coming* [*were about to come, had come*] *to murder them.*

363   4. **Dependent questions as to a matter of fact and de-pendent exclamations take a subjunctive with weakened meaning.**[2]

[1] The subjunctive in these *ut*-clauses is of the same origin as that in clauses of result (§ 360) : compare *id nē fierī posset, obsidiōne fīēbat,* 'that this should not be possible, was brought about by the siege' (Caesar, B. C. i. 19), where *fīēbat* takes *nē* and a *shall*-subjunctive.—*Quīn*-clauses with the subjunctive were originally interrogative. A question like *quīn rogem?* 'why should I not ask?' (Plautus, Mil. 426), or *quīn quod iuvat id semper faciant?* 'why should they not always do what pleases them?' (Sallust, Jug. 85. 41) may be subordinated, like any other question with the subjunctive (§§ 319, 325) ; compare § 331. In the following instance *quīn* preserves its original meaning of 'why not?' and the subjunctive its *shall*-meaning :

Dubitandum nōn existimāvit quīn proficīscerētur. *He thought there ought to be no hesitation as to setting out*: B. G. ii. 2 ; originally 'why should he not set out? He thought there ought to be no hesitation'. It would be impossible here to translate *proficīscerētur* by an English indicative ('was setting out').

[2] The use of the subjunctive in dependent questions as to a matter of fact (which take the indicative in English, French, and Greek) did not become a rule of Latin syntax till the time of Cicero, though it is often found in Old

(*a*) Dependent questions as to a matter of fact:

Quid quisque audierit quaerunt, et cōgunt eōs prōnun-
tiāre quibus ex regiōnibus veniant quāsque ibi rēs cog-
nōverint. *They inquire what each has heard, and compel
them to declare from what country they come and what
they have learned there*: B. G. iv. 5.—Quid fierī velit
ostendit. *He indicates what he wishes to be done*: B. G.
v. 2.—Intellegēbat quā dē causā ea dīcerentur. *He
perceived why those things were said*: B. G. v. 4.—Hinc
intellegī poterat utrum apud eōs pudor an timor plūs
valēret. *Hence could be seen whether honour or fear
had more influence with them*: B. G. i. 40.— Mātrēs
familiae sortibus dēclārābant utrum proelium com-
mittī ex ūsū esset necne. *The matrons used to show by
drawing lots whether it was expedient that a battle should
be fought or not*: B. G. i. 50; contrast § 325, third ex.

(*b*) Dependent Exclamations:

Vidēs ut altā stet nive candidum Sōracte. *You see how
Soracte stands out glistening with deep snow*: Hor.
Od. i. 9. 1 (dependent form of the exclamation *Ut altā
stat nive candidum !*).—Mīrum quantum illī virō fidēs
fuerit. *Strange it is, to what an extent that man was
believed*: Livy i. 16 (dependent form of *Quantum illī
virō fidēs fuit!*).

OBS. 1. In reported speech dependent questions and
dependent exclamations are sometimes expressed by the
accusative with infinitive construction: see § 545.

OBS. 2. In dependent exclamations the indicative is sometimes found in poets:

Aspice ut insignis spoliīs Marcellus opīmīs ingreditur.
*Look how Marcellus steps along conspicuous in a general's
spoils*: Aen. vi. 855, cf. viii. 192, Georg. i. 57.

Latin. It may be connected with the use of the subjunctive to denote the
words or thoughts of another person (§ 364): see note below.

364 **5. Adjective and adverb clauses take the subjunctive when they express the thought of another person or of the speaker himself on some other occasion.**[1]

The adjective or adverb clause may be—

Either (*a*) subordinate to a noun clause which is itself dependent on a verb of 'saying' or 'thinking':

Helvētiī dixērunt sibi in animō esse iter per prōvinciam facere, quod aliud iter **habērent** nullum. *The Helvetii said that they intended to march through the Roman province because they* **had** *no other road*: B. G. i. 7. The adverb clause *quod aliud iter habērent nullum* is part of the thought not of Caesar but of the Helvetii, whose speech Caesar is here reporting. In their original speech they would have used the indicative: *Nōbīs in animō est iter per prōvinciam facere, quod aliud iter* **habēmus** *nullum.*

Caesar dixit haec esse quae ab eō **postulāret.** *Caesar said that these were the things which he* **demanded** *of him*: B. G. i. 35. The adjective clause *quae ab eō postulāret* is part of the thought of Caesar at the time when his speech was made: *Haec sunt quae abs tē* **postulō.**

Or (*b*) subordinate to a main clause (without any noun clause intervening):

Cottae et Titūriī calamitātem, quī in eōdem castellō **occiderint**, sibi ante oculōs pōnunt. *They picture to themselves the misfortune of Cotta and Titurius who* (as they said to themselves) **fell** *in the same fort*: B. G. vi. 37.

---

[1] A use of the English 'should' to denote what was said or thought by another person suggests a possible origin for the Latin subjunctive in this sense. In Elizabethan English instances are found like ' I heard a strange thing reported . . . of a raven that *should build* in a ship of the King's ' (Ben Jonson, *Volpone*, ii. 1), which might be translated *mira res nuntiāta est dē corvo quī in nāve regiā nidificaret.* And the same usage still exists in some dialects of English : e. g. ' He goes about saying that I *should be* a thief.'— Compare also the use of the French Future in the Past in the same sense (see French Grammar, § 310. iv). Thus in the third example above *quī occiderint* might be translated in French *quī auraient péri.*

Rēmī dē suīs prīvātīs rēbus petere coepērunt quoniam cīvitātī consulere nōn **possent**. *The Remi began to entreat about their private affairs because* (as they said) *they* were *not* able *to take thought for the state*: B. G. v. 3.

Obs. 1. This construction is sometimes found in clauses of cause preceded by *nōn* :

Persevērābō, nōn quod confīdam sed quia adhūc spērō. *I shall persevere, not* (as might be supposed) *because I have confidence, but because I still have hopes* ; French *je continuerai, non pas que j'aie confiance, mais j'espère encore* (French Grammar, § 359).

Obs. 2. There is a similar use of the subjunctive in noun clauses introduced by *quod* and depending on verbs of ' rejoicing ', 'grieving ', and 'wondering ':

Mīlitēs indignābantur quod conspectum suum hostēs ferre possent. *The soldiers were indignant that the enemy should be able to face them*: B. G. vii. 19. In such clauses English very often uses 'should' and French the subjunctive (see French Grammar, § 362): compare the following instances from Shakespeare : 'This I wonder at that he *should be* in debt' (Com. of Err. iv. ii. 48) ; 'Alas that love *should be* so tyrannous !' (Rom. and Jul. i. i. 176).

SEQUENCE OF TENSES

365 The tenses of the subjunctive used in subordinate clauses generally *correspond to* or *follow from* the tense of the verb of the main clause. The following rule is illustrated by all the examples of *shall*-subjunctives in subordinate clauses given in §§ 324–46, and by all but one [1] of the examples of subjunctives with weakened meaning in §§ 358–64.

[1] B. G. ii. 21 in § 360. This exception is explained below (Remark 2).

Rule: 1. When the main clause has a tense of present or future time, the subjunctive of the subordinate clause is either Present or Perfect:

> Present to denote action not completed: *e. g.* Quid faciat nescit, *He does not know what he is doing* (§ 363) or *what he is to do* (§ 325):
>
> Perfect to denote completed action: *e. g.* Quid fēcerit nescit, *He does not know what he has done* (or *did*); § 363.

2. When the main clause has a tense of past time, the subjunctive of the subordinate clause is either Past or Past Perfect:

> Past to denote action not completed: *e. g.* Quid faceret nesciēbat, *He did not know what he was doing* (§ 363) or *what he was to do* (§ 325):
>
> Past Perfect to denote completed action: *e. g.* Quid fēcisset nesciēbat, *He did not know what he had done*; § 363.

366 Subordinate clauses with the Present or the Perfect Subjunctive are said to have 'primary sequence'; those with the Past or the Past Perfect Subjunctive are said to have 'secondary sequence'.

Remarks.

367 (1) The Perfect Indicative when used as a Present Perfect is a tense of present time and properly takes primary sequence; when used as a Past Historic it is a tense of past time and properly takes secondary sequence:

> Nē qua cīvitās Rōmānōs suīs fīnibus recipiat ā mē prō-vīsum est. *I have taken precautions that no state shall receive the Romans within their borders*: B. G. vii. 20.
>
> Dixit mihi quid faceret (fēcisset). *He told me what he was doing (had done)*.

But there are exceptions; for even when the Perfect is

used as a Present Perfect it sometimes takes secondary sequence:

Nē vōbīs nocēre possent ego prōvīdī; nē mihi noceant vestrum est prōvidēre. *I have taken precautions that they should not be able to injure you; it is your business to take precautions that they shall not injure me*: Cic. Cat. iii. 27.

In noun clauses introduced by *ut* or *quīn* (§ 362) the Perfect always takes secondary sequence; and the only tense of the subjunctive used is the Past: see the examples in § 362. Perfects which have become Presents in meaning always take primary sequence: *e. g.* Nōvimus [Meminimus] quid proximā nocte ēgerīs. *We know [remember] what you did last night*: cf. Cic. Cat. i. 1.

(2) In clauses of result (§ 360) the tense of the subjunctive is often independent of the point of view of the main clause:

Tam parātus fuit ad dīmicandum animus hostium ut ad galeās induendās tempus dēfuerit. *So eager were the enemy for fighting that time failed our men for putting on their helmets*: B. G. ii. 21. Here the action of *dēfuerit* is marked as having taken place before the time of speaking, not in relation to *fuit*, which would naturally have been followed by *dēesset*.

Siciliam ita perdidit ut ea restituī in antīquum statum nullō modō possit. *He ruined Sicily to such an extent that it can nowise be restored to its ancient condition*: Cic. Verr. Act. I. 12. Here the action of *possit* is marked as going on at the time of speaking, and not in relation to *perdidit*.

(3) The Historic Present (§ 293. ii) is treated sometimes as a tense of past time, sometimes as a tense of present time (this latter usage is the commoner in Caesar):

Speculātōrēs mittit ut quid agerētur scīret.
       „   „   ut quid agātur sciat.

(4) The Historic Infinitive (§ 480) is always treated as a tense of past time:

> Obsecrāre ut Caesar certior fieret. *They entreated that Caesar might be informed*: B. C. i. 64.

(5) In the course of a long passage of reported speech depending on a tense of past time, some of the adjective and adverb clauses may have primary sequence: *e.g.* in B. G. i. 14. 6 the Present Subjunctives depend on *respondit* (not on *consuēsse*, which is a present in meaning). This varied construction is common in Livy.

(6) It follows from the Rule (§ 365) that a sentence like 'I know what he *was doing* last night' cannot be translated literally into Latin; we must say 'I know what he *did* last night', *Sciō quid proximā nocte fēcerit*. And a sentence like 'He did not know how much twice two is' must be translated *Nesciēbat quot bis bīna essent* (literally 'He did not know how much twice two *was*').

IV. CASES AND PREPOSITIONS

THE NOMINATIVE CASE

368 The nominative is the case of the subject:

> Haeduī, gens valida, Rōmānīs amīcī erant. *The Haedui, a powerful tribe* (§ 281), *were friends to the Romans.*— Exercitus salvus et incolumis rediit. *The army returned safe and sound* (§ 274).—Orgetorix dux dēligitur. *Orgetorix is chosen leader* (§ 274).

369 When the subject is indicated only by the inflexion of the verb (§ 251), it is often vague in meaning: Dīcunt. *They say, people say.*—Pluit. *It is raining* ('it' = something, *i. e.* the sky or the rain[1]).—Aliōs effugere saepe, tē numquam potes. *You* (= One) *can often escape from others, but never*

---

[1] Compare in English 'The rain it raineth every day' (Shakespeare).

from yourself (= oneself).—Ferās, nōn culpēs, quod 'mūtārī nōn potest. *One should put up with, not find fault with, what cannot be altered* (§ 289).

370 Verbs which are used only in the 3rd person (generally without a nominative[1]) and in the infinitive are called **impersonal verbs**: e.g.

pluit (-ere), *it is raining*	tonat (-āre), *it is thundering*
lūcescit (-ere), *it is dawning*	fulgurat (-āre), *it is lightening*

371 The following impersonal verbs are either used without any subject expressed, or take as their subject either the nominative of a neuter pronoun or more commonly an infinitive or (in a complex sentence) a noun clause :—

372 (i) *piget, pudet, paenitet, taedet,* and *miseret,* which express the feelings of vexation, shame, regret, weariness, and distress.

These verbs may take an accusative of the person who has the feeling and a genitive of that which causes the feeling (unless this is expressed as the subject); compare 'It repented the Lord that he had made man, and it grieved him' (Genesis vi. 6); 'He is slow to anger and repenteth him of the evil' (Joel ii. 13):

Fatērī pigēbat. *It was annoying to confess* (*To confess was annoying*).—Factōrum meōrum (*or* Haec fēcisse) mē numquam paenitēbit. *I shall never repent of my deeds* (or *of having done these things*).—Nēquitiae tuae mē pudet. *I am ashamed of your wickedness.*—Mē tuī miseret. *I am sorry for you, I pity you.*

373 (ii) *interest* 'it makes a difference' and *rēfert* 'it matters'. These verbs may take a genitive of the person to whom it makes a difference or matters; but instead of the genitive of a pronoun of the 1st or 2nd person, or of the 3rd person

---

[1] A nominative case is sometimes added : Iuppiter pluit, *Jupiter is raining* (i. e. is sending rain); saxa pluunt, *stones are raining down* (*i.e.* coming down like rain); hoc lūcescit, *this is the dawn coming* ; caelum tonat, *the sky is thundering.*

when reflexive, the ablative singular feminine of the possessive adjective is used :[1]

Ad nostram laudem nōn multum interest. *It does not make much difference to our reputation.*—Quid Milōnis intererat interficī Clōdium? *What* (§ 392) *did it concern Milo that Clodius should be killed?*—Meā nihil interest scīre, sed illīus multum. *It matters nothing* (§ 392) *to me to know, but it matters very much* (§ 393, § 77) *to him.*—Quod tuā nihil rēfert nē cūrāverīs. *Do not take thought for what does not concern you* (= Mind your own business).—Illōrum magis quam suā rētulisse crēdunt. *They think that it concerned those persons rather than themselves* (Sallust).—Neque cūiusquam rēfert. *Nor does it concern anyone* (Tacitus).

374 (iii) *libet* 'it pleases', *licet* 'it is allowed', and *liquet* 'it is clear'.

These verbs may take a dative of the person to whom something is pleasing, allowed, or clear :

Licet iīs incolumibus discēdere. *They may depart unharmed* (§ 274).—Hoc fēcī dum licuit. *This I have done, so long as it was permitted.*—Quod cuique libet loquātur. *Let each man say what he likes.*—Hoc nōn liquet, neque satis cōgitātum est. *This is not clear, nor has it been sufficiently pondered.*

375 (iv) *oportet* 'it is fitting', *decet* 'it is seemly', and *dēdecet* 'it is unseemly':

Mē ipsum amēs oportet, nōn mea. *It is fitting [that] you should love* (§ 325. ii) *me myself, not my possessions* (Cic. Fin. ii. 85).—Amīcitiam populī Rōmānī mihi praesidiō, nōn dētrīmentō esse oportet. *It is fitting that the friend-*

---

[1] The origin of this ablative is uncertain, as is also the case of *rē-* in *rēfert. Meā rēfert* comes either from *meā rēs* (nom.) *fert* 'my interest involves', or from *meam rem fert* 'it tends to my interest' (*meam rem* = *ad meam rem*). In either case the *rē-* was misunderstood as an ablative, and the possessive adj. made to agree with it.

ship of the Roman nation should be (§ 466) *a protection, not a disadvantage to me* (cf. B. G. i. 44. 5).—Perge, decet. *Go on, it befits you* (Aen. xii. 153).—Omnēs hominēs ab odiō vacuōs esse decet. *It is seemly that all men should be free from hatred.*

376 The Past Imperfect and the Perfect Indicative of these verbs denote what *ought to have been done*, i. e. what *would have been fitting* (see § 353):

Amīcitiam populī Rōmānī mihi praesidiō esse oportēbat (*or* oportuit). *The friendship of the Roman nation ought to have been a protection to me* (implying that it had not been a protection).

Note that where English has a perfect infinitive with 'ought' Latin has a present infinitive with a past tense of *oportet*. The reason is that the English 'ought' (originally a past tense of 'owe') has come to be used like a present tense, and so there is no means of indicating past time except the perfect infinitive.

377 Verbs which are used intransitively in the active have an impersonal passive use, expressing that an action takes place: ītur, *there is a going, a journey is made*; pugnātum est, *there was fighting, a battle was fought.*

THE VOCATIVE CASE

378 The vocative is the case of the person (or personified thing) addressed:

Dēsilīte, mīlitēs, nisi vultis aquilam hostibus prōdere. *Leap down, fellow soldiers, unless you want to betray the standard to the enemy.*

THE ACCUSATIVE CASE

379 (*A*) THE ACCUSATIVE WITHOUT A PREPOSITION
The accusative without a preposition has two main uses:
(i) as the direct object of a verb used transitively,
(ii) in certain adverbial expressions.

380 (i) **Accusatives of the direct object:**

Commium, rēgem Atrebatem, remittit. *He sends back Commius, the Atrebatian king* (§ 281).—Exercitum salvum et incolumem reduxit. *He brought back the army safe and sound* (§ 274).—Commium rēgem constituerat Caesar. *Caesar had appointed Commius king* (*as king*, § 274).

381 Many verbs which are used intransitively in their uncompounded form acquire a transitive use when compounded with a preposition; *e. g. pugnō* 'I fight', *oppugnō* 'I fight against', 'I attack'. Especially verbs of motion, when compounded with certain prepositions (*circum, per, praeter, trans,* and some others), may be used transitively:

hostem circumvenīre, *to surround an enemy*; agrōs percurrere, *to overrun a country*; aliquem praeterīre, *to overlook* (*pass by*) *some one*; flūmen transīre, *to cross a river*; cīvitātēs adīre, *to approach the states* (literally or figuratively); consilium inīre, *to enter on a plan*; mortem obīre, *to meet death*; perīculum subīre, *to face danger.*

382 Many verbs whose ordinary use is intransitive may be used transitively with an object which is akin in meaning to the verb. Such 'cognate objects' are generally either (*a*) nouns qualified by an epithet, or (*b*) neuter adjectives or pronouns:

(*a*) vītam longam vīvere, *to live a long life*; vītam exsulis vīvere, *to live the life of an exile*; bīduī iter prōgredī, *to advance a two days' march.*

(*b*) pingue et peregrīnum sonāre, *to have a coarse and foreign sound* (*to ring coarse and foreign*); illud laetor, *I am glad of that* (*I have that joy*).

383 Verbs of 'teaching' and 'asking' sometimes take two direct objects, especially when one of them is a neuter pronoun or adjective:

Captīvī Rōmānī Nerviōs haec (= ūsum turrium) docuerant. *The Roman prisoners had taught the Nervii these things* (= *the use of turrets*).—Caesar Haeduōs frūmentum flāgitāvit.—*Caesar demanded corn of the Haedui* (B. G. i. 16; but this construction is rare).— Illud tē ōrō. *I beg that of you.*—Multa deōs ōrans. *Entreating many things of the gods.*—Hoc tē interrogō (*or* rogō). *I ask you this question.*

384 But these verbs more commonly take a phrase formed with a preposition instead of one of the accusatives :

Bōiōs dē adventū suō docet. *He informs the Boii of* (=*about*) *his arrival.*—Dē tē ipsō tē rogō. *I ask you about yourself.*—Auxilium ā populō Rōmānō nōn implōrābimus. *We shall not ask aid of* (*from*) *the Romans.* —Haec Caesar ex Liscō quaerit. *Caesar asks these questions of Liscus.*

385 Some verbs compounded with a preposition (especially *trans*) take two direct objects :

Exercitum Ligerim trādūcit. *He leads his army across the Loire* (B. G. vii. 11. 9).

386 A passive construction is occasionally found, in which the accusative denoting the person becomes the subject of the sentence and the accusative denoting the thing is retained :

Nerviī haec ā captīvīs Rōmānīs docēbantur. *The Nervii were being taught these things by the Roman prisoners* (B. G. v. 42).

Belgae Rhēnum trāductī sunt. *The Belgae were led across the Rhine* (cf. B. G. ii. 4).

387 The accusative after some passive verbs (chiefly in poets) is to be regarded as due to a reflexive use of the passive, in which it denotes an action done to oneself. But the Romans drew no clear line of distinction between this construction and that of a passive verb with a retained accusative (§ 386) :

Induor vestem. *I put on a garment* (= Induō mihi vestem, *or* Induō mē veste).—Exuitur cornua. *She sheds her horns.*—Inūtile ferrum cingitur. *He girds on the useless sword* (= Accingit sibi ferrum).—Antīquum saturāta dolōrem. *Having sated her ancient grudge.*

388 By the omission of the verb of the sentence the accusative of the object sometimes becomes an exclamation :

nūgās ! *nonsense!* (from *nūgās agis*, 'you are talking nonsense'); dī, vestram fidem ! *ye gods, your protection!* (supply *implōrō* 'I entreat'). Cupīdinem Praxitelis H. S. MDC ! *A Cupid by Praxiteles for 1,600 sesterces !* (Cic. Verr. iv. 12). Compare 'A horse ! a horse ! my kingdom for a horse !' (Shakespeare).

(ii) Adverbial accusatives :

389 (*a*) The accusative of a noun denoting a period of time may be used to express duration, answering the question 'How long?'[1]:

Multōs annōs regnāverat. *He had reigned many years* (or *for many years*). French *Il avait régné beaucoup d'ans.*

390 (*b*) The accusative of a noun denoting a measure of space may be used to express extent, answering the question 'How far?'[1]:

Decem mīlia passuum prōgressī sunt. *They advanced ten miles.* French *Ils se sont avancés dix kilomètres.* So with *abesse* 'to be distant'.—Aggerem pedēs cccxxx ātum, pedēs lxxx altum exstruxērunt. *They constructed a rampart 330 feet broad and 80 feet high.*

391 (*c*) The accusative of names of towns and of the words *domus* and *rūs* may be used to express 'to' or 'towards', answering the question 'Whither?'[2]:

Lūtētiam Parīsiōrum proficiscitur. *He marches to Paris.*
—Domum[1] contendērunt. *They hastened home* (or

---

[1] In this usage Latin is exactly like English and French.

[2] A similar use of the accusative of an abstract noun of the 4th declension is the origin of the supine in *um* (§ 136) : spectātum eō, *I am going to the spectacle* = *I am going to see.*

homewards).—Rūs mē recipiam. *I will betake myself to the country.*

392   (*d*) The accusative of neuter pronouns and *nihil* may be used adverbially :

Quid venīs? *Why do you come ?*—Caesar eā rē nihil commovēbātur. *Caesar was not at all moved* (*nothing moved*) *by this.*

393   The accusative singular neuter of many adjectives of quantity has become an adverb : see § 77.

(*B*) The Accusative with a Preposition
General rules.

394   (1) Most prepositions take the accusative. Nine take the ablative (see § 452) and four take either the accusative or the ablative (see § 397).

395   (2) Phrases formed with prepositions are nearly always adverbial, qualifying a verb or an adjective, not adjectival, as they often are in English, *e.g.* 'the camp across the river', 'the soldiers outside the walls'. In most instances where this adjectival use is found in Latin, the noun qualified by the phrase is akin in meaning to a verb, as in *ascensus ad mūnītiōnēs, reditus in patriam*. In other instances the phrase belongs to a noun qualified by an adjective, in which case it stands between them, as in *magna inter Gallōs auctōritās*, 'great authority among the Gauls.' Apart from the above uses and a few special uses mentioned below,[1] English phrases which are adjectival should be translated into Latin by turning them into adverb phrases : *e.g.* castra trans flūmen *sita*; mīlitēs *quī* extrā mūrōs *erant*.

396 **The following prepositions always take the accusative.**

ad : (i) *to* : ad oppidum proficiscī, *to march to a town* (cf. § 391);
         ad locum venīre *or* pervenīre (= *to arrive at*); ad mīlitum salūtem pertinēre (*to relate to*); ad decem

---

[1] E. g. under *ergā*, § 396; *in* (ii), § 397; *ex* (i), § 453 ; *sine*, § 453.

mīlia hominum (*to the number of 10,000*); ad ūnum omnēs (*to the last man*); ad mediam noctem (*till midnight*).

(ii) *to the neighbourhood of*: ad Genavam pervenīre (contrast *Genavam pervenīre*, § 391).

(iii) *at or by, near*: ad portās esse ; pons quī ad Genavam erat; ad sōlis occāsum; ad tempus (*at the right time*) ; ad extrēmum (*at last*).

(iv) *according to*: ad suum arbitrium imperāre ; quem ad modum (= *as*).

(v) *for*: diem ad dēlīberandum sūmere ; satis ad laudem et ad ūtilitātem prōficere.

(vi) *among* (= apud): nōmen ad omnēs nātiōnēs sanctum.

adversus, *towards* : adversus montem prōgredī ; iustitia etiam adversus infimōs servanda est ; adversus hostem cōpiās dūcere (*against the enemy*).

ante, *before*: ante portās ; ante pugnam ; ante hōram sextam.

apud : (i) *among, in the presence of*: apud mīlitēs contiōnārī.

(ii) *in the opinion of*: apud barbarōs multum valēre.

(iii) *at the house of* (French *chez*): apud Cicerōnem vīvere.

circum, circā, and **circiter,** *around, about*: circum urbem hiemāre ; circum mūnicipia mittere ; circum sē habēre ; circā secundam hōram venīre ; circiter merīdiem.

citrā and **cis,** *this side of*: citrā flūmen ; cis Alpēs.

contrā : (i) *against*: contrā hostem pugnāre.

(ii) *opposite to*: regiōnēs contrā Galliam sitae ; contrā opīniōnem (*contrary to expectation*).

ergā, *towards*: perpetua ergā populum Rōmānum fidēs (adjectival, § 395).

extrā, *outside of*: extrā mūnītiōnēs prōcēdere ; extrā ordinem (= *irregularly*).

infrā, *below*: infrā locum ubi pons erat.

inter : (i) *between*: inter montem et flūmen situs.

(ii) *among*: inter omnēs constat ; inter sē bellāre ; inter sē iūs iūrandum dare (*mutually*).

(iii) *in the opinion of* (cf. apud); plūrimum inter suōs
    valēre.

(iv) *during*: inter bellum.

intrā, *within*: intrā portās esse; intrā mūnītiōnēs ingredī (tēla
conicere); intrā paucōs diēs.

iuxtā, *near*: iuxtā mūrum castra pōnere.

ob, *on account of*: ob eam rem; quam ob rem.

penes, *in the power of*: penes eōs victōria est.

per, *through*: per fīnēs Sēquanōrum cōpiās dūcere; per Alpēs
iter est; per agrōs nuntiōs mittere (*over the country*); per
trēs annōs (cf. time how long, § 389); per explōrātōrēs
cognoscere (*by means of scouts*); per aetātem in armīs
esse nōn poterant (*owing to their age*); per vim oppidum
occupāre (*by force, forcibly*).

post: (i) *after*: post pugnam; post diem tertium.

(ii) *behind*: post montem sē occultāre; post tergum.

praeter: (i) *beyond, past*: praeter castra cōpiās dūcere; prae-
    ter spem; alium praeter sē habēre nullum (*in
    addition to himself*).

(ii) *except*: nihil praeter pellēs.

prope, *near, near to*: prope castra esse; castra prope oppidum
pōnere. Similarly the adverbs *propius* and *proximē* (§ 79):
propius tumulum accēdere.

propter, *on account of, because of*: propter fertilitātem locī ibi
consīdere; propter gravitātem armōrum pugnāre nōn
posse.

secundum: (i) *along*: secundum flūmen legiōnēs dūcere.

(ii) *after*: secundum proelium; secundum ea
    (= *next to that*); secundum nātūram flūmi-
    nis (*according to*).

suprā, *above*: suprā pontem (= *in the upper part of the river*).

trans, *across*: trans Rhēnum colōniās mittere; trans Alpēs
habitāre.

ultrā, *beyond*: ultrā Hibērum locum dēligere; ultrā modum
prōgredī.

versus, *towards*: oppidum versus proficiscī.

397 The four following prepositions are used either with the accusative or with the ablative.

in with the accusative corresponds to the English 'into' or 'onto' or 'to', answering the question 'Whither?':

(i) in urbem venīre; in Siciliam iter facere; in fīnēs Treverōrum pervenīre (*to come-through into = to arrive at*); in ūnum locum convenīre (*to come-together into = to assemble in*); in collem confugere (*on to a hill*).

(ii) in a figurative sense: in conspectum agminis venīre; in fidem recipere; hostēs in fugam conicere; in hostēs impetum facere (*upon the enemy*); odium Gallōrum in Rōmānōs (*against the Romans*: adjectival); bonō animō in populum Rōmānum esse (*well disposed towards the Romans*).

sub, *under*, with the accusative answers the question 'Whither?':

(i) sub iugum mittere; sub terram īre; mīlitēs sub mūrōs urbis mittere (*up to the walls*).

(ii) in a figurative sense: Galliam sub imperium Rōmānōrum redigere.

Sub with the accusative is also used of time, denoting *towards*, i. e. *shortly before*: sub occāsum sōlis; sub vesperum.

subter, *under*, and **super**, *over*, with the accusative answer the questions 'Whither?' and 'Where?': subter mūrum advehī; aliōs super aliōs praecipitāre; Nōmentānus erat super ipsum, Porcius infrā (*N. sat above the host, P. below him*: HORACE); super subterque terram pugnāre (LIVY).

THE DATIVE CASE

398 The dative is mainly a *personal* case, *i. e.* words denoting persons (nouns and pronouns) stand in the dative far more commonly than words denoting things.

The dative is never used with a preposition; but it is very frequently used with verbs compounded with a preposition. This is, indeed, the commonest of all its uses.

The uses of the dative may be divided into two main classes : [1]

> (i) those in which it is an object ;
> (ii) those in which it is adverbial.

(i) **Datives used as objects.**

399   (*a*) **as the indirect object of a verb which also takes a direct object in the accusative :**

> Haeduī Bōiīs agrōs dedērunt. *The Haedui gave the Boii lands* or *gave lands to the Boii.*—Caesarī rem renuntiant. *They report the matter to Caesar.*—Alterī negōtium exhibēs. *You are causing your neighbour trouble* (*trouble to your neighbour*).—Iīs auxilium suum pollicitus est. *He promised them his help.*—Trinobantibus XL obsidēs frūmentumque imperat. *He gave orders to the Trinobantes for 40 hostages and corn.*—Mihi honōrem invident. *They envy me my distinction.*—Id iīs suāsit (persuāsit) Orgetorix. *Orgetorix recommended this to them* (*persuaded them of this*).—Sē suaque omnia aliēnissimīs crēdidērunt (commīsērunt). *They trusted themselves and all their possessions to perfect strangers.*—Hoc mihi ignosce. *Pardon me this* (= *this offence*).

400   Many verbs compounded with prepositions take a dative and an accusative, the dative being closely connected in sense with the preposition :

> legiōnī aliquem praeficere, *to put some one in charge of* (*at the head of*) *a legion*; hostibus bellum inferre, *to wage war upon the enemy* (= in hostēs); hostibus metum

---

[1] Many uses of the dative may be regarded as falling under either of these heads. Where the dative is governed by (or 'taken by') a verb it is an object; where it might be removed from the sentence without destroying the construction it is adverbial.

inicere, *to inspire fear in the enemy*; alicui vestem induere, *to put clothing on some one*; mortī aliquem ēripere, *to rescue some one from death* (= ex morte); mortī aliquem offerre, *to expose some one to death*; magnīs parva conferre, *to compare small things with great* (= cum magnīs); voluptātī salūtem antepōnere (posthabēre), *to put welfare before (after) pleasure*; = ante voluptātem, post voluptātem; urbī murum circumdare, *to put a wall round a city* (= circum urbem).

401 Note the verb *adimere* ' to take away ', which takes a dative denoting 'from' (like *ēripere*, § 400), though this meaning is not expressed by the preposition *ad*:

Omnia nōbīs adēmit. *He has taken everything away from us* (lit. *he has robbed us everything*); compare French *il nous a enlevé (arraché) tout*.

402 In the **passive construction** of these verbs (§§ 399–401) the direct object becomes the subject of the sentence and the dative remains:

Agrī datī sunt Haeduīs ā Bōiīs. *Lands were given to the Haedui by th Boii.*—Omnia nōbīs adempta sunt. *Everything has been taken away from us.*

403 (*b*) as the **sole object of certain verbs** :[1]

Some of the verbs which have the dative as a sole object are verbs which may also take a direct object (§ 399), and verbs of similar meaning to these : **imperāre**, *to command*; **ignoscere**, *to pardon*; **parcere**, *to spare*; **indulgēre**, *to be indulgent*; **favēre**, *to favour*; **crēdere**, *to believe*; **confīdere**, *to trust* :

Populus Rōmānus victīs imperāre consuēvit. *The Roman people is wont to give orders to the vanquished.*—parcere

---

[1] A Dative put—remember pray—
With *imperāre* and *obey*,
Studēre, nūbere, nocēre,
Favēre, parcere, placēre;
To these add *envy, trust, forgive,*
Resist, indulge, persuade, believe.

subiectīs et dēbellāre superbōs, *to be merciful to the conquered and to war down the defiant* (Aen. vi. 853).— Ōrābant ut sibi ignosceret. *They begged him to pardon them* : French *pardonner* with dat.—Decimae legiōnī indulserat Caesar et maximē confīdēbat. *Caesar had been indulgent to the tenth legion and he trusted it more than the others.*—Fortūna fortibus favet. *Fortune favours the brave.* — Fīnitimī nōbīs invident. *Our neighbours envy us* (cf. B. G. ii. 31).

404   Others are verbs which cannot take two objects :

verbs of 'obeying' and 'resisting':

   pārēre and oboedīre (a compound of *audiō*, § 405), *to obey*, French *obéir*; servīre and inservīre (§ 405), *to be a slave to, to serve.*

   resistere, repugnāre, adversārī, *to resist, to oppose,* French *résister.*

verbs of 'pleasing' and 'displeasing':

   placēre, *to please*, French *plaire.*

   displicēre, *to displease.*

verbs of 'benefiting' and 'injuring':

   prōdesse (§ 405), *to benefit*; medērī, *to remedy.*

   nocēre and obesse (§ 405), *to injure*, French *nuire* ;

the verbs studēre, *to pursue zealously*;

      nūbere, *to marry* (said only of the bride : virō nūbere, *to marry a husband*; contrast uxōrem dūcere, *to marry a wife*).

Decima legiō Caesarī pārēbat. *The tenth legion obeyed Caesar.*—Cicerō coniūrātiōnī Catilīnae restitit (adversātus est). *Cicero resisted (opposed) the conspiracy of Catiline.*

Cicerō bonīs cīvibus placēre cupiēbat. *Cicero desired to please good citizens.*—Māiōrī partī placuit castra dēfendere. *It seemed good to the majority to defend the camp.* —Id consilium multīs displicēbat. *That plan displeased many.*

Haec rēs aliīs prōderat, aliis oberat (nocēbat). *This was advantageous to some and disadvantageous to others.*—Inopiae reī frūmentāriae medērī cōnābātur. *He was trying to remedy the lack of provisions.*

Dumnorix novīs rēbus studēbat. *Dumnorix was bent on a change of government* (lit. *new things*).

Iūlia, fīlia Iūliī Caesaris, Pompēiō nupsit. *Julia, the daughter of Julius Caesar, married Pompey.* Contrast *Pompēius Iūliam in mātrimōnium duxit.*

405 Many verbs compounded with prepositions take a dative as their sole object, the dative being closely connected in sense with the preposition :

legiōnī praeesse, *to be at the head of a legion* ; alicui subvenīre (succurrere), *to come to the assistance of some one* ; alicui succēdere, *to come after some one,* or *to turn out well for some one* (*e. g.* nulla rēs iīs successerat, *they had not succeeded in anything*) ; alicui occurrere, *to run up against some one* ; alicui praestāre (antecellere), *to surpass some one.*

406 The only **passive construction** which is possible with verbs that take a dative as their sole object is the impersonal passive construction (§ 377) :

Decimae legiōnī ā Caesare indulgēbātur. *Indulgence was shown* (lit. *it was indulged*) *to the tenth legion by Caesar* ; equivalent in meaning to 'The tenth legion was indulged by Caesar'.—Nōbīs ā fīnitimīs nostrīs invidētur. *We are envied by our neighbours.*—Bellovācīs persuādērī nōn poterat ut diūtius morārentur. *The Bellovaci could not be persuaded* (lit. *it could not be made acceptable to the B.*) *to wait any longer* (§ 329).

(ii) **Adverbial datives.**

407   (*a*) **With verbs.**

The dative may denote, as in French, the person in whose

interest (or against whose interest) the action is done. Here the dative may be translated by ' for ':

Quid sibi vult? *What does he want for himself?*—Nōn tibi ipsī sēd tōtī reī publicae vīvis. *You live not for yourself but for the whole state* (Cicero).—Hīs numerum obsidum duplicat. *He doubles the number of the hostages for them* (*i.e.* demands twice the number of hostages from them, B. G. iv. 36).—Sibi quemque consulere (cavēre, prōvidēre) iussit. *He bade each man to take thought for himself.*—Ea rēs legiōnī fēlīciter ēvēnit. *This turned out fortunately for the legion.*—Pugna adversa eī ēvēnit. *The battle fell out adverse for him* (= he was defeated).

.08 In some instances the dative of a personal pronoun marks a person as interested in a statement, command, or question about an action, rather than in the action itself:[1]

At tibi repente vēnit ad mē Canīnius. *But you will be interested to hear that all of a sudden Caninius came to me* (Cicero).—Quid mihi Celsus agit? *What is Celsus doing, I should like to know?*
Compare ' Knock *me* at that door, Sirrah!' (Shakespeare).

09 *Esse* with the dative may denote possession:

Hīs erat inter sē dē principātū contentiō. *They had* (lit. *There was for them*) *a quarrel among themselves about the leadership.*
Est mihi nōmen Antōnius (*or* Antōniō, attracted into the case of *mihi*). *My name is Antony.*

.10 With *esse* or a verb meaning 'to come', 'to send', 'to give', ' to regard ', or the like, the dative singular of certain nouns (mostly abstract) denotes what some one or something *is to be* or *is to serve as*. The meaning of the dative in this construc-

---

[1] In such cases the dative is sometimes called ' ethical ' (i. e. emotional).

tion comes out clearly in a passage of Lucretius (v. 875, with the verb *iaceō*) :

  - Aliīs praedae lucrōque iacēbant. *They lay there to be a prey and a profit to others.*

In this use the dative is generally translatable by a predica-tive noun or adjective :

Alter alterī inimīcus auxiliō salūtīque erat. *The one rival was a supporter and rescuer to the other*: B. G. v. 44. 14 ; lit. *existed to be a support and salvation.*

dōnō aliquid dare, *to give something as a present* (= *to be a present*), *to give something for a gift.*

rēs quae ūsuī sunt, *things which are useful* (lit. *for use*).

411 This dative is generally accompanied by a dative of the person interested :

Amīcitia populī Rōmānī nōbīs ornāmentō et praesidiō nōn dētrīmentō, esse oportet. *The friendship of the Roman people ought to be a distinction and protection, not a loss to us*: B. G. i. 44. 5.

curae (auxiliō, subsidiō, sōlāciō, honōrī, probrō, con temptuī, onerī) esse alicui, *to be a charge (help, support consolation, honour, disgrace, laughing stock, burden) to any one*

auxiliō venīre (mittere) alicui, *to come (to send) as an aid to some one*

legiōnem praesidiō relinquere castrīs, *to leave a legion as a protection for the camp*

laudī esse (habēre, dūcere, &c.) alicui, *to be (to regard) as an honour to some one*

412 In writing Latin two cautions should be borne in mind :

(1) The only nouns which can be used in this construc tion are nouns like the above (mostly abstract). Other English predicative nouns preceded by 'as' agree in case with the noun of which they are predicated (§ 274).

(2) The dative in this construction is never qualified by

any adjective except one of quantity : magnō sōlāciō, *a great consolation.* Expressions like the English 'an everlasting disgrace' are not Latin.

ǀ13 With the gerund adjective, and sometimes with the perfect participle, the dative may denote the agent:

> Sēquanīs omnēs cruciātūs erant perferendī. *The Sequani had to endure all kinds of torture = all kinds of torture had to be endured by the Sequani;* cf. § 453 *ab* (iii).— Quam multa poētae dīcunt quae philosophīs aut dīcenda sunt aut dicta! *How many things the poets say which either ought to be said or have been said by philosophers!* (Seneca).

ǀ14 (*b*) **With adjectives which in English take 'to' or 'for'**, *i. e.* those meaning 'necessary', 'useful', 'pleasant', 'friendly', 'suitable', 'similar', 'equal', and their opposites :

> locus castrīs idōneus, *a place suitable for a camp*
> Helvētiīs inimīcus, *hostile to the Helvetii*
> nostrō exercituī pār, *equal to our army*
> cēterīs similis, *like the rest* (but with *similis* the genitive is commoner, § 424).

ǀ15 The adjectives *propior* 'nearer' and *proximus* 'nearest' generally take the dative; but the corresponding adverbs *propius* and *proximē* take the accus. or *ab* with the abl., like *prope* 'near' when it is a preposition (§ 396):

> Belgae propiōrēs (proximī) sunt Germānīs. *The Belgae are nearer (the nearest) to the Germans.*
> propius (proximē) tumulum accēdere, *to draw nearer (very near) to the mound*
> propius abesse ab aliquō, *to stand nearer to some one*

THE GENITIVE CASE

16 The genitive is chiefly an adjectival case, used to qualify nouns. But it is also used adverbially (§§ 423–6), and as the object of certain verbs (§ 427). It is never used with a pre-position (except with *tenus* sometimes, in poets).

I. Adjectival Genitives.

(a) Answering the question ' What sort of a —— ? '

417 (i) Denoting 'belonging to':

(*a*) in the sense of 'possessed by':

domus Caesaris, *Caesar's house, the house of Caesar.*

This genitive of the possessor may be used predicatively:

Haec domus est Caesaris. *This house is Caesar's.—* Gallia populī Rōmānī nōn Ariovistī est. *Gaul is the property of the Romans not of Ariovistus.*

(*b*) in the sense of 'connected with'. What special kind of connexion is indicated by the genitive depends on the context:

expedītiō Caesaris, *Caesar's expedition*; imāginēs Caesaris *Caesar's images, likenesses of Caesar*; statua Phīdiae *a statue of* (i. e. *made by*) *Phidias*; cīvitātēs Galliae, *the states of* (*belonging to*) *Gaul, the Gallic states*; radiī sōlis *the sun's rays*; facultās itineris faciendī, *the opportunity of making a journey*; signum proelī committendī, *the signal for engaging*; speculandī causā (*or* grātiā), *for the sake of scouting*; cōpiae equitātūs peditātūsque *forces of* (i. e. *consisting of*) *cavalry and infantry*; in iūria retentōrum equitum, *the wrong of* (i. e. *which con sisted in*) *detaining the cavalry.*

Used predicatively: līber sum et līberae cīvitātis, *I am a free man and I belong to a free state* (B. G. v. 7. 8) imperātōris est nōn minus consiliō quam gladiō supe rāre, *it belongs to* (= is the part or duty of) *a genera to prevail by strategy as much as by the sword.*

418 (ii) Used objectively (i. e. as the object of a noun which is akin in meaning to a verb):

interfectōrēs Caesaris, *Caesar's murderers, the murderers of Caesar* (= iī quī Caesarem interfēcērunt); metus mortis, *the fear of death*; amor patriae, *the love of*

country; amor suī, *self-love* (cf. § 101); cupiditās
bellī gerendī, *the desire of waging war*; imperium
tōtīus Galliae, *the command of the whole of Gaul*; spēs
impetrandī, *the hope of obtaining one's request.*

Contrast the genitives in *amor mātris* (in the sense of
amor māternus) 'a mother's love', 'the love felt by
a mother'; *minae Clōdiī* 'the threats of Clodius'
(§ 417 *b*).

19   (iii) Used to describe a person or thing.

In this use the genitive is always qualified by an adjective:

hominēs parvae statūrae, *men of small stature* (= parvī
hominēs, *little men*); bēlua multōrum capitum, *a many-
headed beast*; puer decem annōrum, *a boy ten years old.*

Used predicatively: rēs incertī exitūs est, *the affair is of
uncertain issue.*

(b) Denoting partition.

20 In this use the genitive denotes the whole of which a part
is mentioned; it therefore corresponds to the denominator
of a fraction. This meaning is closely connected with the
idea of 'from' or 'out of'; hence it may generally be expressed in Latin by *ex* or *dē* with the abl.: *ūnus ex multīs*
or *ūnus dē multīs* 'one of many'; *perpaucae ex nāvibus* (or *ex
numerō nāvium*) 'very few of the ships (*or* out of the number of
the ships) '.

21 The English genitive in *s* cannot be used to translate the
Latin genitive when it denotes partition; here it is necessary
to employ a genitive-phrase formed with *of*:

multī Gallōrum, *many of the Gauls*; omnium hominum
doctissimus, *the most learned of all men*; duo nostrum
(*or* vestrum), *two of us* (or *of you*).

22 The genitive of partition is very frequently used after the
neuter singular of a pronoun or adjective of quantity used
as a noun, like *aliquid, id, quid, quicquam, nihil, hoc, quod,*

tantum, quantum, aliquantum, multum, plūs, minus, and after
satis, nimis, parum (adverbs used as nouns):

quid novī?, lit. *what of new?* (gen. of the neuter adj.
novum 'a new thing'), = *what news?*; hoc sōlācī, *this
much consolation*; tantum spatī, *so much distance*; multum aestātis, *much of the summer*; plūs dolōris, *more
pain*; satis ēloquentiae, sapientiae parum, *plenty of
eloquence, but too little wisdom.*

The only *adjectives* which can stand in the genitive in this
construction are those whose genitives end in *-ī* (adjectives
like nouns of the 2nd decl., § 18).

II. Adverbial Genitives.

423 The genitive of some neuter adjectives of quantity and
some words of similar meaning may denote the price at which
a thing is valued or bought, sold, hired, &c.:[1]

Auctōritās Commiī in hīs regiōnibus magnī habēbātur.
The authority of Commius was highly regarded (lit. *was
held at a high price*) *in these quarters.*
Quantī equum ēmit? *At what price did he buy the horse?*
—Tantī quantī voluit. *At the price which he wished.*

Note the comparative and superlative of *magnī* and *parvī*:

magnī, plūris, plūrimī, *at a high* (*higher, very high*) *price.*
parvī, minōris, minimī, *at a low* (*lower, very low*) *price.*

424 The genitive may be used with adjectives which in English
take 'of', and a few others of similar meaning: *e.g.*

plēnus fīdūciae, *full of confidence* (cf. abl. § 437).
cupidus (avidus, studiōsus) bellandī, *desirous of making
war.*
memor (immemor) praeceptōrum, *mindful* (*unmindful*) *of
the precepts.*
gnārus (ignārus, inscius) omnium rērum, *aware of* (*ignorant of*) *everything.*
perītus (imperītus) bellī, *experienced in* (*ignorant of*) *war.*

[1] Compare the similar use of the ablative (§ 438).

similis (dissimilis) meī, *like (unlike) me.* Here English
uses the dative; and the Latin *similis* may also take
the dat. (§ 414), but less commonly.

25 The genitive may be used with the impersonal verbs *piget,
pudet, paenitet,* and *taedet* to denote the cause of the vexation
(§ 372).

> Piget taedetque mē mōrum cīvitātis. *I am annoyed at
> and sick of the manners of the state* (Sallust).—Pudet mē
> stultitiae meae. *I am ashamed of my folly.*—Gallōs
> consiliōrum suōrum saepe paenitet. *The Gauls often
> repent of their resolutions.* Compare French *se re-
> pentir de.*

26 The genitive of nouns denoting a charge or accusation may
be used with verbs of 'accusing', 'acquitting', 'condemning':

> aliquem prōditiōnis accūsāre (insimulāre, arguere, reum
> facere, &c.), *to accuse some one of treachery*; aliquem
> inertiae nēquitiaeque condemnāre, *to condemn some one
> on the charge of idleness and profligacy.*

These genitives, like the corresponding genitive-phrases
formed with 'of' in English, are to be explained as qualifying
a noun in the ablative understood, *i.e.* as originally adjectival:
crīmine furtī accusātus est 'he was accused on the charge of
theft'. The genitive *capitis*, which is sometimes used with
these verbs, is to be explained in the same way: *capitis dam-
nātus est* 'he was condemned on a charge involving his *caput*'
(a capital charge).

III. Genitives used as objects.

27 Most verbs meaning 'to pity', 'to remember', or 'to forget'
take a genitive as their object:

> Miserēre meī. *Pity me.*
> Hōrum hominum mē miseret. *I pity these people* (§ 372).
> Meminī neque umquam oblīviscar illīus noctis. *I remem-
> ber and shall never forget that night.*

So too with the impersonal expression *venit mihi in mentem*, lit. 'it comes into the mind to me ' = ' I call to mind '.

But (i) *miserārī* ' to pity ' (1st conj.) takes the accusative :

Commūnem Galliae fortūnam miserantur.

(ii) with verbs of ' remembering ' and ' forgetting ' the object may stand in the accusative if it denotes a thing :

Hoc meminī neque oblīviscī possum.   Iniūriās meminisse nōlō.

THE ABLATIVE CASE

428   The ablative is mainly an adverbial case, used to qualify verbs, adjectives, and adverbs.   The particular kind of adverbial meaning which it expresses depends partly on the meaning of the noun which stands in the ablative, partly on the meaning of the verb, adjective, or adverb with which it is used.[1]

The ablative is used either (*A*) without a preposition, or (*B*) with a preposition.

(*A*) THE ABLATIVE WITHOUT A PREPOSITION

I. Adverbial ablatives.[2]

429   (i) The ablative may denote ' from ' :

(*a*) answering the question ' Whence ? ', when the noun is the name of a town, or *domus, rūs* :

Rōmā (domō, rūre) proficiscī, *to start from Rome* (*from home, from the country*).

---

[1] The meanings of the Latin ablative are derived from three different cases of the parent language : (1) an ablative proper, denoting *from* ; (2) an instrumental or sociative case, denoting *by, with* ; (3) a locative case, denoting *at, in, on*.   This fact explains how it is that the Latin ablative has such different meanings.   But it is not always certain from which of these original cases a particular Latin usage is derived ; and it is probable that some Latin usages have been formed by contributions from more than one of these sources.

[2] The first five of these adverbial ablatives (§§ 429-41) correspond to adverb-phrases formed with *de* in French.   See French Grammar, §§ 417-28.

|30   (*b*) when used with a verb which itself denotes separation :[1]
patriā cēdere, *to withdraw from one's native land* ; cōnātū
dēsistere, *to desist from an attempt*; aliquem equō dēi-
cere, *to unhorse some one* ; oppidum obsidiōne līberāre,
to free a town from siege; alicui aquā atque ignī inter-
dīcere, *to cut some one off from water and fire*; aliquem
urbe expellere, *to drive some one from the city*; cīvēs
calamitāte prohibēre, *to keep the citizens out of harm's
way*: Cic. pro leg. Man. 18.   [For the construction of
adimere 'to take away' see § 401.]

431   (*c*) when used with a verb of 'depriving' or an adjective
meaning 'deprived' the abl. is translated by 'of' :
armīs aliquem spoliāre, *to strip some one of his armour*;
oppidum vacuum dēfensōribus, *a town deprived of de-
fenders.*

432   (ii) The ablative may denote 'owing to', 'because of'
('from' in a figurative sense).   The noun whose ablative is
so used is generally abstract :
inopiā pābulī perīre, *to perish from (owing to) want of
food*; sīve cāsū, sīve consiliō deōrum, *whether owing
to accident, or to the design of the gods* (B. G. i. 12. 6);
nōn voluntāte suā sed coactū cīvitātis, *not owing to his
free will but through the compulsion of the state* (B. G.
v. 27. 3); temeritāte hostium, *owing to the rashness of
the enemy*; studiō pugnandī aut spē praedae, *through
zeal for fighting or hope of booty.*—This use of the abl.
is often found with verbs denoting emotion or the
expression of emotion: dēlictō dolēre, correctiōne
gaudēre, *to feel pain at having done wrong and to rejoice in punishment* (Cic. Amic. 90); victōriā glōriārī, *to
boast of a victory.*

433   (iii) The ablative may denote 'by', when the verb is
passive and the noun denotes something not living :
ventō tenērī, *to be detained by the wind*; flūmine tegī, *to*

[1] There are not many verbs of this kind. The verb *sēparō* itself takes *ab, ā*.

be covered *by the river*; onere armōrum opprimī, *to be burdened by a weight of armour*; religiōnibus impedīrī, *to be hampered by scruples*.

[Contrast *ab, ā* with the abl. of nouns denoting living agents, § 453.]

434 (iv) The ablative may denote manner or means, answering the question 'How?': the English 'with' often serves as a translation.[1]

(*a*) when the noun (generally qualified by an epithet) denotes attendant circumstances—often something connected with the body or mind:

magnā vōce exclāmāre, *to cry with a loud voice*, French *crier d'une voix forte*; passīs manibus pācem petere, *to sue for peace with outstretched hands*; omnibus cruciātibus aliquem adficere, *to visit some one with every kind of torture*; impetum magnō animō sustinēre, *to resist an attack with great resolution (very resolutely)*; summō studiō et alacritāte nītī, *to strive with the greatest zeal and eagerness (very zealously and eagerly)*; magnā dīligentiā, *with great diligence (very diligently)*.

435 (*b*) when the noun denotes an instrument or something which can be used as an instrument:

armīs contendere, *to fight with arms*; castra vallō fossāque mūnīre, *to fortify a camp with a rampart and a ditch*; nāvibus transīre, *to cross by ship (by means of ships)*; sagittāriīs et fundātōribus hostem terrēre, *to frighten the enemy by means of archers and slingers*;[2] magnīs praemiīs aliquem adlicere, *to attract some one by means of great rewards*; sē aliōrum cōpiīs alere, *to*

---

[1] But when 'with' means 'together with' it is expressed by *cum* with the abl., § 453. So too when the noun denotes attendant circumstances and is not qualified by an epithet; see ex. in § 453 *cum*.

[2] 'By means of' followed by a noun denoting a person is ordinarily expressed by *per* with the accusative: *litterās per nuntium mittere*, 'to send a letter by a messenger.'

support oneself·on the supplies of others (B. G. iv. 4);
piscibus vescī *or* vīvere, *to live on fish, to support life
by means of fish* (B. G. iv. 10).

436   (*c*) when the noun denotes a road or route:

eōdem itinere revertī, *to return by the same road*; essedāriōs omnibus viīs ēmittere, *to send out charioteers by
all routes.*

437   (*d*) when used with a verb of 'filling' or 'equipping' or
an adjective meaning 'filled' or 'equipped':

nāvigia mīlitibus complēre, *to man the ships with soldiers*
(cf. French *remplir de*); dōnāre aliquem cīvitāte, *to
present some one with the citizenship*; omnibus rēbus in-
structus (ornātus), *equipped with everything*; singulārī
audāciā praeditus, *gifted with unique effrontery.*

The adj. *plēnus* sometimes takes an abl.: nāvis frūmentō
plēna, *a ship filled with corn*; but cf. § 424.

438   (*e*) when the noun denotes price or cost and the verb
denotes 'buying', 'selling', 'hiring', or 'costing':[1]

parvō pretiō redimere, *to purchase (redeem) at a small
cost*; patriam aurō vendere, *to sell one's country for
gold*; magnō dētrīmentō constāre, *to be secured at a great
loss*; victōria multō sanguine constābit (*or* stābit), *victory
will cost much blood.* Compare the use of the genitive
of neuter adjectives of quantity, § 423.

439   (*f*) when used with the adjectives *dignus* and *indignus*
(cf. French *digne de*):[2]

memoriā dignum, *a thing worthy of mention*; vox populī

---

[1] With verbs of 'buying' the price paid is the means of acquisition.
The other verbs of this group took the same construction by imitation of
verbs of 'buying'.

[2] The abl. with *dignus* is perhaps connected with the abl. of price; cf.
'worthy' and 'worth' in English: *sextante sāl Rōmae erat* 'salt cost (was
worth) a sixth of an as at Rome' (Livy xxix. 37. 3). Others connect *dignus*
with *decet*: *corōnā dignus* 'adorned with a garland', hence 'worthy of
a garland'.

Rōmānī māiestāte indigna, *a speech unworthy of the dignity of the Roman people.*

440　　(*g*) in expressions like the following, in which the abl. answers the question 'In what respect?' (a modification of 'How?'):

> pār virtūte, *equal in valour*; nāvēs numerō LX, *ships 60 in number*; magnitūdine paulō infrā elephantōs, *in size a little below elephants*; meō arbitrātū vir iustus, *in my judgement (opinion) a just man*; nōmine Bibrax, *Bibrax by name.*

441　　(v) With comparatives the ablative may denote two distinct things:

(*a*) the degree of difference (English 'by'[1]); the words which stand in the abl. are neuter adjectives of quantity or pronouns or nouns denoting measurement:

> carīnae aliquantō plāniōrēs, *keels considerably* (lit. *by a considerable amount*) *flatter*; multō gravior, *much heavier* (lit. *heavier by much*); multō gravius, *much more seriously*; paulō hūmāniōrēs, *a little more civilized*; eō minus, *so much the less*; hōc (*or* tantō) angustior, *so much the narrower*; quō facilius, *whereby the more easily*; nihilō magis, *none the more*; Hibernia dīmidiō minor est quam Britannia, *Ireland is smaller by a half than Britain*; decem pedibus altior, *higher by ten feet*; multīs partibus māior, *many times as great.* Similarly with *ante* and *post*, used as adverbs or as prepositions: vīgintī annīs ante, *twenty years before* (adv.); paucīs ante diēbus, *a few days before* (adv.); paulō post mediam noctem, *a little after midnight.*[2]

---

[1] This meaning is connected with the meaning 'by means of' (§ 435 ff.).

[2] The meaning 'ago' may be expressed by *abhinc*, but with the accusative: *abhinc annōs quattuordecim mortuus est* 'he died fourteen years ago'.

442 (*b*) 'than':[1]

Ubiī cēterīs Germānīs paulō hūmāniōrēs sunt, *the Ubii are a little more civilized than the rest of the Germans* (= quam cēterī Germānī); Caesar mīlitum vītam laude suā habēbat cāriōrem, *Caesar held the lives of his soldiers dearer than his own glory* (= quam laudem suam); amplius hōrīs sex pugnābātur, *the fight went on for more than six hours* (= quam hōrās sex, accusative of time how long).

443 The ablative *may* always be used instead of *quam* with a nominative or accusative (except where it would cause ambiguity), and *must* be used instead of *quam* with the nom. or acc. of a relative pronoun:

Mīsēnum Aeolidēn, quō nōn praestantior alter. *Misenus the Aeolid, than whom none other was more excellent* (Aen. vi. 164).

The English accusative *whom*, which is always used instead of *who* after *than*, is an imitation of this Latin abl. But the abl. cannot be used instead of *quam* with other cases: e. g. in *tibi plūs quam mihi dedit*. Ambiguity would arise if the abl. were used in *Brūtum plūs amō quam Cassium*; for *Cassiō* might mean *quam Cassius amat*. But there is no ambiguity in *nī tē plūs oculīs meīs amārem* 'if I did not love thee more than my eyes' (Catullus).

444 (vi) The ablative may denote 'at', 'on', 'in', or 'within'. These meanings are closely connected with the meaning of the locative case (§ 55).

(*a*) When the noun denotes a period of time, its ablative may answer the question 'When?':

vēre, *in the spring*; aestāte, *in the summer*; autumnō, *in the autumn*; hieme, *in the winter*.

---

[1] The meaning 'than' was probably derived from the meaning 'from', 'starting from' (§ 429): *hūmāniōrēs cēterīs Germānīs* 'more civilized starting from the rest of the Germans *as a standard*'.

The ablative of the words *hōra, diēs, nox, mensis, annus, tempus* is generally accompanied by an epithet:

> hōrā sextā, *at the sixth hour*; diē quartō, *on the fourth day*; Īdibus Martiīs, *on the Ides of March*; proximō annō, *in the next year*; eō tempore, *at that time*.

445 The ablative of words which do not properly denote a period of time, such as *pueritia* 'boyhood', *bellum* 'war', *proelium* 'battle', *adventus* 'arrival', are sometimes used to answer the question 'When?', but only when accompanied by an epithet or preceded by the preposition *in*:[1]

> extrēmā pueritiā, *at the end of his boyhood* (Cic. pro leg. Man. 28); in pueritiā, *in boyhood* (Cic.); hōc proeliō, *in this battle*; equestribus proeliīs, *in cavalry battles* (B. G. iv. 2); in bellō, *in time of war*; Lūcullī adventū, *on the arrival of Lucullus*.

446 (*b*) The ablative of nouns denoting a period of time and some other nouns of similar meaning may answer the question 'Within how long a time?':

> xxv diēbus aggerem exstruere, *to construct a rampart within 25 days* (= intrā xxv diēs); hīs decem diēbus, *within the last ten days*; eō bīduō, *within two days from then*; patrum nostrōrum memoriā, *within the memory of our fathers*.

447 (*c*) The ablative of the nouns *terra, mare, locus* and a few others of less importance may answer the question 'Where?':

> terrā marīque pollēre, *to be powerful on land and at sea*; idōneō (aequō, inīquō) locō pugnāre, *to fight in a convenient (favourable, unfavourable) position*; hōc (eō, eōdem, quō) locō esse, *to be in this (that, the same, which) place*; suō locō esse, *to be in one's proper place*: scrībae locō aliquem habēre, *to have some one as secretary* (lit. *in place of a secretary*). So too nouns denoting place with the epithet *tōtus*: tōtā urbe, *throughout the city*; tōtā Italiā, *throughout Italy*.

[1] Exceptions are rare.

148   (*d*) With verbs of 'relying' and the adjective *frētus* the ablative of any noun may answer the question 'On what?':

> virtūte suā nītī, *to rely on one's own valour*; nātūrā locī confīdere, *to rely on the nature of the ground*; superiōribus victōriīs frētus, *relying on previous victories*.

For the ablative absolute construction see Participles, §§ 494–7.

II. The adjectival ablative.

149   The adjectival ablative describes a person or thing. The noun which stands in the ablative generally denotes a feature of body or mind, and (as in the corresponding use of the genitive, § 419) is always qualified by an adjective:

> hominēs magnā statūrā, *men of great stature* (=*tall men*); hominēs capillō prōmissō, *men with long hair* (= *long-haired men*); summā virtūte adulescens, *a young man of great courage*; simulācra immānī magnitūdine, *images of vast size*.
>
> Used predicatively: Britannī capillō prōmissō erant, *the Britons were long-haired*; bonō animō esse vidēbantur, *they seemed to be of good disposition* (= *well disposed*).

III. Ablatives used as objects.

150   The ablative is used as an object—

(*a*) With the deponent verbs *ūtor, fruor, fungor, potior*— verbs which express the kindred ideas, 'enjoying,' 'getting possession of':[1]

> nāvibus (iūmentīs, &c.) ūtī, *to employ ships* (*beasts of burden*, &c.); suō iūre ūtī, *to exercise one's right*; vestītū ūtī, *to wear clothing*; commodīs vītae fruī, *to enjoy the comforts of life*; eōdem mūnere fungī, *to perform the same task*; ter aevō functus, *having enjoyed a triple life* (Horace).

---

[1] With these verbs the abl. originally denoted means (§ 434): ūtī nāvibus, *to serve oneself with ships*, French *se servir de*.

451 (*b*) With the verbs *careō, egeō* — verbs of 'lacking' or 'needing' (the opposite ideas to those of § 450)—and the impersonal expressions *opus est* and *ūsus est* 'there is need':[1]

> cibō carēre, *to lack food, to be without food*; omnibus rēbus necessāriīs egēre, *to be destitute of all necessities*; auxiliō nōbīs opus est, *we need aid* (lit. *there is need to us of aid*); nāvibus consulī nōn ūsus erat, *the consul had no need of ships* (lit. *there was not use of ships to the consul*).

(*B*) THE ABLATIVE WITH A PREPOSITION

452   I.   **ab, cum, sine, ex** (or **ē**),
          cōram, tenus, prae, prō, dē.

Phrases formed with these, as with other prepositions (§ 395), are nearly always adverbial. Exceptional instances of adjectival phrases formed with *cum, sine,* and *ex* are given below.

453 ab, or (only before a consonant) **ā,** or (only before *tē*) **abs** :

> (i) *from* : ab Haeduīs venīre ; octō mīlia passuum ā castrīs abesse ; ab oriente ad occidentem ; nōn longē ā marī ; aliquid ab aliquō accipere ; abs tē ratiōnem reposcent (B. G. v. 30) ; ā prīmā lūce ad vesperum.
>
> (ii) *on the side of* (i. e. regarded *from* . . .): ā Septentriōnibus (*on the north*) ; ab hāc parte (French *de ce côté*) ; ā fronte ; ā tergō.
>
> (iii) *by*, with passive verbs, the ablative denoting a living agent (person or animal): ab equitibus (*or* equitātū) repellī ; ab duce et ā Fortūnā dēserī (*Fortūna* is here personified) ; ā lupā nūtrīrī (*to be fed by a she-wolf*; contrast the abl. without a prep. § 433).

---

[1] For the origin of the abl. with these verbs see verbs of 'depriving' (§ 431). *Ūsus est* followed the construction of *ūtor* (§ 450), from the stem of which the noun *ūsus* is derived.

cōram, *in the presence of* : cōram populō.[1]

cum, *with* :

(i) denoting accompaniment : cum omnibus cōpiīs exīre ; legiō quam sēcum habēbat ; lēgātōs cum mandātīs mittere ; cum hostibus bellum gerere (*or* pugnāre) ; pācem facere cum Helvētiīs ; cum dignitāte ōtium, *peace with honour* (adjectival).

(ii) denoting manner : cum cruciātū necārī (*with torture*) ; *cum* is used here because there is no epithet ; cf. § 434.

dē : (i) *about, concerning* : dē aliquā rē dīcere (*or* loquī, *or* docēre) ; dē aliquā rē audīre (*or* cognoscere *or* certiōrem fierī) ; lēgātōs dē pāce mittere ; dēspērāre dē salūte (*of deliverance*) ; cf. French *de* with verbs of 'speaking' and 'thinking'.[2]

(ii) *down from* or *from* : dē mūrō iacere ; dē nāvibus dēsilīre.

(iii) *of*, denoting partition : paucī dē nostrīs (*few of our men* ; cf. genitive, § 421).

(iv) *owing to, according to* : quā dē causā (*for which reason*) ; dē mōre ; cf. *ex* (iv), below.

ex or (only before consonants) ē :

(i) *out of, from* : ex nāvī (or *ē nāvī*) dēsilīre ; ex omnibus partibus venīre ; ex equīs conloquī (*from horseback*) ; ex captīvīs quaerere (*or* comperīre *or* invenīre) ; quīdam ex Hispāniā (*a person from Spain*, adjectival) ; ferventēs ex argillā glandēs (*red-hot balls made out of clay*, adjectival ; B. G. v. 43).

---

[1] *Cōram* is often an adverb (= 'face to face'). Conversely the adverbs of kindred meaning, *palam* 'openly' and *clam* 'secretly', are sometimes used as prepositions : *palam populō* (Livy), *clam mē* 'without my knowledge'.

[2] A phrase formed with *dē* is sometimes nearly equivalent to an object : inīquum est dē stipendiō recūsāre, *it is unreasonable to refuse about the tribute* (B. G. i. 44. 4) is almost = *it is unreasonable to refuse the tribute.* Compare *significāre dē fugā*, nearly = *significāre fugam* (vii. 26. 4) ; *addunt dē Sabīnī morte* (v. 41. 4).

(ii) *after* : ex terrōre ac fugā sē recipere (*to recover after their alarm and flight,* B. G. ii. 12).

(iii) *of,* denoting partition : quattuor et septuāgintā ex equitibus (B. G. iv. 12) ; ūnus ex captīvīs ; ex omni bus hūmānissimī : paucae ex numerō nāvium ; cf *dē* (iii), above, and the genitive, § 421.

(iv) *according to* : ex commūnī consensū (*by common con sent*) ; ex consuētūdine suā.

prae : (i) *in comparison with* : Gallīs prae magnitūdine cor porum suōrum brevitās nostra contemptuī est.

(ii) *for = owing to* (in negative sentences) : collis prae multitūdine hostium vix cernī poterat.

prō : (i) *in front of* : prō portīs castrōrum in statiōne esse prō oppidō conlocāre.

(ii) *for = instead of* : innocentēs prō nocentibus.

= *on behalf of* : prō patriā morī.

= *in return for* : prō beneficiīs grātiam referre.

= *as* : prō amīcō habēre (*to regard as a friend*).

(iii) *according to* : prō tempore et prō rē.

sine : *without* : sine ullō labōre et perīculō ; nōn sine aliquā spē ; gladius sine mūcrōne (*pointless,* adjectival).

tenus (placed after its noun) *as far as* : pectore tenus Aethiopiā tenus.

2. in, sub, super, subter.

[For the accusative with these prepositions see § 397.]

454 **in** with the ablative corresponds to the English *in* or *on* answering the question ' Where ? ' (cf. the locative § 55) :

(i) in urbe esse ; in Siciliā habitāre ; in Treverīs esse (*i the country of the Treveri*) ; in colle consistere (*o a hill*) ; in ponte turrim constituere praesidiumqu pōnere ; sua in silvīs dēpōnere.

(ii) in a figurative sense : in celeritāte posita est salū (*deliverance depends on swiftness*) ; in repentīnō ho tium adventū multum fortūna potest (*in the case of the sudden arrival of the enemy*).

sub, *under*, with the ablative answers the question ' Where ? ' :

(i) sub aquā esse ; sub terrā habitāre ; sub mūrō stāre ; sub monte consīdere (*at the foot of a mountain*).

(ii) in a figurative sense : sub oculīs omnium pugnāre ; sub imperiō Rōmānōrum esse ; sub umbrā amīcitiae Rōmānae latēre.

super with the ablative generally means *about, concerning* : super aliquā rē dīcere (scrībere, rogāre). In poets it sometimes means *over, above*; cui ensis super cervīce pendet (*over whose neck hangs a sword* ; Horace).

subter, *under*, with the ablative (rare) answers the question ' Where ? ' : subter densā testūdine (*beneath a close shed of shields* ; Aen. ix. 514).

V. VERB-NOUNS AND VERB-ADJECTIVES

 Verb-nouns and verb-adjectives are nouns and adjectives formed from the stems of verbs. They therefore denote acts or states, like some other nouns and adjectives connected with verbs. Compare *morī* ' to die ' and *mortuus* ' dead ' with *mors* ' death '.

But verb-nouns and verb-adjectives are like verbs in three respects :

(1) They have tenses and voices.

(2) They take the same case as the verb from which they are formed :

légibus pārēre, *to obey the laws*
légibus pārendō, *by obeying the laws*
légibus pārens, *obeying the laws*

(3) They are qualified by adverbs (not adjectives) :

légibus semper pārēre (pārendō, pārens), *always to obey (by always obeying, always obeying) the laws.*

USES OF THE INFINITIVE

I. The Infinitive as an Object

456 The chief use of the infinitive is as an object :

(i) as the sole object of certain verbs (chiefly verb denoting some activity of the mind).

The same kind of verbs take an object-infinitive in Latin a in English :

(*a*) verbs of 'desiring', 'resolving', 'striving', and th like :

> volō, *I will*; nōlō, *I will not*; mālō, *I prefer*; cupiō, *desire*; studeō, *I am eager*; audeō, *I dare*
> statuō, constituō, dēcernō, animum indūcō, *I resolve*
> cōnor, contendō, intendō, *I strive*
> cogitō, in animō habeō, *I intend*
> festīnō, mātūrō, properō, *I hasten*
> cunctor, moror, *I delay*
> dubitō, vereor, *I hesitate*
> nōn cūrō, *I do not care*; nōn recūsō, *I do not refuse*

(*b*) verbs of 'being able' and 'being bound' :
> possum, *I can*; nequeō, *I cannot*
> sciō, *I know how* (= I have the ability) ; nesciō, *I kno not how*
> discō, *I learn*; dēdiscō, *I unlearn*
> dēbeō, *I ought*

(*c*) verbs of 'beginning', 'ceasing', 'continuing', 'beir accustomed', and the like :
> coepī, incipiō, īnstituō, *I begin*
> dēsinō, dēsistō, mittō (intermittō, praetermittō), *I ceas* neglegō, *I neglect*
> pergō, persevērō, *I go on, I persevere*
> soleō, cōnsuēvī, *I am accustomed*, assuēscō, cōnsuēsc *I accustom myself*

' EXAMPLES.

(*a*) Scrībere volō. *I will write or I wish to write.*
Scrībere nōlī. *Will-not to write* (= Please do not
write, § 316).
Sapere audē. *Resolve (Dare) to be a wise man.*

(*b*) Eōs longius prōsequī nōn potuērunt. *They could not
pursue them further*: B. G. iv. 26.
Vincere scīs, Hannibal, victōriā ūtī nescīs. *You understand how to win a victory, Hannibal, but you do not
understand how to use it*: Livy xxii. 51. 4.

(*c*) Nostrōs lacessere coepērunt. *They began to attack our
men.*
Fugere dēstitērunt. *They ceased to run away.*

For the agreement of predicative adjectives and nouns
attached to an object-infinitive (e. g. with *esse*) see § 275:
Cīvis Rōmānus esse cupiō. *I desire to be a Roman
citizen.*

} CAUTIONS.

1. This use of the infinitive as an object must be carefully
distinguished from the adverbial uses of the infinitive
which are common in English and French but which are
not found in classical Latin prose. Thus in sentences
like 'Come to see me' (infin. of purpose, French *viens
me voir*), 'He is worthy to be loved' (infin. qualifying the
adj. 'worthy', French *digne d'être aimé*), 'It is easy to
do' (French *facile à faire*), Latin generally employs some
other construction: see §§ 484, 485.

2. The Latin infinitive is not often used alone as the object
of verbs of 'hoping' and 'promising', as in the English
'I hope to see him' (French *j'espère le voir*), 'I promise
to come'. Here Latin uses the construction of the
accusative with the future infinitive (§ 470): *spērō mē eum
vīsūrum esse*; *prōmittō mē ventūrum esse.*

459 (ii) **as one of two objects after certain verbs** (verb;
which denote some activity of the mind) :

(*a*) verbs of 'teaching' and 'accustoming':
doceō, *I teach*; assuēfaciō, *I accustom*

(*b*) some verbs of 'bidding', 'forbidding', and 'permitting'
iubeō, *I bid* (but not *imperō*, which takes a clause witl
the subjunctive, § 329); vetō, *I forbid*; prohibeō, .
forbid, or *I prevent*[1]
sinō, patior, *I permit*

(*c*) verbs of 'perceiving':
videō, *I see*; audiō, *I hear*

460 Examples.

(*a*) Doceō tē Latīnē scīre. *I am teaching you to understan*
Latin.

Equōs eōdem remanēre vestīgiō assuēfēcērunt. *The*
have accustomed their horses to remain on the sam
spot : B. G. iv. 2.

(*b*) Mīlitēs conscendere nāvēs iubet. *He bids the soldier*
embark : B. G. v. 7.—Teutonōs intrā fīnēs suō
ingredī prohibuērunt.—*They forbade the Teutons*
enter (or *prevented the T. from entering*) *their territory*
B. G. ii. 4.

(*c*) Ubi praeter spem quōs fugere crēdēbant infestīs signī
ad se īre vīdērunt, impetum nostrōrum ferre nō
potuērunt. *When contrary to expectation they saw thos*
whom they believed to be retreating advance in batt
array, they could not withstand the attack of our men
B. G. vi. 8. 6.—Classica canere audiērunt. *The*
heard the trumpets sound.[2]

---

[1] Other verbs of 'preventing' generally take a clause with the subjuncti\
(see § 330); and that construction is also found with *prohibeō*, though le:
commonly than the infinitive.

[2] Cf. Necdum etiam audierant inflārī classica, necdum . . . crepitāre ensē

61 The above are simple sentences containing two objects—the first an accusative, the second an infinitive (or a phrase formed with the infinitive), denoting the action which is taught, bidden, or perceived :

doceō, *I teach* {tē, *you* (1st object)
Latīnē scīre, *to understand Latin* (2nd object)

iubet, *he bids* {mīlitēs, *the soldiers* (1st object)
conscendere nāvēs, *embark* (2nd object)

audiērunt, *they heard* {classica, *the trumpets* (1st object)
canere, *sound* (2nd object)

62 Out of this construction there grew a usage of great importance in Latin. The accusative and the infinitive, instead of being two separate objects of the main verb grew together so as to form a single object, in which the infinitive acquired a predicative meaning and the accusative played the part of its subject. This usage is rightly called the **accusative with infinitive** construction ; for the accusative goes strictly *with* the infinitive as its subject and not with the main verb as its object.

> Iubet nāvēs dēdūcī. *He bids the launching of the ships =* He bids that the ships be launched. (The sentence does not mean that he gave an order to the ships.)
>
> . Hostēs castra movēre ex perfugīs audit. *He hears from deserters about the enemy striking their camp =* He hears that the enemy are striking their camp. (He did not hear the enemy striking their camp.)

In the course of time, when the accusative with infinitive had come to be regarded as a separate clause of a complex sentence, it began to be used in dependence on verbs which could not take an accusative alone, e. g. *oportet* 'it is fitting', *constat* 'it is well known' (see §§ 466, 472).

63 French has this construction ; but it is only used when the accusative is a relative pronoun.[1] English has it also ; though

Nor as yet had they heard the signal given on trumpets nor swords ring on anvils : Virg. Georg. ii. 539 f.

[1] See French Grammar, § 463.

there are not many verbs on which it can depend in modern English : e. g. ' He believed them to be retreating', ' He declared himself to be an honest man '.[1]

464 When a predicative adjective or predicative noun is attached to the infinitive it always agrees with the accusative-subject (cf. § 275):

Cicerō dixit Balbum cīvem Rōmānum esse. *Cicero said that Balbus was a Roman citizen.*

Oportet Balbum cīvem Rōmānum esse. *It is fitting that Balbus should be a Roman citizen.*

465 The construction of the accusative with infinitive is used with two different meanings :

(i) **as equivalent to an English ' that '·clause with the subjunctive or the equivalent of a subjunctive** (denoting that something *is to be done.* or *was to be done*).[2] In this usage the only tense of the infinitive which is employed is the Present.

(*a*) as object, depending on certain verbs of:

' willing' : volō, nōlō, mālō, cupiō (§ 456)
' bidding' and ' forbidding' : iubeō, vetō, prohibeō (§ 459)
' permitting' : sinō, patior (§ 459)
' compelling' : cōgō

and the like.

The infinitive may be either active or passive :

Iubet {mīlitēs pontem rescindere.
He orders {*that the soldiers shall cut down the bridge.*
{pontem ā mīlitibus rescindī.
{*that the bridge be cut down by the soldiers.*[3]

[1] There is no sufficient reason for regarding this English construction as an imitation of the Latin. It was well-established in Old English.

[2] Instead of the acc. with infin. a clause with the subjunctive (as in §§ 329, 330) is occasionally used with some of these verbs. *Cōgō* generally takes *ut* with the subjunctive when the verb of the subordinate clause is active.

[3] Note the subjunctive ' be' in the translation. It would be impossible to translate by an indicative (' that the bridge *is* cut down ').

Plūribus praesentibus eās rēs iactārī nōluit. *He was unwilling that that matter should be discussed in the presence
of several persons* : B. G. i. 18.—Lēgēs duo ex ūnā familiā
magistrātūs creārī vetābant. *The laws forbade that two of
the same family should be appointed magistrates* : B. G. vii.
33. 3.—Cīvem Rōmānum capitis condemnārī coēgit.
He caused a Roman citizen to be condemned to death
(Cicero).

66   (*b*) as subject of certain impersonal expressions :

oportet, *it is fitting*; decet, *it is seemly*; licet, *it is
allowed*

placet, *it is approved*; displicet, *it is disapproved*

aequum est, *it is fair*; inīquum est, *it is unfair*

interest, *it is important*; necesse est, opus est, *it is
necessary*

and the like.

Amīcitiam populī Rōmānī mihi praesidiō esse oportet.
It is fitting that the friendship of the Romans be[1] (= the
friendship of the Romans ought to be) *a protection
to me* : B. G. i. 44. 5.—Consiliōrum eōs paenitēre
necesse est. *It is necessary that they repent* (= they
must necessarily repent) *of their resolutions* : B. G.
iv. 5. 3.

67   (ii) **as equivalent to an English 'that'-clause with the
indicative** (denoting that something *is being done* or *was done*
or *will be done*).   In this usage all the three tenses of the
infinitive are used, marking the action as *going on* (Pres.
Infin.) or *completed* (Perf. Infin.) or *in prospect* (Fut. Infin.) at
the time denoted by the verb of main clause, which may be
present, past, or future.   For the use of the Future Participle
with *fuisse* to denote what *would have happened* see § 471.

---

[1] Note the subjunctive 'be' (active voice) = 'should be'.   The translation
'is' would be impossible.   Similarly 'repent' in the next example is a subjunctive, though it does not differ in form from an indicative.

468 This construction is found—

(*a*) as object, depending on certain verbs which denote some activity of the mind :

> verbs of 'perceiving' : sentiō, intellegō, *I perceive*; animadvertō, *I observe*; videō, *I see*; audiō, *I hear*; cognoscō, discō, *I learn*
>
> arbitror, iūdicō, existimō, *I judge, I think*; cōgitō, *I reflect*; opīnor, putō, *I fancy*
>
> crēdō, *I believe*; confīdō, *I am confident*; spērō, *I hope*; suspicor, *I suspect*
>
> nōvī, sciō, *I know*; nesciō, *I do not know*; meminī, *I remember*
>
> and the like.
>
> verbs of 'saying' : dīcō, *I say*; negō, *I deny*; respondeō, *I answer*; doceō, *I show*; fateor, *I confess*; nuntiō, trādō, *I report*; glōrior, *I boast*; queror, *I complain*; simulō, *I pretend*
>
> prōmittō, polliceor, *I promise*; minor, *I threaten*
>
> and the like (including equivalent expressions such as *scrībō*, 'I write to say', *certiōrem faciō* 'I inform') ;
>
> verbs of 'feeling'[1] : gaudeō, laetor, *I rejoice*; doleō, *I grieve*; indignor, *I am indignant*; mīror, *I am surprised*
>
> and the like (including aegrē ferō, *I am annoyed*).

469 EXAMPLES.

Crēdunt
They believe
> nōs cōpiās dēdūcere *us to be withdrawing* (that we **are withdrawing**) *our forces*.
>
> nōs cōpiās dēduxisse *us to have withdrawn* (that we **have withdrawn**) *our forces*.
>
> nōs cōpiās dēductūrōs esse *us to be about to withdraw* (that we **shall withdraw**) *our forces*.

---

[1] These verbs may also take a *quod*-clause, corresponding to a *that*-clause in English or a *que*-clause in French : Gaudent quod cōpiās dēdūcimus (dēduximus, dēductūrī sumus, &c.). *They rejoice that we are withdrawing (have withdrawn, are about to withdraw, &c.) our forces.*

Crēdēbant
They believed

$\left\{\begin{array}{l}\text{nōs cōpiās dēdūcere } \textit{us to be withdrawing } \text{(that} \\ \quad \text{we } \textbf{were withdrawing}\text{) } \textit{our forces.} \\ \text{nōs cōpiās dēduxisse } \textit{us to have withdrawn } \text{(that} \\ \quad \text{we } \textbf{had withdrawn}\text{) } \textit{our forces.} \\ \text{nōs cōpiās dēductūrōs esse } \textit{us to be about to with-} \\ \quad \textit{draw } \text{(that we } \textbf{should withdraw}\text{) } \textit{our forces.}\end{array}\right.$

Sē fīnēs angustōs habēre arbitrābantur. *They considered themselves to have* (that they had) *a narrow territory*: B. G. i. 2.—Dixit sē scīre illud esse vērum. *He declared himself to know it to be true* (He said that he knew that it was true): B. G. i. 20.—Nostrōs indīligentius servātūrōs esse crēdiderant. *They had believed our men to be likely to keep* (that our men would keep) *a less careful watch*: B. G. ii. 33.

470 The Future Infinitive is the tense generally required in dependence on verbs of 'hoping' and 'promising':

Spērābant (Prōmīsimus) nōs cōpiās dēductūrōs esse. *They hoped (We promised) that we should withdraw the forces.*

471 To express that something *would have happened* under certain imagined conditions the Future Participle with the Perfect Infinitive *fuisse* is employed:

Crēdēbant nōs proeliō victōs cōpiās dēductūrōs fuisse. *They believed that we having been defeated* (= if we had been defeated, *cf.* § 487) *in a battle should have withdrawn our forces*: dēductūrōs fuisse, lit. *to have been likely to withdraw* (cf. § 352).

Titūrius dixit sē arbitrārī Caesarem profectum in Italiam; neque aliter Carnutēs interficiendī Tasgetiī consilium fuisse captūrōs, neque Eburōnēs, sī ille adesset, tantā contemptiōne Rōmānōrum ad castra ventūrōs. *Titurius said that he considered that Caesar had started for Italy; that otherwise the Carnutes would not have adopted the measure of putting Tasgetius to death, nor would the Eburones have come to the camp with such contempt for*

the Romans, if Caesar had been there: B.G. v. 29.—Crēdō
veterēs hāc rē ūsūrōs fuisse, sī nōta esset. *I believe that
the ancients would have made use of this thing, if it had
been known*: Cic. Orator 169.

472 (*b*) as subject of certain impersonal expressions:

constat, *it is well known*; appāret, *it is apparent*;
manifestum est, *it is manifest*;
and the like (including equivalent expressions such as
fāma est, *there is a report*; spēs est, *there is hope*).
Multa genera ferārum in eā silvā nascī constat. *It is an
established fact that many kinds of wild beasts are produced in that forest*: B. G. vi. 25.

473 When a clause of comparison is subordinated to an accusative
with infinitive, it also takes the accusative with infinitive construction:

Scīpiō nihil difficilius esse dīcēbat quam **amīcitiam** usque ad
extrēmum vītae diem **permanēre**. *Scipio used to say that
nothing was more difficult than that friendship should endure
right on to the last day of life*: Cic. Amic. 33.

When the same verb belongs to both of the subordinate clauses
(as in ' I don't believe that you can stand on one leg as long as I
[can]'), it is generally omitted in the clause of comparison; but its
subject still stands in the accusative:

Nōn crēdō tē tantum temporis in ūnō pede stāre posse
quantum mē.
Decet cāriōrem esse patriam nōbīs quam **nōsmēt ipsōs**. *It is
seemly that our country should be dearer to us than we ourselves* [*are*].

Contrast the following, in which the comparative clause has
a different verb: Quis crēdit tantum esse sōlem quantus vidētur?
Who believes that the sun is only just as big as it appears?

474 **Nominative with infinitive.** Sentences containing an
accusative with infinitive may often be thrown into passive
form. The accusative then becomes the subject of a simple
sentence in which the infinitive is retained (cf. the retained

accusative in § 386). Compare the following sentences with those in § 469 :

Crēdimur [1] (Dīcimur) cōpiās dēdūcere (dēduxisse, dēductūrī esse). *We are believed (said) to be withdrawing (to have withdrawn, to be about to withdraw) our forces.*

The predicative adjective or noun then stands in the nominative (cf. § 275):

Homērus caecus fuisse trāditur. *Homer is reported to have been blind.*

475 This construction (called 'nominative with infinitive') is generally preferred in Latin to that of a complex sentence like 'It is believed (It is said) that we are withdrawing our forces', though that construction is sometimes found (*e.g.* with *vērē dīcitur* and with compound forms like *nuntiātum est, dīcendum est*):

Vērē dīcitur nōs cōpiās dēdūcere. *It is said with truth that we are withdrawing our forces.*

476 An exceedingly common use of the nominative with infinitive construction is with the verb *videor* 'I seem', which is a kind of passive of *videō* 'I see':

Vidēmur	cōpiās dēdūcere.
Vidēbāmur	cōpiās dēduxisse.
Vidēbimur	cōpiās dēductūrī esse.

II. Infinitive as Subject and as Predicative Noun

477 The infinitive without an accusative may stand as the subject of a sentence, chiefly with the verb *est* and a few impersonal verbs, such as *interest* 'it is important', *decet* 'it is seemly', *praestat* 'it is better', *licet* 'it is allowed':

Cīvitātibus maxima laus est quam lātissimē circum sē sōlitūdinēs habēre. *It is the greatest glory to the states*

---

[1] When *crēdō* means 'I take it on trust', as distinct from 'I trust', it does not take a dative (as in §§ 399 and 403); hence the personal passive construction is used, not the impersonal passive construction (§ 406).

*to have uninhabited country around them to as great
a distance as possible*: B. G. vi. 23.—Magnī interest
oppidō potīrī. *To get possession of the town is very
important*: B. G. i. 21.—Accipere quam facere iniūriam
praestat. *It is better to suffer than to inflict an injury*:
Cic. Tusc. v. 56.—Nōn longius annō unō in locō remanēre licet. *To stay longer than a year in one place
is not permitted*: B. G. iv. 1.

Infinitive as predicative noun:

Loquor dē homine doctō, cui vīvere est cōgitāre. *I speak
of an educated man, to whom to live is to think* (= life is
thought): Cic. Tusc. v. 111.

478 When a predicative adjective or noun is attached to the subject-
infinitive (e. g. to *esse* or *fierī* or *vidērī*), it stands in the accusative
case. The explanation is that it agrees with an accusative (subject
of the infinitive, § 462) *understood*; epithets, too, of this unexpressed
subject may stand in the accusative:

Est aliquid, fātōque suō ferrōque **cadentem** | in solidā moriens
pōnere corpus humō, | et mandāre suīs aliqua, et spērāre
sepulcrum, | et nōn aequoreīs piscibus esse **cibum**. *It is
something, when falling by decree of fate and by the sword to
lay one's dying body on solid earth, and to give some last com-
missions to one's friends, and to hope for a tomb, and not to be
food* (predicative noun) *for the fishes of the sea*: Ovid, Trist.
i. 2. 53-6. Supply *aliquem* ' some one '.

479 But after *licet* with a dative the predicative adj. or noun attached
to the infinitive generally stands in the dative (cf. § 274):

Licet vōbīs incolumibus discēdere. *You may depart unharmed*:
B. G. v. 41. 6.

III. The Historic Infinitive

480 The Present Infinitive may be used in lively narrative as
equivalent to a finite verb in a simple sentence (Historic Infinitive):

Cottīdiē Caesar frūmentum flāgitāre; diem ex diē dūcere
Haeduī. *Caesar kept demanding the corn daily: the Haedui kept
putting him off day by day*: B. G. i. 16. In origin the historic
infinitive may have been adverbial, with the verb understood
(cf. § 252): *flāgitāre* [*erant*], 'they were for demanding':

hence 'they proceeded to demand' or 'they kept demanding'; compare *être à* with the infinitive in French, and the
English idiom 'What are you at?' Or the usage may have
originated in a verb-less sentence of which the infinitive was
the subject.

IV. The Infinitive in Exclamations

481 The infinitive is sometimes used in exclamations and indignant
questions (depending on a verb of emotion understood):[1]

Tē nunc, mea Terentia, sīc vexārī! idque fierī meā culpā! *To
think that you, my Terentia, are thus troubled! and that this is
due to my fault!* (Cicero.) Understand *doleō* 'I grieve' or
indignor 'I am indignant'.

Mēne inceptō dēsistere victam? *I desist from my purpose
baffled?* (Aen. i. 37.) Equivalent to *egone dēsistam?* · 'Am
I to desist?' (§ 319.) Here the infinitive is probably adverbial,
as in § 480: *dēsistere* 'for desisting'. English has the same
use; for sentences like 'I desist?' 'I honour thee?' contain
infinitives, not indicatives.

The original meaning of the infinitive.

482 In origin the infinitive is a dative or locative case: for example
regere 'to rule' is formed from the stem *reges-*, meaning 'the act of
ruling'; dative or locative *reges-ī* or *-e* 'for (or in) the act of ruling'.
Compare *gener-ī*, dative of *genus*, from the stem *genes-*, which
became *gener-* (§ 37).[2] The passive infinitives show the original
dative or locative ending more clearly: *darī* 'to be given', from
das-ī, lit. 'for the giving'. The passive meaning was acquired
later. In the passive infinitive of the 3rd conjugation the inflexion
ī was added directly to the root (*reg-ī*).

483 Many uses of the infinitive show traces of its original meaning.
In most constructions it stands nearer in meaning to a dative, in
some to a locative. The following instances come mainly from
poets; for infinitives with their original datival or locatival meaning
are for the most part avoided in classical prose, where some other
construction is generally substituted (especially *ut* or *quī* with the
subjunctive, the genitive of the gerund, *ad* with the accusative of
the gerund, or in a few cases the supine in *ū*).

---

[1] Compare the accusative of exclamation, § 388.
[2] By the change of *s* into *r* between two vowels.

484   The original meaning of the infinitive is **adverbial**:

(i) with verbs :

Libycōs populāre penātēs nōn vēnimus. *We have not come to lay waste the Libyan homes*: Aen. i. 527 f. (cf. Hor. Od. i. 2. 7 ; iii. 8. 11). *Populāre* here denotes purpose, which would be expressed in classical prose by *ut populēmus* or *ut populēmur* (deponent).

Argentī magnum dat ferre talentum. *He gives them a great talent of silver to carry away*: Aen. v. 248. *Ferre* ' for carrying away '; classical prose *quod ferant*.

Intereā soror alma monet succēdere Lausō Turnum. *Meanwhile his kindly sister warns Turnus to take the place* (classical prose *ut succēdat*) *of Lausus* : Aen. x. 439.

Flectere iter sociīs imperat. *He commands his comrades to change* (classical prose *ut flectant*) *their course*: Aen. vii. 35.

Hortāmur fārī. *We exhort him to speak* (classical prose *ut loquātur*): Aen. ii. 74.

Quid habēs dīcere? *What have you to say?* (classical prose *quod dīcās*): Cic. Balb. 33.—From this usage of the infinitive with *habeō* comes the French Future : *diras* from *dire as*, Lat. *dīcere habēs*, ' you have to say ', hence ' you will say '.

485   (ii) with adjectives :

avidus committere pugnam, *eager to join* (for joining) *the fray* : Ovid, Met. v. 75. Classical prose *avidus pugnae committendae*.

bonus dīcere versūs, *good at composing verses* (locatival meaning of infin.) : Virg. Ecl. v. 2. Classical prose *perītus* with gen.

dignus amārī, *worthy to be loved*: ibid. 89. Classical prose *quī amētur*.

parātus dēcertāre, *ready to fight* (for fighting), is found in Caesar, B. G. i. 44 ; but would more commonly be expressed by *parātus ad dēcertandum*.

vultus lūbricus aspicī, *a countenance hazardous to behold* (in the beholding, locatival meaning): Hor. Od. i. 19. 8. Classical prose *lūbricus vīsū* (supine). Constructions like *facilis facere* (= *facilis factū*) are common in Propertius.

USES OF THE PARTICIPLES

6 The participles are used

(1) as epithets (§ 256):

> gladiātor moriens, *a dying gladiator* ;
> gladiātor mortuus, *a dead gladiator.*

7 The epithet participle may be appositive (cf. § 258):

> Orgetorix, regnī cupiditāte inductus, coniūrātiōnem fēcit. *Orgetorix, prompted by the desire of being king, formed a conspiracy*: B. G. i. 2.

A phrase containing an appositive participle may often be translated by a clause of time, cause, condition, or concession, according to the context: thus *inductus* in the above example might be translated 'when he had been prompted' or 'because he had been prompted'; and in other contexts by 'if he had been prompted', 'though he had been prompted'.

> Hanc adeptī victōriam, in perpetuum sē fore victōrēs confīdēbant. *If they gained this victory, they felt sure that they would be victorious for ever*: B. G. v. 39. 4 (*adeptī* for *adeptōs*; cf. vii. 56. 2).

> In conloquium venīre invītātus gravāris. *You refuse to come to a conference, though invited*: cf. B. G. i. 35. 2.

8 But more commonly the participle denotes attendant circumstances :[1]

> Flens mē obsecrāvit. *Weeping he entreated me* = He entreated me with tears in his eyes.—Aquilifer fortissimē pugnans occīditur. *The eagle-bearer falls, fighting bravely*: B. G. v. 37.—Centuriōnēs armātī Mettium circumsistunt. *The centurions in arms surround Mettius*: Livy i. 28.

---

[1] This meaning is often expressed by *cum* with the subjunctive : see §§ 358, 359.

P

489 (2) as predicative adjectives (§ 254):

> Invēnī eum morientem. *I found him dying.*
> Invēnī eum mortuum. *I found him dead.*

490 Often with verbs of 'perceiving':

> Sedentem in saxō cruōre opplētum consulem vīdit. *He saw the consul sitting on a rock covered with blood*: Livy xxii. 49. 6.—Tībīcinem cantantem audiō. *I hear the piper playing.*

Here the participle is nearly equivalent to the infinitive in the use mentioned in § 459 (*c*).

491 The nominative of the Perfect Participle Passive, used predicatively with a tense of *esse*, forms the tenses of completed action of the passive voice : *vocātus sum,* 'I have been called' or 'I was called' (§ 153); *vocātus eram,* 'I had been called'; *vocātus erō,* 'I shall have been called'.

492 The nominative of the Future Participle Active, used predicatively with a tense of *esse*, forms an equivalent for three active tenses :

> Moritūrus sum. *I am likely to (about to) die = I shall die* (Future Indic.).
> Moritūrus eram (*or* fuī). *I was likely to (about to) die :* equivalent to a Future in the Past of French or English when used to denote futurity from a past point of view : 'je mourrais,' 'I should die.'
> Moritūrus erō. *I shall be likely to (about to) die.*

493 The nominative of the Present Participle Active is never used predicatively with a tense of *esse*, except when the participle has acquired the character of an ordinary adjective or noun (§ 498): *dīligens est* 'he is diligent', *sapiens erat* 'he was wise (*or* a philosopher)', *excellens erit* 'he will be eminent'; *dictō audiens sum* 'I am obedient to command'. So too in French: *il est savant* 'he is learned', but not *il est lisant* 'he is reading' (French Gram. § 481).

494 A very important use of the participle as a predicative adjective is that which is found in the construction called the **ablative absolute**,[1] which corresponds to the English nominative absolute construction :

> Pōnuntque ferōcia Poenī corda, volente deō. *And the Carthaginians lay aside their haughty temper, a god willing it* (= because a god willed it): Aen. i. 303. Compare the English nom. abs. in 'God willing (= if God wills it), I shall do it'.
>
> Paucīs dēfendentibus, oppidum expugnāre nōn potuit. *He could not take the town by storm, few defending it* (= though few defended it): B. G. ii. 12.
>
> Omnibus rēbus comparātīs diem dīcunt. *Everything having been got ready* (= when everything had been got ready), *they appoint a day*: B. G. i. 6.
>
> Signīs in ūnum locum collātīs mīlitēs sibi ipsōs impedīmentō esse vīdit, quartae cohortis omnibus centuriōnibus occīsīs, signiferō interfectō, signō āmissō. *He saw that the soldiers were an impediment to themselves, the standards having been crowded together in one place* (= because the standards had been crowded together), *all the centurions of the fourth cohort having been killed and the standard-bearer having been slain and his standard lost*: B. G. ii. 25.

495 In this construction the ablative is an adverbial ablative and the participle is predicated of it, so that the ablative and its participle together form an equivalent of an adverb-clause (as is indicated by the translations given in brackets above). On the predicative character of the participle depends the difference between the ablative absolute construction and other ablatives with adjectives attached to them. Contrast *signīs collātīs* 'the standards having been crowded together' (§ 494) with *infestīs signīs* 'with hostile standards' (= in battle

---

[1] *Ablatīvus absolūtus* ' ablative set free ', ' dissociated ablative '—so called because the ablative and its participle form a group by themselves.

array ; see example in § 460 c). In the latter case the adjective is an epithet; in the former it is predicative. Similarly *volente deō* in § 494 means not 'owing to a willing god' but 'owing to a god willing it'.

496   The ablative in this construction denotes attendant circumstances (cf. § 434); it may generally be translated by the English 'with'.[1] Thus *paucīs dēfendentibus* 'with few defending it', *omnibus rēbus comparātīs* 'with everything got ready'. Compare the following sentences in English, where the omission of 'with' would leave an absolute construction : 'But Marlborough *with the rapture of the fight still dancing in his blood* pulled up his horse on a little rustic bridge and scribbled a dozen lines to his wife to tell her of the great event.'[2] 'The latter plan would relieve the British communications from danger, and *with this accomplished* Lord Roberts could deal with the Transvaalers east of Pretoria at his leisure.'[3] But this construction may assume various shades of meaning according to the context in which it stands. Thus the abl. abs. may be equivalent to a clause of—

(i) time (cf. the abl. of time when, § 444) :

signō datō, *the signal having been given* = when the signal was given ; crescunt loca dēcrescentibus undīs, *the land comes into view as the water subsides* : Ovid, Met. i. 345.

(ii) cause (cf. the abl. of cause, § 432) : see examples § 494.

(iii) condition or concession :

Prohibentibus nostrīs hostēs sine perīculō vītae flūmen adīre nōn possent. *If our men made opposition the enemy would not be able to approach the river without risking their lives* : B. G. viii. 40. 4.

---

[1] The preposition *cum* is sometimes added in Latin : *cum dīs bene iuvantibus arma capite* 'arm yourselves, with the gods graciously assisting you' : Livy xxi. 43. 7 (so the MSS.). There are several examples in Old Latin.

[2] *Fights for the Flag* (Blenheim), by W. H. Fitchett, p. 16.

[3] *Birmingham Daily Post*, June 15, 1900.

Obs. In writing Latin the abl. abs. construction should be avoided when the subject of the English subordinate clause is repeated by a noun or pronoun in the main clause : e. g. 'When the hostages had been received, he put *them* under close custody', 'As he was saying this, *he* expired'; in such sentences an appositive participle (§ 487) should be used : *obsidēs acceptōs custōdīvit*; *haec dīcens, vītam exspīrāvit*. In this last instance the abl. abs. would be as awkward in Latin as the nom. abs. in English : 'he saying this, he expired.'[1]

497 Instead of the participle in the abl. abs. construction a predicative noun or adjective may be used :

Cicerōne et Antōniō consulibus, *with Cicero and Antony as consuls* = in the consulship of Cicero and Antony.

mē invītō, *with me unwilling* = against my will.

498 Some participles have acquired the character of ordinary adjectives or nouns : e. g. *absens* 'absent', *praesens* 'present', which are present participles of *esse* 'to be' (see other examples in § 493) ; *amans* 'a lover' ; *adulescens* 'a young man (*or* young woman)' :

In improbī praesentis imperiō māior est vīs quam in bonōrum absentium patrociniō. *In the command of a wicked man who is on the spot there is more force than in the protection of honest men who are far away*; praesens tempus, *the present time* ; in praesentī, *at present* (Cicero).

So too some perfect participles, e. g. *certus* 'certain', *factum* 'a deed', *impensa* (sc. *pecūnia*) 'expense' :

Factō non consultō opus est. *There is need of action, not of deliberation.*

Participles so used may be compared : *amans, amantior, amantissimus ; optātus, optātior, optātissimus.*

[1] There are some examples in Latin writers (Caesar, Cicero, and others) of the abl. abs in sentences like ' When the hostages had been received, he put them into close custody '; see B. G. vi. 4. 4 : but it would be difficult to find an abl. abs. in sentences like ' He saying this, he expired '.

499 Many words that look at first sight like participles are not really such : for participles are *verb*-adjectives and formed from the stems of verbs. But adjectives like the following are formed (by means of the same suffix as is used in verb-adjectives [1]) from the stems of nouns or adjectives : *barbā-tus* 'beard-ed', *aurī-tus* 'ear-ed' (e.g. *leporēs aurītī* 'long-eared hares'), *togā-tus* 'dressed in a *toga*', *tunicā-tus* 'dressed in a tunic', *candidā-tus* 'dressed in a *candida (toga)*', &c.

USES OF THE GERUND ADJECTIVE

500 The gerund adjective is a passive verb-adjective (§ 133), which has two uses :

(1) denoting what *is to be done*. Here the gerund adjective is a passive participle with the sense of obligation or necessity : [2]

(*a*) as an epithet :

vir laudandus, *a man to-be-praised, a laudable man*
homō contemnendus, *a person to-be-despised, a contemptible person*

(*b*) as a predicative adjective :

Hic vir laudandus est. *This man is to be praised.*
Aciēs erat instruenda. *The line of battle was to be formed* (had to be formed): B. G. ii. 20.
Urbem inflammandam Cassiō attribuit. *He handed over the city to Cassius to be set on fire* : Cic. Cat. iv. 13.

---

[1] See note on the suffix *t* in § 148.

[2] The name given to the gerund adjective by the Roman grammarians was *participium futuri passivi* 'future participle passive'. This term is applicable to the usages treated in §§ 500 and 501 above, though the idea of obligation or necessity is more prominent in them than that of futurity ; but to the usage treated in § 502 the name 'future participle passive' is not applicable. Here the gerund adjective (like the subjunctive in certain of its usages) loses the sense of obligation and becomes equivalent to a *present* participle passive

Pontem in Ararī faciendum cūrat. *He orders a bridge to be made on the Arar*: B. G. i. 13.

;01 The nominative neuter of the gerund adjective, with the sense of obligation, is often used with a tense of *esse* in the impersonal passive construction (§ 377). The person by whom the action is to be done is generally denoted by a dative:

Pugnandum est nōbīs. *We must fight* (lit. *fighting is to-be-done by us*).

Mīlitibus dē nāvibus dēsiliendum erat. *The soldiers had to leap down from the ships*: B. G. iv. 24.

Iuvenī parandum, senī ūtendum est. *A young man ought to get, an old man to employ*: Seneca, Epist. xxxvi. 4.

Oblīviscendum est nōbīs iniūriārum acceptārum. *We ought to forget injuries received.*

Aguntur bona multōrum cīvium, quibus est ā vōbīs consulendum. *The property of many citizens is at stake, whose interests you ought to consult*: Cic. pro leg. Man. 6. Here *ā vōbīs* is substituted for the dative *vōbīs* in order to avoid ambiguity: *quibus vōbīs consulendum est* might have meant 'who ought to consult your interests'.

The personal and the impersonal constructions may be used side by side:

Nunc est bibendum, nunc pede līberō pulsanda tellūs. *Now we must drink, now the earth must be struck with free step*: Hor. Od. i. 37. 1.

;02 (2) without the sense of obligation or necessity.

In this use the gerund adjective is like a present participle passive:

Facultātem itineris per prōvinciam faciendī dare nōlēbat. *He was unwilling to grant an opportunity of a journey being made through the Roman province*: B. G. i. 7.

This passive construction is equivalent in meaning to that of an active verb-noun with an object : *facultātem itineris faciendī* = 'the opportunity of making a journey'.　Thus—

cupiditās bellī gerendī, lit. *the desire of war being waged* = the desire of waging war : B. G. i. 41.

Suī mūniendī, nōn Galliae oppugnandae causā id facit. lit. *He does so for the sake of himself being protected* (= of protecting himself), *not of Gaul being attacked* (= of attacking Gaul) : B. G. i. 44.

Lēgātōs suī purgandī grātiā mittunt.　*They send envoys for the sake of clearing themselves* : B. G. vii. 43.

OBS.—Note that in the last instance *suī* is plural, in the one before it is singular : yet the gerund adjective is singular in both cases.　The reason is that the gerund adjective always agrees with the *form* of this pronoun, whether its meaning be singular or plural.

USES OF THE GERUND

503　The gerund is an active verb-noun, corresponding to the English verb-noun in -*ing*.[1]　Its genitive and ablative cases are used very much like the genitive and ablative of any other noun ; but its accusative is used only after certain prepositions (chiefly *ad*).　Its dative is not much used, because the meaning 'for . . . ing' is usually expressed by *ad* with the accusative. The gerund has no nominative.

Gen.　studium pugnandī, *a desire of fighting*: B. G. i. 46.— difficultās nāvigandī, *the difficulty of sailing*: B. G. iii. 12.—hiemandī causā, *for the sake of wintering* : B. G. iii. 1.—hominēs bellandī cupidī, *men desirous of going to war* : B. G. i. 2.

Abl.　Vēnērunt ut dē indūtiīs fallendō impetrārent.　*They came in order that they might get their way about the truce by deceiving* : B. G. iv. 13.

---

[1] The gerund (verb-noun) probably grew out of certain usages of the gerund adjective, which is to be regarded as the older form.

Reperiēbat in quaerendō. *He found in the course of inquiry*: B. G. i. 18.—Malignitātis auctōrēs quaerendō rem arbitriī suī ad senātum reiēcerat. *While* (lit. *in*) *seeking for supporters of his meanness he had referred to the senate a matter which lay in his own discretion*: Livy v. 22. 1. Compare *tālia fandō*, Aen. ii. 6.[1]

Accus. Diem ad dēlīberandum sūmam. *I will take a day for deliberating*: B. G. i. 7.

Nostrōs alacriōrēs ad pugnandum fēcerant. *They had made our men more keen for fighting*: B. G. iii. 24.

504   The cases of the gerund supply a genitive and an ablative to the infinitive (which is also equivalent to an English verb-noun in *-ing*): thus the infinitive might be declined as follows:

Nom. discere, *to learn*: ingenuās didicisse fidēliter artēs ēmollit mōrēs, *to have studied the liberal arts conscientiously refines the character* (Ovid).

Acc. discere, *to learn*: discere cupiō, *I desire to learn.*

Gen. discendī, *of learning*: discendī cupidus sum, *I am desirous of learning.*

Dat. discendō, *to learning*: discendō operam dō, *I devote myself to learning.*

Abl. discendō, *by learning*: discendō ēmolliuntur mōrēs, *the character is refined by learning.*

505   As a verb-noun the gerund may take an object in the same case as the verb from which it is formed. Thus *causā parcendī victīs* 'for the sake of sparing the conquered'; *parcendō victīs* 'by sparing the conquered'. But the gerund with an object in the **accusative** case is for the most part avoided in the best prose.[2]

---

[1] From these uses (with and without *in*) comes the French gerund with *en*: e. g. *en demandant, en cherchant.*

[2] The gerund with an accusative-object begins to be fairly common in later prose (e. g. in Livy, see ex. quoted in § 503, Abl.) and in the poets of the Augustan age. It is chiefly the genitive and the dative of the gerund that takes an accusative-object in these writers: e. g. *spēs urbem capiendī*

Instead of this construction the passive construction of the gerund adjective is generally employed (see above, § 502), and *must* be employed after a preposition, such as *ad* or *in*:

> Nōn modo ad insignia accommodanda sed etiam ad galeās induendās tempus dēfuit. *Time failed them not only for fitting on their badges but even for putting on their helmets*: B. G. ii. 21 (not *ad insignia accommodandum, ad galeās induendum*).

506 But in some cases the gerund with an accusative object is almost necessary:

(i) when the object is a neuter pronoun; for here any other case than the accusative would be indistinguishable from a masculine:

> studium aliquid agendī, *the desire of doing something* (not *alicūius agendī*); tālia fandō, *in speaking of such things* (not *tālibus fandīs*), see ex. in § 503.

(ii) in order to avoid the repetition of the clumsy endings *ōrum, ārum*:

> neque consiliī habendī neque **arma** capiendī facultāte datā, *no opportunity having been given either of holding counsel* (passive construction with gerund adjective) *or of taking arms* (active constr. with gerund, instead of *armōrum capiendōrum*); cf. B. G. iv. 14.

USES OF THE SUPINES[1]

507 The supine in *-um* is the accusative of a verb-noun of the 4th declension in *-tus* or *-sus*, used adverbially to answer the question 'Whither?' (cf. § 391), chiefly with verbs of motion; it thus denotes the end in view or purpose (§ 136):

> Lēgātī grātulātum vēnērunt. *The envoys came to offer*

' the hope of capturing the city '(instead of *urbis capiendae*), *mens alitur artēs discendō* 'the mind is nurtured by studying the arts' (instead of *artibus discendīs*,.

[1] The curious name 'supine' chosen by the Roman grammarians to describe these forms means literally 'lying on its back', *i. e.* out of action.

their congratulations: B. G. i. 30.—Nunc venīs ultrō
inrīsum dominum. *Now you actually come in order to
laugh at your master*: Plaut. Amph. 587.

Lūdōs spectātum eō. *I am going to see the games.* The
supine with *eō* is sometimes (not always) equivalent to
a Future Participle with *sum* (§ 492): *spectātum eō =
spectātūrus sum.* Compare the French *je vais* with the
infinitive, denoting immediate futurity: *je vais voir* ' I
am just going to see ' (French Gram., § 298).

Out of the last-mentioned usage grew the most important
use of the supine in *-um*, viz. that in which it is joined with
īrī to form the Future Infinitive Passive (§ 137). In this construction *īrī* is impersonal :

Titūriō ipsī nihil nocitum īrī respondit. *He answered that
no harm would be done to Titurius himself*; lit. *that
there was-a-going* (īrī) *to do no harm* (nihil nocitum) *to
Titurius himself*: B. G. v. 36.

The supine in *ū* is the ablative or dative or locative of
a verb-noun of the 4th decl. in *-tus* or *-sus*. But very few
verbs form a supine in *-ū*: the most important are those
which denote ' saying ', ' perceiving ', or ' doing '.

The supine in *ū* is used chiefly with certain adjectives
meaning ' easy ', ' difficult ', ' wonderful ', ' best ', and the like.
It may generally be translated by the English infinitive (sometimes active, sometimes passive):

facile factū, *an easy thing to do*: B. G. i. 3.—optimum
factū, *the best thing to do* or *to be done*: B. G. iv. 30.—
mīrābile dictū, *strange to say*: Aen. i. 439.—rēs nefāria
vīsū, *a thing awful to behold*: Cic. Planc. 99.

Difficile dictū est. *It is difficult to say*: Cic. Tusc. ii. 19.—
Hōc horridiōrēs sunt aspectū. *They are all the more
dreadful to look upon*: B. G. v. 14.—Macedonia dīvīsuī
facilis est. *Macedonia is easy to partition* or *to be par-
titioned*: Livy xlv. 30. 2.

VI. PRONOUNS AND INDICATING ADJECTIVES

The reflexive pronoun and adjective.

510   The reflexive pronoun **sē, suī, sibi, sē** and the reflexiv₁
possessive adjective **suus, a, um** have two chief uses :

(i) referring to the subject of the clause in which they stand
Catō sē pūgiōne suō occīdit. *Cato slew himself with h₁
dagger.*—Dēserēbantur ab amīcīs suīs. *They were bein₁
deserted by their friends.*

Caesar temeritātem mīlitum reprehendit quod sibi ips
iūdicāvissent quid agendum esset. *Caesar blamed th₁
rashness of the soldiers, on the ground that they ha₁
themselves judged for themselves what was to be done*
B. G. vii. 52.—Constat Dioclem sē suspendisse. *It i*
well known that Diocles hanged himself (accusative witl
infinitive = noun clause): Cic. Verr. v. 129.—Suīs in
commodīs graviter angī sē ipsum amantis est. *To b₁*
seriously troubled by one's own misfortunes is the mar₁
of one who loves himself (amantis = ēius quī amat): Cic
Amic. 10.

511   With certain impersonal verbs the accusative denotes th₁
logical subject : Paenitet eōs consiliōrum suōrum. *It repent₁*
them (= *They repent*) *of their plans*: B. G. iv. 5.

(ii) referring to the subject of a different clause of a complex sentence, as in an English example like 'God ha₁
brought man into being in order that he may know *Himself*'.

Rule.   The reflexive pronoun and the reflexive adjective,
standing in a **clause of purpose,** or in a **dependent state-**
ment, **dependent question,** or **dependent clause of desire,**
may refer to the subject of the main clause :[1]

Caesar castella constituit nē hostēs suōs circumvenīre

---

[1] For the exact meaning of the term 'dependent' in this rule see
Classification of Sentences and Clauses, §§ 523, 524. A dependent clause is
one particular kind of subordinate clause.

possent. *Caesar built forts in order that the enemy might not be able to surround his (i.e.* Caesar's) *men*: B. G. ii. 8.

Caesar statuit sibi Rhēnum esse transeundum. *Caesar decided that the Rhine must be crossed by him*: B. G. iv. 16 (sibi = Caesarī). Contrast *constat Dioclem sē suspendisse*, § 510.

Quid suī consiliī sit ostendit. *He indicates what his plan is*: B. G. i. 21.

Germānī petēbant ut sibi trīduī spatium daret. *The Germans asked that he should grant them a period of three days*: B. G. iv. 11 (sibi = Germānīs).

͵ But such sentences are sometimes ambiguous; for a pronoun or adjective referring to the subject of the subordinate clause is also expressed by *sē* or *suus*; see § 510:

Ariovistus dixit nēminem **sēcum** sine **suā** perniciē contendisse. *Ariovistus said that no one had fought with him* (Ariovistus) *without disaster to himself (i.e.* to the fighter): B. G. i. 36.

Such ambiguity is sometimes unavoidable; sometimes, though avoidable, it is not avoided; sometimes it is avoided by using *ipse* to indicate the subject of the main clause:

Cūr dē suā virtūte aut dē ipsīus dīligentiā dēspērārent? [Caesar asked the centurions] *why they despaired of their own valour or of his* [Caesar's] *zeal*: B. G. i. 40.

͵ The possessive adjective **suus, a, um** is sometimes used with reference to a noun which is not the subject of any clause of the sentence, especially when the possessive adjective has emphasizing force (= 'his own', 'their own'):

Gallīs prae magnitūdine corporum suōrum brevitās nostra contemptuī est. *To the Gauls the short stature of the Romans is contemptible in comparison with the great size of their own bodies*: B. G. ii. 30.

Hirtium suī mīlitēs interfēcērunt. *It was his own men who killed Hirtius.*

514 'One another' is expressed in Latin either by a phrase formed with *inter* or by *alter . . . alterum*, when two persons are spoken of, or *alius . . . alium*, when more than two persons are spoken of:

Amīcōs inter sē prōdesse oportet. ⎫
Amīcōs alterum alterī (*or* alium aliī) ⎬ *Friends ought to help one another.*
prōdesse oportet. ⎭

Demonstrative pronouns and adjectives.

515 The Latin demonstratives are never used like the English demonstratives in expressions like 'My house is larger than *that* of my neighbour' = 'the house of my neighbour', nor before a participle in expressions like 'those standing by' = 'the bystanders', 'those in Rome' = 'the people who are (or were) in Rome'. In these usages the English demonstrative is equivalent to the definite article; but the Latin demonstratives are never used with this weakened meaning:

Domus mea māior est quam vīcīnī. *My house is larger than my neighbour's* = that of (the one of) my neighbour
iī quī adstant (adstābant) ⎫ *the bystanders*
or adstantēs (*without* iī) ⎭
iī quī Rōmae sunt (erant), *those in Rome*

The following sentence is no exception to this rule, for *eōrum fugientium* does not mean 'of those fleeing', but 'of them as they fled':

Hī novissimōs adortī magnam multitūdinem eōrum fugientium concīdērunt. *These, attacking the rearguard, cut to pieces a great number of them as they fled*: B. C. ii. 11. 4; cf. v. 9. 8 (*eōs fugientēs*), vi. 27. 4 (*eārum stantium = arborum stantium*).

Interrogative pronouns and adjectives.

516 The interrogatives are sometimes strengthened by *nam, quisnam* 'who in the world?'

Ecquis, ecquid is an interrogative form of the indefinite *quis, quid* ' any one ', 'anything' (§ 111):

Ecquis fuit quīn lacrimāret? *Was there any one who did not weep?* (quīn = quī nōn, § 360, Obs.)

Indefinite pronouns and adjectives.

7 For the distinctions in meaning between the indefinite pronouns and adjectives see §§ 112–18.

A good example to illustrate the meaning of *quīvīs* and *quīlibet* (§ 114) is—

Cūiusvīs est errāre, nullīus nisi insipientis in errōre persevērāre. *Every one makes mistakes, but no one excepting a fool persists in a mistake* (Cicero).

Quisquam (§ 115) is sometimes used in sentences which are neither negative nor interrogative :

Cuivīs potest accidere quod cuiquam potest. *What can happen to any one at all can happen to every one* : Publilius Syrus.

Indignor quicquam reprehendī quia nūper compositum sit. *I am indignant that anything should be blamed merely because it has been recently written.* ·Hor. Epist. ii. 1. 76. Similarly with *sī* 'if' and *quam* 'than'.

Quisque ' each ' (§ 117) is sometimes used with superlatives and ordinals :

Optimus quisque confitētur. *Every good man* (lit. *each best man*) *confesses = All good men confess.*

Decimus quisque interfectus est. *Every tenth man was killed.*

Quotus quisque iūris perītus est ! *How few are skilled in the law !*

Relative pronouns.

18 Latin has two **generalizing** relative pronouns and adjectives, corresponding to the French *quiconque* 'whoever':

quīcumque m., *quaecumque* f.,.*quodcumque* n. } whoever
quisquis m., f., *quicquid* n.

Both of them ordinarily take the indicative mood :

Coercēre quibuscumque rēbus poterat Dumnorīgem cōnā-
tus est. *He tried to keep Dumnorix in check by whatever
means he could.*

Quicquid circuitūs ad molliendum clīvum accesserat, id
spatium itineris augēbat. *Whatever amount of détour
(§ 422) was added with a view to making the ascent easier,
increased the length of the journey*: B. G. vii. 46.

519 *Quīcumque* is also used in certain phrases as an indefinite
adjective, *i.e.* without a verb (like the French *quelconque*) :

Quī quācumque dē causā ad eōs vēnērunt, ab iniūriā pro-
hibent. *Those who have come to them for any reason,
they protect from injury*: B. G. vi. 23.

VII. CLASSIFICATION OF SENTENCES AND CLAUSES

520 Sentences are of the following kinds—

(1) **Statements** :

Sīc est. *It is so.*—Vēra dīcō. *I speak the truth.*

(2) **Questions** :

(*a*) Questions which may be answered with ' Yes ' or
' No '. These questions are generally introduced in Latin by
the interrogative words *num* [1] or *-ne* :

Num sīc est ? *Is it so ?*—Dīcisne vēra ? *Are you speaking the truth ?*

But sometimes no interrogative word is used :

Vīs pugnāre ? *Do you want to fight ?* or *You want to
fight ?*

In negative questions of this class the word *-ne* is attached
to the negative, which is put first in the sentence :

Nōnne vēra dīcēbam ? *Was I not speaking the truth ?*
Nōnne argentum redderem ? *Was I not to pay back the
money ?* (§ 319).

---

[1] When *num* is used the answer ' No' is generally expected.

The answer 'Yes' is expressed in Latin by *etiam* or *ita* or *ita vērō*, or by repeating the question in the form of a statement :

Vēra dīcis. *You are speaking the truth* (= yes).

'No' is generally expressed by *minimē* or *minimē vērō*, or by a repetition :

Nōn vēra dīcēbās. *You were not speaking the truth* (= no).
—Nōn redderēs. *No* (§ 319).

(*b*) Questions which cannot be answered with 'Yes' or 'No' are introduced, as in English, by interrogative pronouns, interrogative adjectives, or interrogative adverbs :

Quis dixit? *Who said it ?*—Quae erant verba ēius? *What were his words ?*—Quandō dixit ? *When did he say it ?*—Quam saepe dixit ? *How often did he say it ?* —Ut valēs ? *How do you do ?*
Quid faciam ? *What am I to do ?* (§ 319).

(3) **Desires** (including commands, requests, entreaties, and wishes) :

Aut 'etiam', aut 'nōn' respondē. *Answer either 'yes' or 'no'* (Cicero); § 313.
Sīs fēlīx. *Be thou fortunate* (§ 321).

The negative of all desires is *nē* :

Nē transierīs Hibērum. *Do not cross the Ebro.*

(4) **Exclamations :**

Quam pulcher est ! *How handsome he is !*—Quae erit laetitia ! *What a joy it will be !*—Ut periī ! *How I was undone !*

21 Two or more coordinate parts of a sentence may be connected by one of the following coordinating conjunctions :

et, -que, atque, āc, *and*
sed, at, autem, vērum, *but*
nam, namque, enim, *for*
aut, vel, -ve, *or*; neque, nēve, *nor*;

or by a coordinating relative.

Q

The words *autem* and *enim* stand after the first word in the sentence, though they are not attached to it like -*que* and -*ve*. Two conjunctions cannot stand together, but *enim* in the sense of 'indeed' (a sentence-adverb) may follow *sed*, *et*, or *at*.

522 Double questions may be introduced by

utrum } *whether . . . an* or:
-ne }

Utrum vērum est an falsum ? *or* Vērumne est an falsum ? [*Whether*] *is it true or false ?*
Utrum vērum est an nōn ? *Is it true or not?*
Ēloquar an sileam? *Am I to speak or am I to keep silence ?* Aen. iii. 39.

523 **Subordinate clauses** are of the following kinds—

(1) **Noun Clauses :**

(*a*) Dependent Statements :

Opportūnissima rēs accidit, quod Germānī ad Caesarem suī purgandī causā vēnērunt. *A most fortunate thing happened, namely that the Germans came to Caesar for the sake of clearing themselves* (§ 266).
Dīviciācus dixit sē scīre illud esse vērum. *Diviciacus said that he knew that it was true* (§ 469).

(*b*) Dependent Questions :

Quid fierī velit ostendit. *He points out what he wishes to be done* (§ 363 *a*).
Utrum vēra an falsa dīcerēs (Utrum vēra dīcerēs necne), nesciēbam. *I did not know whether you were speaking truth or falsehood (whether you were speaking the truth or not).*—*Necne* is used in dependent questions in place of *an nōn*.
Nesciō an mīrabilior adversīs quam secundīs rēbus fuerit. *I know not whether* (= I am inclined to think that) *he was more admirable in adversity than in prosperity :*

Livy xxviii. 12. 2. Similarly *haud sciō an* = 'probably' or 'perhaps'.

Quid faciam nesciō. *What I am to do I don't know* (§ 325. i).

(*c*) Dependent Desires:

Hortātur ut populī Rōmānī fidem sequantur. *He exhorts them to place themselves under the protection of the Roman people* (§ 326).

(*d*) Dependent Exclamations:

Vidēs ut altā stet nive candidum Sōracte. *You see how Soracte stands glistening with deep snow* (§ 363 *b*).

Mīrum quantum illī virō fidēs fuerit. *It is strange how much people trusted that man* (§ 363 *b*).

524 Dependent questions must be carefully distinguished from adjective clauses introduced by a relative pronoun without an antecedent (§ 289), and from adverb clauses introduced by a subordinating conjunction.

Observe —

(i) The verb (or other word) in the main clause on which a dependent question depends always denotes some activity of the mind; the main clause to which an adjective or adverb clause belongs may contain any kind of verb: *Dīc mihi quae ēmerīs* 'Tell me what you have bought' (dep. quest.), *Dā mihi quae ēmistī* 'Give me what you have bought' (adj. cl.); *Quid velim sciēs* 'You shall know what I want' (dep. quest.), *Quod quaeris [scīre] sciēs* 'You shall know what you want [to know]', adj. cl.

(ii) An adjective clause may be replaced by a noun denoting a person or thing: *quae ēmistī = ea quae ēmistī*, e. g. *pōma, vīnum*, &c. A dependent question cannot be so replaced; the answer to it must always be a sentence, containing a subject and a predicate: *Dīc mihi quae ēmerīs* 'Tell me [the answer to the question] What have you bought?' The answer would be 'I have bought apples, wine, &c.'

(iii) The English 'whether' may be either interrogative or a subordinating conjunction meaning 'if on the one hand': *Quaerō num medicum adhibitūrus sīs necne*, 'I ask whether you are going to call in a doctor or not' (dep. quest.); *Sīve medicum adhibueris*, *sīve nōn adhibueris, nōn convalescēs* 'Whether you call in a doctor or not, you will not recover' (adverb clause).

Dependent exclamations, which are introduced by an exclamatory word, differ in meaning from dependent questions, which are introduced by an interrogative word. But the subjunctive mood is used in both : see § 363.

525   (2) Adjective Clauses:

Duās viās occupāvit quae ad portum ferēbant. *He seized the two roads which led to the harbour.*

Quid est quod rīdēs ? *What is it that you are laughing at ?* (Contrast *Quid est quod rīdeās ?*, § 335.)

Omnēs quī tum eōs agrōs ubi hodiē haec urbs est incolēbant illī pārēbant. *All who then occupied the land where* (= on which) *this city now stands submitted to him* (Romulus) : Cicero de Rep. ii. 4.

Circumscrībit nōs terminīs quōs nōn excēdāmus. *He confines us within limits which we are not to pass over* (§ 334).

For other *quī*-clauses with the subjunctive see §§ 335, 337, 338, 341, 343, 344, 346, 355, 360, 361, 364.

526   (3) Adverb Clauses:

(*a*) **Clauses of Time,** introduced by the subordinating conjunctions *ubi, ut,* 'when', *postquam, posteāquam,* 'after', *simul atque,* 'as soon as', *antequam, priusquam,* 'before', *dōnec, dum, quoad,* 'while', 'until', *cum,* 'when' :

Quod ubi Caesar animadvertit, nāvēs removērī iussit. *When Caesar observed this, he ordered the ships to be withdrawn* : B. G. iv. 25. For tense see § 311.

Posteā vērō quam equitātus noster in conspectum vēnit, hostēs terga vertērunt. *But after our cavalry came in sight, the enemy fled* : B. G. iv. 37.

Hostēs simul atque sē ex fugā recēpērunt, statim lēgātōs mīsērunt. *As soon as the enemy recovered from their flight, they immediately sent envoys* : B. G. iv. 27.

Neque prius fugere dēstitērunt, quam ad flūmen Rhēnum pervēnērunt. *Nor did they stop their flight before they reached the Rhine*: B. G. i. 53.

Dum haec geruntur, quī erant in agrīs reliquī disces-sērunt. *While these events were taking place* (§ 312), *the others who were in the fields went away*: B. G. iv. 34.

Ipse, quoad potuit, fortissimē restitit. *He resisted most bravely, as long as he could*: B. G. iv. 12.

Dē comitiīs, dōnec redjit Marcellus, silentium fuit. *Nothing was said about the elections until Marcellus returned*: Livy xxiii. 31.

Cum in spem vēnerō aliquid mē conficere, statim vōs certiōrēs faciam. *When I become* (lit. *shall have become*, § 310) *hopeful that I am producing some effect, I will let you know*: Caes. ap. Cic. ad Att. ix. 13.

Cum equitātus noster sē in agrōs ēiēcerat, essedāriōs ē silvīs ēmittēbat. *Whenever our cavalry had sallied out into the fields, he sent the charioteers out of the woods*: B. G. v. 19.

Infēlix Dīdō, nunc tē facta impia tangunt? Tum decuit, cum sceptra dabās. *Unhappy Dido, does thy disloyalty now come home to thee? It should have done so at the time when thou wast offering thy sceptre*: Aen. iv. 596.

For *antequam, priusquam, dōnec, dum, quoad* with the subjunctive see §§ 339, 340. For *cum* with the subjunctive see § 358 a.

527   (*b*) **Clauses of Place,** introduced by the subordinating conjunctions *ubi* ' where ', *quā* ' by what route ', *quō*, 'whither ', *unde*, ' whence':

Aliae nāvēs eōdem, unde erant profectae, referēbantur. *Other ships were being carried back to the place from which they had started*: B. G. iv. 28.

528   (*c*) **Clauses of Cause,** introduced by the subordinating conjunctions *quia, quod, quoniam*, ' because.'

Reliquōs sēcum dūcere dēcrēverat, quod mōtum Galliae

verēbātur. *He had decided to take the rest with him, because he feared a rising in Gaul*: B. G. v. 5.

For *cum* ' since ' with the subjunctive see § 358 *b*.

529 (*d*) **Clauses of Purpose**, introduced by the subordinating conjunctions *ut* 'in order that ', *nē* 'in order that . . . not ', *quō* 'whereby ', with the subjunctive (§ 338) :

Labiēnum in continentī relīquit, ut portūs tuērētur.

530 (*e*) **Clauses of Result**, introduced by the subordinating conjunction *ut* 'that ' with the subjunctive:

Ita currūs collocant ut expedītum ad suōs receptum habeant (§ 360).

531 (*f*) **Clauses of Condition**, introduced by the subordinating conjunctions *sī* 'if ', *nisi* 'unless ', with the indicative or the subjunctive, or by *dum*, *dummodo* 'provided that' with the subjunctive (§ 343).

A complex sentence containing a clause of condition is called a 'conditional sentence'.

The indicative mood is used in the *if*-clause in instances like the following :

Sī peccat, poenam meret. *If he is doing wrong* (= if it is a fact that he is doing wrong), *he deserves punishment.*

Sī peccāverit, poenam merēbit. *If he does* (lit. *shall have done*, § 310) *wrong, he will deserve punishment.*

Sī peccāvit (*or* peccābat), poenam meruit (*or* merēbat). *If he did wrong, he deserved punishment.*

Sī peccāvit, pūniātur. *If he has done wrong, let him be punished.*

These clauses of condition may be called 'open ' as distinct from the clauses of condition which take the subjunctive (§§ 349, 350). *Sī peccat* means simply ' If it is a fact that he is doing wrong '; the speaker does not imply that it *is* a fact or that it is not.

RULE.—Open clauses of condition take the indicative mood, and the main clause is free in regard to tense and mood.

532 (*g*) **Clauses of Concession,** introduced by the sub-ordinating conjunctions *etsī* 'even if', 'although', with the indicative or the subjunctive, *quamquam* 'although' with the indicative :

> Etsī in hīs locīs mātūrae sunt hiemēs, tamen in Britan-niam contendit. *Although the winters are early in these parts, yet he hastily crossed to Britain* : B. G. iv. 20.

For *quamvīs, ut,* 'although', with the subjunctive, see § 343 ; for *cum* 'although' with the subjunctive see § 358 *b*.

533 (*h*) **Clauses of Comparison:**

(i) denoting *manner,* introduced by the subordinating con-junctions *ut, sīcut, quemadmodum, quam,* 'as' :

> Valeant precēs apud tē meae, sīcut prō tē hodiē valuērunt. *May my prayers be as effectual with you, as they have been for you to-day!* Livy xxiii. 8.

For *quasi, velut sī, tanquam, tanquam sī,* 'as if,' 'as though', with the subjunctive, see § 337.

(ii) denoting *degree,* introduced by the subordinating con-junction *quam* 'than', or by words meaning 'as' :

> Est Hibernia dīmidiō minor quam Britannia. *Ireland is smaller than Britain by half.*

For *quam ut* 'than that' with the subjunctive see § 337.

OBS. After adjectives and adverbs that denote likeness or difference (*pār, pariter; similis, similiter; aequē, perinde; alius, aliter; contrārius, contrā, secus*) the clause of comparison is introduced by *atque* or *āc* :

> Similī ratiōne (*or* Aliā ratiōne) āc ipse fēcī iniūriās vestrās persequiminī. *Avenge your wrongs in the same way as* (or *otherwise than*) *I have done* : B. G. vii. 38.

VIII. REPORTED SPEECH

534 Instead of *quoting* the words used by a speaker, an historian may *report* what was said.

Reported speech takes the form of subordinate clauses depending on a verb of 'saying' (called the **leading verb**), expressed or understood.

ORIGINAL SPEECH:

Dēsilīte, mīlitēs, nisi vultis aquilam hostibus prōdere: ego certē meum reī publicae atque imperātōrī officium praestiterō (= praestābō). *Leap down, soldiers, unless you want to betray the eagle to the enemy : I at any rate shall do my duty to the commonwealth and to the general.* Quoted by Caesar, B. G. iv. 25.

REPORTED SPEECH:

Dēsilīrent, nisi vellent aquilam hostibus prōdere: sē certē suum reī publicae atque imperātōrī officium praestātūrum esse. *They were to leap down* (§ 325, ii) *unless they wanted* (§ 363) *to betray the eagle to the enemy : he at any rate would do his duty to the commonwealth and to the general* (§ 467).

535 **Simple sentences** and **main clauses** of the original speech become noun clauses in the reported speech (§ 523).

536 **Statements** in the indicative become dependent statements in the accusative with infinitive construction (§ 467):

Ego certē officium meum praestābō.

sē certē officium suum praestātūrum esse.

537 **Desires** become dependent desires with the subjunctive (§ 329):

Dēsilīte, mīlitēs, nēve aquilam hostibus prōdiderītis (*or* nōlīte aquilam hostibus prōdere).

Dēsilīrent, nēve aquilam hostibus prōderent.

The vocative is generally omitted; but it may appear as a nominative in the reported speech, if necessary for the sake of drawing a distinction between one section of the persons addressed and another: e. g. *dēsilīrent mīlitēs decimae legiōnis; cēterī in nāve manērent.*

538 **Questions** generally become dependent questions with the subjunctive (§§ 363, 325); but see below, § 541:

Num aquilam hostibus prō-dere vultis ?	Num aquilam hostibus prō-dere vellent ?
Hīs barbarīs cēdāmus? Hō-rum condiciōnēs audiāmus? Cum hīs pācem fierī posse crēdāmus ? [1]	Cēderentne illīs barbarīs ? Audīrentne eōrum condi-ciōnēs ? Pācemne cum iīs fierī posse crēderent ?

539 **Exclamations,** if immediately dependent on a verb like *meminissent* 'let them remember', or *reputārent* 'let them reflect', become dependent exclamations with the subjunctive (§ 363); otherwise they are expressed by the accusative with infinitive (see below, § 545):

Quantō dēdecorī est aquilam hostibus prōdere! *How great a disgrace it is to betray the eagle to the enemy!*	(Meminissent) quantō dēde-corī esset aquilam hostibus prōdere. (*Let them remem-ber*) *how great a disgrace it was to betray the eagle to the enemy.*

540 **Adjective and adverb clauses** of the original speech remain adjective and adverb clauses in the reported speech; but they always take the subjunctive mood, whatever the mood of the original speech may have been (§ 364).

nisi vultis aquilam hostibus prōdere, quī nōs circum-stant, *unless you wish to be-tray the eagle to the enemy who surround us.*	nisi vellent aquilam hostibus prōdere, quī sē (§511) circum-stārent, *unless they wished to betray the eagle to the enemy who surrounded them.*

[1] Questions as to what *is to be done* (§ 325). Compare Cicero, Philippic xiii. 16.

541 Noun clauses of the original speech remain noun clauses in the reported speech : e, g.

Ego certē prōmittō mē officium meum reī publicae praestātūrum esse. *I at any rate promise that I will do my duty to the commonwealth.*	sē certē prōmittere sē officium suum reī publicae praestātūrum esse, *that he at any rate promised that he would do his duty to the commonwealth.*

But the indicative of a *quod*-clause becomes a subjunctive :

Haec est causa victōriārum nostrārum quod quisque officium suum praestitit. *This is the reason of our victories, that each man has done his duty.*	hanc esse causam victōriārum suārum quod quisque officium suum praestitisset, *that this was the reason of their victories, that each man had done his duty.*

542 In dependence on a tense of past time (such as *dixit* 'he said ') all the subjunctives of the reported speech are, as a general rule, in the Past or the Past Perfect tense—in the Past when the action is to be marked as not completed, in the Past Perfect when the action is to be marked as completed. Note that a Future or a Future Perfect Indicative of the original speech is represented in the reported speech by a prospective subjunctive (Past or Past Perfect, § 341) :

Magnō dēdecorī erit, sī aquilam hostibus prodētis (*or* prōdideritis). *It will be a great disgrace, if you betray the eagle to the enemy.*	magno dēdecorī fore sī aquilam hostibus prōderent (*or* prōdidissent), *that it would be a great disgrace, if they betrayed the eagle to the enemy.*

For the use of tenses of the infinitive see §§ 467-9.

543 When the leading verb is of the 3rd person, pronouns and possessive adjectives referring to the subject of the leading verb, or denoting a person addressed by the subject of the leading verb, are of the 3rd person in reported speech ;

ego and *meus*⎫ become *sē* and *suus* (§ 511); but *ipse* is
nōs and *noster*⎰ sometimes used in order to avoid ambiguity (§ 512).

tū and *tuus* become *is* and *ēius*, or *ille* and *illīus*.

vōs and *vester* become *iī* and *eōrum*, or *illī* and *illōrum*.

544 When the leading verb is in a tense of past time, the
demonstrative *hic* 'this' and such adverbs as *nunc* 'now',
hodiē 'to-day', *herī* 'yesterday', *crās* 'to-morrow', generally
become in reported speech *ille* 'that', *tum* 'then', *eō diē* 'on
that day', *prīdiē* 'on the day before', *posterō diē* 'on the next
day'. But Caesar often retains *hic* and *nunc* of the original
speech.[1]

Notes.

545 **Rhetorical questions** (*i. e.* questions which are equivalent
to statements expressing surprise or indignation) occurring
in the middle of a passage of reported speech are generally
expressed by the accusative with the infinitive, especially when
the verb is of the 1st or 3rd person:

Num quandō in exercitū Caesaris admissum est dē-decus ? *Has dishonour ever been sustained in Caesar's . army ?*	Num quandō in exercitū Caesaris admissum esse dēdecus ? *Had dishonour ever been sustained in Caesar's army ?*

So too **exclamations** occurring in the middle of a passage
of reported speech :

Quantō dēdecorī est aquilam hostibus prodere !	Quantō dēdecorī esse aquilam hostibus prōdere !

546 A **command** standing immediately after the leading verb
may be introduced by *ut* 'that': e. g. *imperāvit ut mīlitēs
desilīrent* 'he commanded that the soldiers should leap down';
but commands in the middle of reported speech have no
conjunction (see example above, § 537).

[1] For example, B. G. i. 14. 5; i. 31. 5; i. 32. 4; v. 27. 5; v. 29. 5;
vii. 20. 6; vii. 14. 10; vii. 14. 5.

547 Relative clauses which are coordinate (*quī = et is* or *sed is* or *nam is*, § 120) generally[1] stand in the accusative with the infinitive : for example the sentence quoted in § 120 might be reported as follows :

> Magnum numerum obsidum sē imperāvisse : quibus adductīs sē Morinōs in fidem recēpisse.

548 The Present and the Perfect Subjunctive are sometimes used for the sake of variety in the course of a long passage of reported speech depending on a leading verb in a tense of past time (see § 366) :

> (Respondit) nōn sēse Gallīs sed Gallōs sibi bellum intulisse ... Sī iterum experīrī velint, sē iterum parātum esse dēcertāre ; sī pāce ūtī velint, inīquum esse dē stīpendiō recūsāre, quod suā voluntāte ad id tempus pependerint. *He answered that it was not he who had made war upon the Gauls, but they upon him. . . . If they wanted to try again, he was ready to fight to a finish; if they desired to enjoy peace, it was unreasonable to make difficulties about the tribute, which they had paid without grumbling up to that time* : B. G. i. 44. 3, 4.

549 **Comments** of the reporter added parenthetically and forming no part of the report do not come under the above rules :

> Interim Caesarī nuntiātur Sulmōnensēs, quod oppidum ā Corfīniō vii mīlium intervallō abest, cupere ea facere quae vellet. *Meanwhile it is reported to Caesar that the people of Sulmo, a town which is seven miles away* (this is a comment of Caesar, not part of what was reported to him), *were desirous of doing what he wanted* : B. C. i. 18.

For the forms which conditional sentences take in dependence on a verb which requires the accusative with infinitive construction see § 471.

---

[1] For exceptions see Prof. Reid's note on Cicero, Amic. § 45.

550 Conversion of Reported Speech into the speech which it represents.

(1) *Report of proposals made by Ambiorix to Sabinus and Cotta.*

Apud quōs Ambiorix ad hunc modum locūtus est: *Sēsē* prō Caesaris in *sē* beneficiīs plūrimum eī *confitērī* dēbēre,[1] quod ēius operā stīpendiō *līberātus esset,* quod Aduatucīs, fīnitimīs suīs, pendere *consuēsset,* quodque *eī*[2] et fīlius et frātris fīlius ā Caesare *remissī essent,* quōs Aduatucī obsidum numerō missōs apud sē in servitūte et catēnīs *tenuissent;* neque id quod *fēcerit* dē oppugnātiōne castrōrum aut iūdiciō aut voluntāte *suā fēcisse,*[1] sed coactū cīvitātis; *sua*que esse ēius modī imperia, ut nōn minus *habēret* iūris in *sē* multitūdō quam *ipse* in multitūdinem. Cīvitātī porrō *hanc fuisse* bellī *causam,* quod repentīnae Gallōrum coniūrātiōnī resistere nōn *potuerit.* Id *sē* facile ex humilitāte *suā* probāre *posse,* quod nōn adeō *sit* imperītus rērum, ut *suīs* cōpiīs populum Rōmānum superārī posse *confīdat.* Sed *esse* Galliae *commūne consilium:* omnibus hībernīs Caesaris oppugnandīs *hunc esse dictum diem,* nē qua legiō alterī legiōnī subsidiō venīre *posset.* ... *Monēre,*[1] *ōrāre*[1] *Titūrium*[3] prō hospitiō, ut *suae* ac mīlitum salūtī *consulat. Magnam manum* Germānōrum conductam Rhē-

Speech represented.

Apud quōs Ambiorix ' *Ego* (or *Equidem*)' inquit 'prō Caesaris in *mē* beneficiīs plūrimum eī *confiteor* mē dēbēre, quod ēius operā stīpendiō *līberātus sum,* quod Aduatucīs, fīnitimīs meīs, pendere *consuēvī,* quodque *mihi* et fīlius et frātris fīlius ā Caesare *remissī sunt,* quōs Aduatucī obsidum numerō missōs apud sē[1] in servitūte et catēnīs *tenuerant;* neque id quod *fēcī* dē oppugnātiōne castrōrum aut iūdiciō aut voluntāte *meā fēcī,* sed coactū cīvitātis: *mea*que sunt ēius modī imperia, ut nōn minus *habeat* iūris in *mē* multitūdō quam *ego* in multitūdinem. Cīvitātī porrō *haec fuit* bellī *causa,* quod repentīnae Gallōrum coniūrātiōnī resistere nōn *potuit.* Id facile ex humilitāte *meā* probāre *possum,* quod nōn adeō *sum* imperītus rērum, ut *meīs* cōpiīs populum Rōmānum superārī posse *confīdam.* Sed *est* Galliae *commūne consilium:* omnibus hībernīs Caesaris oppugnandīs *hic est dictus diēs,* nē qua legiō alterī legiōnī subsidiō venīre *possit.* ... *Moneō, ōrō tē* prō hospitiō, ut *tuae* ac mīlitum salūtī *consulās. Magna manus* Germānōrum conducta Rhēnum *transiit; haec aderit* bīduō. *Vestrum*[2] *ipsōrum*

num *transīsse*; *hanc adfore* bīduō.
*Ipsōrum esse consilium, velint*ne,
prius quam fīnitimī sentiant,
ēductōs ex hībernīs mīlitēs aut
ad Cicerōnem aut ad Labiēnum
dēdūcere. ... Illud *sē polbcērī* et
iūre iūrandō *confirmāre*, tūtum
sē iter per *suōs* fīnēs datūrum.[4]
(B. G. v. 27.)

[1] The accusative-subject *sē* is
understood.
[2] For *sibi*, as several times in
Caesar : *cf.* B. G. i. 6. 3; i. 11. 3.
[3] For *illum* or *eum*.
[4] For *datūrum esse.*

(2) *Report of the debate in the
Roman camp.*

Contrā ea Titūrius sērō *factū-
rōs*[1] clāmitābat, cum māiōrēs
manūs hostium adiunctīs Germānīs *convēnissent,* aut cum aliquid calamitātis in proximīs
hībernīs *esset acceptum. Brevem*
consulendī *esse occāsiōnem.*
Caesarem *sē arbitrārī* profectum
in Italiam; neque aliter Carnutēs
interficiendī Tasgetiī consilium
fuisse captūrōs, neque Eburōnēs,
sī ille adesset, tantā contemptiōne nostrī[2] ad castra *ventūrōs.*[3]
Sēsē nōn hostem auctōrem, sed
rem *spectāre* : *subesse Rhēnum*;
magnō *esse* Germānīs dolōrī
Ariovistī *mortem* et *superiōrēs
nostrās victōriās*; *ardēre Galliam*
tot contumēliīs acceptīs sub
populī Rōmānī imperium *redac-
tam,*superiōre glōriā reī mīlitaris
exstinctā. Postrēmō quis hoc

*estconsilium, velītis*ne,prius quam
fīnitimī sentiant,[3] ēductōs ex hībernīs mīlitēs aut ad Cicerōnem
aut ad Labiēnum dēdūcere. ...
Illud *polliceor* et iūre iūrandō
confirmō, tūtum *mē* iter per *meōs*
(or *nostrōs*) fīnēs datūrum.'

[1] Referring to the subject of *tenuerant* (cf. § 512).
[2] Possessive adjective = ' of you ',
emphasized by *ipsōrum.*
[3] Prospective subjunctive (§ 340)

Speech represented.

Contrā ea Titūrius ' Sērō
faciēmus' inquit ' cum māiōrēs
manūs hostium adiunctīs Germānīs *convēnerint,* aut cum aliquid calamitātis in proximīs
hībernīs *erit acceptum. Brevis*
consulendī *est occāsiō.* Caesarem
arbitror profectum in Italiam ;
neque aliter Carnutēs interficiendī Tasgetiī consilium *cēpis-
sent,* neque Eburōnēs, sī ille
adesset, tantā contemptiōne
nostrī ad castra *vēnissent.* Nōn
hostem auctōrem,sed rem *spectō* :
subest Rhēnus; magnō *est* Germānīs dolōrī Ariovistī *mors* et
*superiōrēs nostrae victōriae ; ardet
Gallia* tot contumēliīs acceptīs
sub populī Rōmānī imperium
redacta, superiōre glōriā reī mīli-
tāris exstinctā. Postrēmō quis
hoc sibi *persuādeat,* sine certā

sibi *persuādēret*, sine certā spē Ambiorīgem ad ēius modī consilium dēscendisse? *Suam sententiam* in utramque partem *esse tūtam* : sī nihil *esset* dūrius, nullō cum perīculō ad proximam legiōnem *perventūrōs*[1]; sī Gallia omnis cum Germānīs *consentīret, ūnam esse* in celeritāte *positam salūtem.* Cottae quidem atque eōrum, quī *dissentīrent consilium* quem *habēre* exitum? in quō sī nōn praesens perīculum, at certē longinquā obsidiōne famēs *esset* timenda. (B. G. v. 29.)

spē Ambiorīgem ad ēius modī consilium dēscendisse? *Mea sententia* in utramque partem *est tūta* : sī nihil *erit* dūrius, nullō cum perīculō ad proximam legiōnem *perveniēmus*; sī Gallia omnis cum Germānīs *consentit, ūna est* in celeritāte *posita salūs.* Cottae quidem atque eōrum quī *dissentiunt consilium* quem *habet* exitum? in quō sī nōn praesens perīculum, at certē longinquā obsidiōne famēs *est timenda* '.

[1] The accusative-subject *se* is understood.

[2] *nostri* is here used because the reporter (Caesar) is writing as a Roman to Romans. He might have used *suī*, which would have expressed the meaning from the point of view of Titurius. So, too, *nostrās* below might have been reported by *suās.* [3] Supply *fuisse.*

IX. ORDER OF WORDS

Rules of Normal Order.

551 RULES 1 and 2. The two most important rules of normal order
have already been given (§ 3). In the following sentence the
position of every word except *populus* and the conjunctions
is determined by these two rules, which apply to phrases
(§ 260) as well as to single words.[1]

Populus Rōmānus   urbēs   sociōrum suōrum,
The nation Roman   *the cities* *of allies   its*

imperiō suō infestās, aut vī aut obsidiōne in potestātem
to rule   its   hostile,   either by force or by siege to sway
suam redēgit :
its   reduced:

   i. e. *The Roman nation reduced to its sway, either by force or
by siege, the cities of its allies hostile to its rule.*

552   But there is **one exception** :

Demonstrative, interrogative, and numeral (cardinal and
ordinal [2]) adjectives, together with adjectives denoting quantity
or size (*i. e.* words meaning 'all', 'some', 'many', 'few', and
words denoting 'big', 'little', and the like) generally stand
before their nouns :

hic homō, is homō, tanta rēs, alia rēs, quae rēs?, utra

---

[1] Thus the adjective phrase *imperiō suō infestās* comes after *urbēs* ; and in
that phrase the adverbial dative *imperiō suō* (§ 414) comes before *infestās*.
The phrases *aut vī aut obsidiōne* and *in potestātem suam* are both adverbial
to *redēgit*, and therefore precede it.

[2] The ordinal numerals generally stand *after* the words *diēs*, *hōra*, and
annus, e. g. *ante diem quartum Kalendās Māiās*, 'the fourth day before the
Calends of May' = April 28th ; *annus millensimus nōngentensimus nōnus*
'the year 1909' ; otherwise they precede their nouns, e.g. *prīma et
secunda aciēs* 'the first and the second line', *prīmum agmen* 'the head of
the column' ; *decima legiō* 'the tenth legion', *quarta pars cōpiārum* 'the
fourth part of the forces'.

pars ?, quanta multitūdō ? , quota hōra ? ; duae nāvēs, vīgintī mīlia hominum.

omnēs (nōn nullī, multī, paucī) hominēs, magnus numerus, magnō animō, parva rēs, parvum spatium.

553 RULE 3. Relative pronouns, relative adjectives, and relative adverbs stand at the beginning of the clause which they introduce :

Hae sunt arborēs quārum in umbrā iacēbat. *These are the trees in the shade of which* (or *in whose shade*) *he was lying.* Not *in umbrā quārum* nor *in quārum umbrā.*

Thus a co-ordinating relative takes precedence of a subordinating conjunction :

Quod ubi Caesar animadvertit, nāvēs longās rēmīs incitārī iussit. *When Caesar observed this, he ordered the ships of war to be set in motion by means of oars* : B. G. iv. 25.

The only words which can stand before a relative are prepositions ; and even a preposition may be placed after the relative, especially *cum* :

Proximī sunt Germānīs, quibuscum continenter bellum gerunt. *They are the nearest to the Germans, with whom they continually wage war* : B. G. i. 4.

quā dē causā, *for which reason* ; quāpropter, quōcircā, *wherefore* (compounds of a preposition with an adverbial ablative of the relative pronoun).

554 RULE 4. Five exceedingly common co-ordinating conjunctions

-que, *and*	autem, vērō, *however.*
-ve, *or*	enim, *for*

always stand immediately *after* the word, or the first word of the group, which they connect :

pedites equitēsque ; senātus populusque Rōmānus ; terram attigit omnēsque incolumēs nāvēs perduxit (B. G. v. 23. 6 ; here -*que* connects the two parts of the double sentence) ; prospera adversave fortūna ; ā nullō vidēbātur, ipse

901 R

autem omnia vidēbat; eō tempore timēbam, nunc vērō timēre nōn dēbeō; cīvis enim Rōmānus erat.

Obs. Several sentence-adverbs,[1] like *quoque* 'too', 'also', *igitur* 'therefore',[2] and *-ne* (used in asking questions) stand after the word, or the first word of the group, to which they belong:

> tū quoque aderās; quid igitur respondeam?; pācemne hūc fertis an arma?

555 Rule 5.—Most adverbs stand immediately before the word which they qualify (and therefore come after objects, cf. Rule 2):

> Hoc saepe dixī.

Especially the adverb *nōn*:

> Hoc nōn dixī.   Hoc dīcere nōn possum.   Hoc nōn saepe dixī.   Nōn omnēs hoc dīcunt.

Order of clauses in complex sentences.

Rules 1 and 2 are applicable, to some extent, to adjective and adverb clauses.

556 (1) Adjective clauses usually come **after** the word to which they are adjectival; see § 525.

557 (2) The following kinds of adverb clause usually come **before** the clause whose verb they qualify:

> *cum*-clauses (temporal or causal or concessive) and clauses of time introduced by *postquam, posteāquam, ubi, ut, simul atque*; see § 358 and § 526.
>
> clauses of condition and concession; see § 350 and §§ 531, 532.

So, too, the ablative absolute construction (equivalent to an adverb clause); see § 494.

---

[1] Sentence-adverbs are adverbs which qualify the sentence as a whole, and not any particular word in it. But they sometimes have the effect of emphasizing a particular word in the sentence.

[2] *Igitur*, however, generally stands at the beginning of its clause in Sallust and Tacitus.

But prospective clauses and clauses of purpose and result usually come **after** the clause whose verb they qualify; see §§ 338, 340, 360, and §§ 529, 530.

558 As to noun clauses, the only generally applicable rule is that noun clauses introduced by *ut, nē, quōminus* or *quin* usually stand after the clause on whose verb they depend (whether as subject or object): see §§ 326-33 and § 523.

559 **Complication of clauses.**—The Latin writers sometimes go very far in putting one clause inside another, like Chinese boxes :

Quī cum ex equitum fugā *quō in locō rēs esset* cognōvissent, **nihil ad celeritātem sibi reliquī fēcērunt**. Lit. *Who, when from the flight of the cavalry what was the position of affairs they had learned, left nothing undone in the way of speed* : B. G. ii. 26. 5.

Sī **quis,** quī, *quid agam,* forte requīret, **erit,** vīvere mē dīcēs. Lit. *If there shall be any one, who, what I am doing, perchance shall inquire, say that I am alive* : Ovid, Trist. i. 1. 18.

In these instances each clause comes exactly in the position which would be expected from Rules 1 and 2 ; but such sentences are complicated and rather obscure. In writing Latin the beginner will do well, as a rule, to finish off one clause before beginning another. It is not necessary that the relative pronoun should come *immediately* after its antecedent. For instance, 'I know the man whom you say you saw yesterday' may be translated *Hominem nōvī quem tē herī vīdisse dīcis* as well as *Hominem quem tē herī vīdisse dīcis nōvī,* and the simpler order is often clearer.

Departures from normal order.

560 In no language is the order of words rigidly fixed ; and in Latin the order is more elastic than in English, owing to its wealth of inflected forms. Thus we find that the normal order is frequently changed for various reasons.

(1) To put a word in an *unexpected* position often makes it prominent and emphatic :

> **Rōmānum** imperium **vestrā** fidē, **vestrīs** vīribus reten-tum est. *It is by your loyalty, by your might, that the empire of Rome herself has been upheld* : Livy xxiii. 5 (epithets placed before their nouns).

(2) A group of words is often divided by putting compara-tively unimportant words in the middle of it. The effect of this arrangement is to make the divided phrase, or one part of it, emphatic :

> Magnus ibi numerus pecoris repertus est. *A great number of sheep were found there* : B. G. v. 21 (*ibi* between *magnus* and *numerus*).
> Omnis accūsātōris ōrātiō in duās dīvīsa est partēs. *The whole speech of the prosecutor was divided into two parts* : Cic. Cluent. i. 1.
> Aliud iter habēbant nullum. *Other road they had none* : B. G. i. 7.

(3) Words are sometimes thrown in, as it were by an after-thought, at the end of a sentence. This may be called tag-order. For instance, instead of 'I am always glad to see you' we may say in English 'I am glad to see you—always':

> Zēnōnem, cum Athēnīs essem, audiēbam frequenter. *When I was in Athens I used to attend the lectures of Zeno—constantly* : Cic. Nat. Deor. i. 59.

(4) The verb *est*, in the sense 'there is', often stands at the beginning of a sentence :

> Erant in eā legiōne duo virī fortissimī. *There were in that legion two very brave men* : B. G. v. 44.

It may also be put before a predicative adjective or noun :

> Haec gens est longē maxima et bellicōsissima : B. G. iv. i.

(5) Imperatives are often put at the beginning of the sen-

tence or clause, as in French and English, with adverbs and objects after them :

> Ēgredere aliquandō ex urbe . . . Ēdūc tēcum etiam omnēs tuōs . . . Purgā urbem : Cic. Cat. i. 10.

(6) In a group of words consisting of a noun + adjective + adverb phrase, the adverb phrase stands between the adjective and the noun, and the adjective often comes first :

> magna inter Gallōs auctōritās, *great influence among the Gauls* (§ 395) ; suum reī publicae atque imperātōrī offi-cium, *his duty to the commonwealth and to the generai* (§ 534).

(7) The order of words in a sentence or clause is to a con-siderable extent influenced by the sentence or clause which precedes and by that which follows.

(*a*) The speaker or writer often begins with a word or phrase which is closely connected in meaning with some-thing which has been said in the preceding sentence or clause : thus after a description of a battle, ending with *Hominum enim multitūdine receptus impediēbātur*, Caesar goes on as follows (B. C. iii. 64. 3) :

> **In eō proeliō** cum gravī vulnere esset adfectus aquilifer et iam vīribus dēficerētur, conspicātus equitēs nostrōs ' Hanc ego' inquit ' et vīvus multōs per annōs magnā dīligentiā dēfendī et nunc moriens eādem fidē Caesarī restituō. Nōlīte, obsecrō, committere, quod ante in exercitū Caesaris nōn accidit, ut reī mīlitāris dēdecus admittātur, incolumemque ad eum dēferte. **Hōc cāsū** aquila conservātur.

Here *in eō proeliō* and *hōc cāsū* have the effect of conjunc-tions or co-ordinating relatives ; for they connect what follows with what precedes.

(*b*) The speaker or writer often ends with a word which prepares the way for something that is to be said in the fol-lowing sentence or clause : thus in the first sentence of the Gallic War Caesar writes *Gallia est omnis dīvīsa in partēs*

trēs (not *in trēs partēs dīvisa*), because he is going to describe
these three parts in detail in the next sentence : ' The divisions
of Gaul are three—as follows.'   And in § 5 of the same
chapter he writes *initium capit ā flūmine Rhodanō,* because he
is going to speak of other boundaries of this part of Gaul.
This principle will explain many instances in which an
adverb phrase or an object is placed after the verb.   In many
examples the effect of the transposition is to bring a noun
into immediate contact with a relative pronoun, as in the first
instance above (*in partēs trēs* immediately before *quārum*),
and in the following :

> Relinquō haec omnia ; quae sī velim persequī, *etc.*: Cic.
> Verr. v. 21.

(8) The normal order is often changed in order to make
the sentence more rhythmical or in other ways more pleasing
to the ear.   This is true of prose as well as verse, though in
verse (English as well as Latin) the normal order is often
changed more than would be permissible in prose.   But it
must not be supposed that the words can stand in *any* order,
even in verse.

INDEX

The references are to the sections

abbreviations, App. XL

abhinc 441, note

ablative 12 ; adverbial 429-448 ; adjectival 449 ; as object 450, 451 ; with a preposition 452-454 ; ablative absolute 494-497

ac ' than ' 533, obs.

accent 10

accusative 11 ; as object 379-388 (retained, in the passive construction 386) ; adverbial 389-393 ; with a preposition 394, 395 ; with infinitive 462-473 (in reported speech 536, 545, 547)

adjectives 18-21, 31-33, 46-50 ; numeral 80-95 ; comparison of 66-72 ; possessive 103 ; demonstrative 104-109, 124, 515 ; interrogative 110, 516 ; indefinite 111-118, 517, 519 ; relative 119-121, 124 ; reflexive 103, 511-514

adjective clauses 525 ; with subjunctive 334, 335, 337, 338, 341, 343, 344, 346, 355, 360, 361 ; in reported speech 364

adverbs, formation of 73-77 ; comparison of 78, 79 ; numeral 84 ; demonstrative 124 ; relative 124, 525

adverb clauses 526-533 ; with subjunctive 335-346, 358-360, 364 ; of time 339, 340, 358 *a*, 526 ; of place 527 ; of cause 358 *b*, 528 ; of purpose 338, 529 ; of result 360, 530 ; of condition 343, 349, 350, 531 ; of concession 343, 358 *b*, 532 ; of comparison 337, 533 ; in reported speech 364, 540

agreement, of verb 270-273 ; of predicative adjective and predicative noun 274-276 ; of verb-adjectives 277 ; of epithets 279-281 ; of pronouns 282-289

aiō 248

aliquis 112

alius 109

alter 91

an 522

analysis of sentences 250-268, 520-533

antequam 340, 526

apposition 258, 281

audiō, conjugated 149-151, 156-158

bōs App. XIII

calendar, App. XXXVIII

canis App. IX

capiō, conjugated 159-163

carō App. XIII

cases, general meanings of 10-12 ; nominative 368-377 ; vocative 378 ; accusative 379-397 ; dative 398-415 ; genitive 416-427 ; ablative 428-454

celer App. XVII

cīvitās App. XII

clause, subordinate 261, 523-533 ; main 266. *See* adjective clauses, adverb clauses, noun clauses

coepī 249

commands 313-316, 320-322 ; dependent 326-329, 523

comparative clauses 533 ; subordinate to accus. with infin. 473

comparison of Latin with modern languages 2

comparison of adjectives 66-72 ; of adverbs 78, 79

complex sentences 265-268

compound verbs, principal parts of, App. XLI

conditional sentences 531, 350 ; in subordination 355, 471

conditioned futurity, subjunctives of 347-356

CPSIA information can be obtained
at www.ICGtesting.com
Printed in the USA
LVOW13*1432311017

554452LV00012B/215/P

9 781298 936264